RE/MAX

Home Buyer's Survival Guide

Home Buyer's Survival Guide

Bridget McCrea

Foreword by
Dave Liniger, Cofounder and Chairman of
RE/MAX International, Inc.

Sterling Publishing Co., Inc.
New York

RE/MAX is proud to donate all its proceeds from the sale of this book to the family of RE/MAX charitable organizations.

Library of Congress Cataloging-in-Publication Data Available

10 9 8 7 6 5 4 3 2 1

Published by Sterling Publishing Co., Inc.
387 Park Avenue South, New York, NY 10016
© 2007 by RE/MAX International
Distributed in Canada by Sterling Publishing
c/o Canadian Manda Group, 165 Dufferin Street
Toronto, Ontario, Canada M6K 3H6
Distributed in the United Kingdom by GMC Distribution Services
Castle Place, 166 High Street, Lewes, East Sussex, England BN7 1XU
Distributed in Australia by Capricorn Link (Australia) Pty. Ltd.
P.O. Box 704, Windsor, NSW 2756, Australia

Manufactured in the United States of America
All rights reserved

Sterling ISBN-13: 978-1-4027-3541-7
        ISBN-10: 1-4027-3541-3

For information about custom editions, special sales, premium and corporate purchases, please contact Sterling Special Sales Department at 800-805-5489 or specialsales@sterlingpub.com.

RE/MAX

Home Buyer's Survival Guide

CONTENTS

ACKNOWLEDGMENTS

Bridget McCrea would like to thank the dozens of RE/MAX agents who provided insights for this book, the trade organizations that provided information and statistics, and the editors and copyeditors who helped make the content valuable and relevant for home buyers.

RE/MAX would like extend their recognition and gratitude to the following:

Meredith Peters Hale, our editor at Sterling Publishing—for her patience and professionalism throughout the development of this work.

Bridget McCrea—for her untiring efforts in making the information understandable and easy to read.

The millions of home buyers and sellers who have selected RE/MAX brokers and sales associates to assist in one of the most important decisions in their lives—buying or selling a home.

The thousands of RE/MAX brokers and sales associates who daily dedicate their lives to providing professional assistance and expertise to home buyers and sellers around the world.

Those RE/MAX agents who assisted in providing information, suggestions, and guidance in the preparation of this work and whose ideas are included.

Michele Blay, former Corporate Counsel at RE/MAX International, for her untiring efforts in reviewing this book.

Geoff Lewis, RE/MAX Chief Legal Officer, for his final review and valuable input.

Dave and Gail Liniger for co-founding RE/MAX in 1973 and nurturing it to become the most dynamic real estate organization in the world.

Building the American Dream— One Home at a Time

What is the American Dream? It's building something valuable from scratch, making things better for yourself and your family, investing in your community. And part of achieving the American Dream has always been buying a home of your own.

Home is more than just a house—it's the place where we build other dreams, showcase our passions, and make lasting memories, too. Because a house is such an integral part of our lives—and because that home purchase may also be the most important financial decision most of us ever make—buying a home requires careful consideration. In 2005, over eight million people joined the homeownership club, buying new and existing homes nationwide at a record-setting pace. Buying a home represents a large investment of money, effort, and hope, so it only makes sense to choose wisely and to draw on the expertise of the best professionals out there to help make that dream of homeownership a reality.

Whether you are a first-time home buyer or an experienced buyer, you face the same challenges and stumbling blocks—from finding the right home to securing financing to deciphering contracts. In addition to these hurdles, increased demand for housing in recent years has driven prices higher in most areas. But during four consecutive record years for home sales, buyers have shown that they refuse to be stymied by such issues. In the first quarter of 2005, the national homeownership rate stood at 69.1 percent, just about even with the all-time high of 69.2 percent, reached in the fourth quarter of 2004. Based on current trends and underlying demand, it's estimated that the overall U.S. homeownership rate could well exceed 70 percent by 2013.

Many factors contribute to the growth in national homeownership. Pride of ownership and tax advantages are just two reasons renters are choosing to buy, even though home-rental rates may appear to be lower than home-purchase and -ownership costs. In addition, mortgage companies are offering creative new ways to help even more people become homeowners. Whether these programs represent a real benefit to consumers remains an open question, but few would argue that they provide prospective home buyers with more mortgage options than they had just five years ago.

Low interest rates, increased mortgage choices, and the lure of tax savings that come from mortgage interest and property tax deductions all make homeownership very appealing, but the process of buying a home is a complex undertaking. The Internet, while a powerful source of information for home buyers, does not make this process simpler, easier, or less prone to pitfalls. Informed buyers continue to rely on real estate agents as trusted advisors to guide them through.

According to the 2005 National Association of REALTORS® Profile of Home Buyers and Sellers, home buyers continue to use real estate professionals to help them navigate the complexities of gathering information, evaluating that information for credibility and relevance, and applying the knowledge they gain to choose a home that fits their needs and financial resources. Among those who turned to the Internet first as a research and information tool, 81 percent chose to retain a real estate professional when purchasing a home, compared to 66 percent of non-Internet users.

The independent real estate professionals who form the RE/MAX franchise network are thoroughly familiar with all the details and considerations that potential buyers face when searching for the right home at the right price. This book, written with input from the field—from our corps of skilled and experienced real estate agents, is designed to give you valuable, real-world insights based on everything these agents know about the home-buying process. Although no one book can provide all the information you'll need in order to buy a home, the *RE/MAX Home Buyer's Survival Guide* is designed to provide you with some straight facts and practical, real-world advice from these agents, who work on the front lines every day with buyers just like you.

This book covers five main areas: getting ready to buy, selecting a real estate professional to work with, obtaining a mortgage, finding your home, and closing the deal. Each chapter contains detailed, easy-to-understand information that you can start using right away to buy your first—or next—home.

The American Dream of homeownership is still very much alive and well. By reading this book and following the information that's offered here, you'll be better equipped to achieve it.

Good luck! Enjoy your exciting journey into the world of homeownership.

—Dave Liniger
Chairman of the Board and Cofounder,
RE/MAX International, Inc.

Survival 101

No two homes—and no two home buyers—are exactly alike, which means that every home purchase is unique. However, most real estate sales do have certain steps in common. Buyers generally begin by deciding that the time is right to invest in a new place to live, and then they look at neighborhoods, amenities, types of housing, commute times, and housing size. Next, buyers usually choose a real estate professional to help them narrow down their choices, to gather information on home prices and availability, and to compare home-financing options. Once a buyer finds one or two possible homes, she negotiates a purchase price on her top choice and investigates the home's condition, title (or ownership), and property boundaries. The buyer completes the process by arranging to finance the purchase. The property is then transferred from the seller to the buyer, who moves in shortly thereafter.

This apparently simple list of steps can be accomplished in any number of ways, depending on a buyer's circumstances. Your favored home styles, your finances, the time you have available for house-hunting, and your preferred location all affect your house hunt. In addition, both the U.S. housing market and the financial market offer more options to today's home buyers than ever before. How do you sort through it all? How do you know when to use a real estate agent—if at all? How do you choose a mortgage? How can you put yourself in the strongest position to win a bidding war on your perfect house in a hot real estate market? (And how do you know if a real estate market is "hot"?) How does the Internet help—and when can it hurt—your research process?

Getting Down to Basics

Knowing the answers to the questions posed above (and more) constitutes basic "home-buying survival." If you have a good grasp of the housing markets where you'd like to move, the home-financing options available today, and research strategies to find out what you need to know, you'll be in a better position to locate a home that fits your lifestyle and to help your real estate agent work efficiently on your behalf.

The home-buying steps noted above generally occur in three major stages: conducting initial research into home types and prices; visiting a limited number of houses with real potential; and then completing the home sale. During your initial research, you evaluate what you're really looking for, honestly assessing your lifestyle and your family's needs, and narrowing your search accordingly (see chapter 1). You might also do some background research, driving around potential neighborhoods, gathering information online, or reading local newspapers for insights into the overall area. Next, you determine what you can afford (chapter 2). You gather documents to support your home-mortgage application and get preapproved for a loan amount. To help you navigate all these tasks, you'll want to retain a local, knowledgeable real estate agent who can guide you through the overall process (chapter 4).

In the second stage—the search itself—you narrow down the characteristics that you want in a home or a neighborhood (chapter 8). For example, do you want a four-bedroom home within walking distance of schools, a Victorian house nestled in a secluded area, or a condominium in a complex with tennis courts and a lively social scene? Must your home have an open floor plan, be handicapped-accessible, or have a fence around the yard for your dog? Your agent schedules appointments for you to see specific homes. After these showings, you may modify or refine your search criteria, based on what's available in your price range and target neighborhood. And then, after looking around at several properties, you find the one that's just perfect. At that point, you negotiate a purchase price with the seller and agree on a closing timetable (chapter 9).

In the third stage—the closing process—you conduct your due diligence on the home. Your agent helps you to arrange for a professional home inspection and to establish which repairs will be made by the seller and which will be your responsibility (chapter 10). The property's past ownership is researched to make sure that ownership can legally pass to you from the seller. (Called a title search, this is performed by a title company.) You arrange for financing to cover the purchase and start making preparations to move (chapter 11). Finally, you and the seller sign the sale documents at the closing table, and the seller gives you the keys (and maybe a garage-door opener) to your new home.

Because mortgage financing, home inspection, and property repairs all take time, most home-purchase transactions take between thirty and sixty days to close. The closing date could be extended by agreement between the parties; maybe the sellers want extra time so that their family can move when the school year ends. Closing also might take longer if the buyers must sell their existing home, or if unexpected significant problems with the property surface. For example, a title search may reveal that a lien (or a legal claim) has been filed against the property, and you may have to wait to close on the home until the lien is paid off and removed.

Finding Your Way Home

These steps, and more, are all spelled out in the pages of this book. And to make the process simpler, we've included a glossary at the end of the book that defines specialized real estate terms (boldfaced at the first reference) that you might find confusing. The information that's presented here is augmented by the expertise of real estate agents and brokers affiliated with the RE/MAX franchise network. Let their experience be your guide. Beginning with the basics of why you want to purchase a home, and then walking you through the fundamentals of home selection and financing, the *RE/MAX® Home Buyer's Survival Guide* will help you understand what to expect during a home-purchase transaction.

Right now, the home-buying process may seem daunting. But if you do your research and understand how the process works, buying your new home can actually be an exciting adventure—one that millions of Americans undertake each year. If you're ready to start your own journey down this path, all you have to do is turn the page. . . .

CHAPTER ONE

Choices, Choices

As you prepare to search for a home, first ask yourself a few questions: What kind of home do you envision yourself coming back to each day? In what sort of neighborhood? Do you want to be near a city or in the country? Is your ideal home near parks and other open spaces?

Buying a home is a highly personal decision, one that should be approached with significant preparation. Your personal preferences have their roots in the types of homes you grew up in, homes that your friends own, homes you've read about in the newspaper or seen online, and homes you pass in the course of your day. You may not even realize what factors make a particular house appealing to you. So before jumping in, stop and figure out why particular home styles capture your fancy.

Think about your current lifestyle. Are you willing to change it in order to buy a home? What aspects of your lifestyle do you need to retain to stay sane? Do you need to be near restaurants, museums, and shops in order to feel active and engaged? Will an hour-and-a-half commute each day drain your energy and lead you to dream ever more fondly of an early retirement?

Then, consider any life changes that you expect to undergo during the next few years—for example, taking a new job, getting married, or having children (or more children). Before you read any further, you might want to take a few minutes to quickly jot down a few factors that you consider important in a home right now. Put a date on the sheet. You'll probably change your mind about what's important to you as your home search proceeds, and you might want to look back from time to time at what you thought you wanted when you first decided to buy.

Let's get started.

Housing Options

Are you looking for a **single-family** home or a **multifamily** home? Single-family homes are stand-alone dwellings designed for occupancy by one or more members of one family who share a single living space. Such homes differ from multifamily developments, where two or more residences are attached together to form one structure. Multifamily home options available for purchase include condominiums, townhouses, duplexes, and cooperatives.

Most housing markets offer both types of homes, but often one home type predominates in a particular area, and this can affect your home search. In densely populated cities, such as New York, Chicago, and San Francisco, where land is at a premium, you are more likely to find multifamily residences; rural and suburban areas generally have more single-family homes. As a result, if it's important to you to live in the heart of a particular city, your home search may need to encompass multifamily housing options.

Single-Family Homes

Single-family homes are **detached,** meaning that they don't physically touch another similar structure. This is the predominant form of housing stock found in the suburbs, exurbs (the areas immediately surrounding the suburbs), and rural areas.

The biggest difference between these homes and their multifamily counterparts is the ownership structure. The single-family homeowner not only owns the building itself but also the land it's on (to the predetermined property lines). As such, the owner is solely responsible for all real estate taxes, as well as all the upkeep and maintenance of that building and land. Multifamily homeowners generally share ownership and upkeep of certain structures and land that all residents use.

Some single-family neighborhoods mimic the shared-upkeep aspect of multifamily housing by establishing a homeowners' association that sets rules and regulations (also known as neighborhood covenants) to maintain the neighborhood's amenities and appearance. The **homeowners' association** usually collects fees (annually, quarterly, or monthly) to handle upkeep of any **"common areas"** in the neighborhood, including lawns, security facilities, pools, or playgrounds. In such neighborhoods, single-family homeowners are also responsible for the cost of keeping their land in compliance with the association's rules.

Advantages of single-family homes include privacy, more outside land and space around the home itself, and a more independent way of living because you don't share walls with other homeowners. On the downside, owning a single-family home may involve assuming sole responsibility for maintenance of the property, including all fees and costs associated with keeping up the interior and exterior of the home. It can also be more isolating, depending on where the home is located and how many other dwellings are nearby.

Multifamily Homes

Multifamily homes come in a variety of shapes and sizes, and include **attached** properties such as condominiums, townhouses, cooperatives, and villas. Such homes are considered "attached" because they are connected to one or more other residences (called units) by sharing one or more walls. Owners of the units also share the use and upkeep of common areas, which can include surrounding landscaping and amenities, such as a pool, a gym, or a tennis court. Some home buyers are pleased that a group of owners share the cost of upkeep of the common grounds and amenities, in part because this may mean that they have access to better amenities than they would if they had to bear the entire cost themselves. Others don't want to share a wall or upkeep decisions with a neighbor. In certain housing markets, multifamily homes are also more affordable, making them more accessible to buyers who lack the resources for a substantial down payment and high monthly housing costs.

The differences between multifamily housing options are also based on ownership structure and the extent of one unit's attachment to another. Certain multifamily options offer more shared control than others do. In a condominium, for example, owners share more of the fee responsibility and decision making than, say, the owners of a townhouse complex would. Here's a look at a few multifamily options on the market today and how they differ from one another.

Condominiums

A condominium or "condo" is a development where individuals own units, but share common-area ownership (including the surrounding land that the building sits on) with other unit owners within the complex. Common area ownership is often expressed as a percentage of the whole common area. However, condominium common-area ownership is undivided, which means that the common area is shared, and no one condo owner can monopolize these areas for his exclusive use. Owners must abide by a declaration of Covenants, Conditions, and Restrictions (commonly known as a CC&R), which spells out how a property may be used and any protections put in place for the benefit of all owners.

Typically, an association or a corporation creates a condominium development and files appropriate documents with the state. These documents establish the condo owners' rights and responsibilities. For example, in most condos, the bylaws state that the association or corporation is responsible for the maintenance and repair of the common areas. In turn, the association charges individual unit owners a share of the costs involved in this upkeep, sometimes called an **association fee.** The condo owner is responsible for maintaining her unit, paying her own utility bills, obtaining homeowner's insurance for her unit, and paying the monthly association fee to the condominium association. In addition, from time to time the condominium association might require a one-time extra payment from homeowners, known as an **assessment,** to pay for particular expenses, such as unexpected roof repairs. Association fees and assessments can vary greatly, so multifamily home buyers should note carefully the amount of monthly payments and ask about any upcoming, anticipated repairs that may result in an assessment. Condo owners are responsible for the payment of property taxes to the municipal tax assessor on an annual basis.

Many buyers like the low-maintenance aspect of condo living: Unit owners have little or no responsibility for tasks such as yard care or snow shoveling. In addition, in areas where home prices are high or housing inventory is low, buyers may be attracted to condos as an affordable homeownership alternative.

Townhouses

Townhouses are a popular choice for the home buyer who is torn between a single-family home and a condo. For some buyers, townhouses (sometimes referred to as "townhomes") provide the best of both. Often two or three stories high, townhouses are attached residences and, as such, share many of the characteristics of condominiums. However, while condominiums are generally units within a single building or set of buildings, a townhouse is usually a semi-separate structure that is minimally attached to another townhouse. Owners of townhouses generally own both the townhouse structure (even though it is attached) and the land that it sits on, which often has a front and back yard. Townhouse owners pay taxes on this individually owned property.

If only two townhouses are attached to each other, they may be called a duplex (and three may be called a triplex). Townhouse developments may range from several dozen attached buildings to hundreds. Like condominiums, townhouse development common areas and amenities (such as swimming pools and playgrounds) are maintained jointly by all townhouse owners in the complex, who pay dues to a homeowners' association that is charged with maintaining the common areas of the development.

Cooperatives

A housing cooperative is typically an apartment building or a group of dwellings owned by a not-for-profit corporation, the stockholders of which are the residents of the dwellings themselves. This home type is more common in cities like New York. Cooperatives (or "co-ops") are operated for the stockholders' benefit by their elected board of directors. In a cooperative, the corporation or association holds title in the real estate, and a resident purchases "stock" in the corporation, which allows him to occupy a unit in the building or property owned by the cooperative. The resident does not own his unit, but does have an absolute right to occupy his unit for as long as he owns the stock. Each month, the co-op's owners pay an amount that covers their share of the corporation's operating expenses.

According to the National Association of Housing Cooperatives (NAHC), the primary distinction between a housing co-op and other forms of homeownership is that owners in a housing co-op don't own real estate directly. Instead, you're buying shares or a membership in a cooperative housing corporation. The corporation owns or leases all real estate and pays the real estate taxes. All costs to operate the building are shared by the shareholders. An administrative board of directors, made up of representative owners, usually must approve any new shareholders (that is, you must apply to the board before you can purchase a co-op unit in the building).

The purchase price of a co-op will vary depending on what kind of neighborhood it is in, how big the unit is, whether the co-op's rules and regulations place limits on resale prices, and whether the co-op has an underlying mortgage for the entire property. This makes the financing process much different for co-op buyers than, say, for buyers of a single-family home or a condo. In most cases, you may apply for what is known as a **share loan** from a lender who specializes in such financing (you can find some listed on the NAHC's Web site at www.coop-housing.org). A share loan provides you with borrowed funds to buy the share(s) from the seller. You then make monthly payments on the share loan to the lenders and monthly carrying charge (maintenance) payments to the co-op association.

Other Multifamily Home Options

Some homeowners with busy lives or physical limitations may opt for a multifamily home in order to minimize the amount of maintenance they must perform to keep up the home's yard or the exterior of the structure. Multifamily homes typically offer the perfect solution for such homeowners, since a wide range of multifamily homes have been designed with limited or no yards to maintain. Multifamily homes called patio homes feature a small yard that usually consists of an outdoor

Figuring out the differences between condos, townhouses, and co-ops can be a daunting task for homeowners, who can't always rely on industry lingo to be clear and concise. Here's a quick cheat sheet to help you distinguish between the different types of ownership structures and physical attributes:

Multifamily Homes at a Glance

CONDOMINIUM

Description: Usually comprised of multiple units that are owned by individual residents. Condos are often found in high-rise structures, although they can also be part of lower-profile buildings.

Ownership structure: Condos use a type of joint ownership of real property in which portions of the property (such as hallways) are commonly owned and other portions (the interior units themselves, for example) are individually owned.

Fees: Condo owners pay a monthly or quarterly fee to cover the maintenance and upkeep of common areas, and usually pay as a group for utilities such as water, garbage removal, and cable television.

TOWNHOUSE

Description: Aside from the fact that owners share a wall or two with their next-door neighbors, townhouses are usually two-story structures that closely mimic single-family homes in terms of physical attributes and ownership.

(continued)

LUXURY HOMES

Ownership structure: Residents own the land under their townhouses, plus the structures themselves,

Fees: Owners typically pay a quarterly or annual fee for the maintenance and upkeep of common areas (such as lawns and swimming pools).

CO-OP

Description: Co-ops look like condos from the outside, but internally these entities are set up much differently.

Ownership structure: Residents become "shareholders" of a corporation, and not actually owners of the property itself. They buy shares in a housing corporation, and in return earn the right to reside in the building.

Fees: The shareholders elect a governing board, which determines an annual operating budget, collects monthly maintenance fees, and allocates funding for property improvements.

stone- or concrete-floored area. This kind of patio is easier to maintain than a large yard, but provides some space for outdoor entertaining and relaxation. In the United States, an attached home that is only one story is often called a villa. The single level and limited outside maintenance offer a flexible living option for a homeowner who cannot manage the stairs of a two-story home. The ownership structure of a patio home or villa is usually similar to that of a townhouse.

New Homes

Your home-buying options also include newly constructed homes (as opposed to properties that are currently occupied or were previously occupied). New homes are divided into two types: custom-built homes that buyers contract to have built to their specifications, and homes that are already under construction or completed but have not yet been occupied. The latter are sometimes called **spec homes.** Many times, new homes are offered for sale by new home builders who work with real estate agents to find buyers. As such, your real estate agent can help you locate the best new developments in your area and walk you through the whole process to make that new home your own.

If you're looking to purchase a new home, you should check out which builders are doing the most construction in your area, and which are most reputable and reliable. You can turn to your local Better Business Bureau for some of this information, but you should also speak with each builder's references before signing a contract. A check through your local newspapers' archives (usually available online) can also help you ferret out any questionable practices on a builder's record (such as shoddy workmanship, construction delays, and the like), as well as learn about any awards and accolades your local builders have received.

New homes typically have updated architectural designs, floor layouts, building features, fixtures, and appliances. They may be priced higher than older homes of the same size and configuration in a particular area. If you choose a new home in a completely new development, you may have to be patient while neighborhood trees and other landscape features grow in. You may want to devote more time early on to community activities or to getting to know your neighbors, in order to establish a neighborhood feel.

With a new home, you may have the opportunity to choose from a number of different lots with different views. For example, if having a living room that overlooks your pool and patio is important to you, be sure to request a floor plan that incorporates that element.

Keep in mind that *new* doesn't necessarily mean "maintenance-free" or "low upkeep." You may have to address such issues as poor or incomplete workmanship, the need to make changes in landscaping once shrubs and trees start to grow in, or equipment repairs to furnaces and air-conditioning units. Shaun Tracy, a broker at RE/MAX of Boise, Idaho, frequently works with buyers who are looking at newly constructed homes and notes that new homes pose different challenges than existing homes. Here he outlines five key areas that new-home buyers should consider before making a buying decision:

- **Location:** It is important for home buyers to like what they have chosen as a location and not buy in haste. He advises buyers to consider seemingly small issues, such as the direction in which the sun comes up and which rooms face that light, before the building process even begins. "Otherwise, they'll never be satisfied once the home is built," says Tracy.

- **Your time frame:** It takes significantly longer for a new home to be ready for occupancy, compared to an existing home. For this reason, buyers need to keep their time frame in mind when purchasing, factoring everything from weather to material-procurement problems into the equation. "The waiting process isn't easy," says Tracy, "and can be very hard for the buyer to accept."

- **Your builder:** Choose your builder wisely, based on reputation in the marke place, home styles and offerings, and referrals from other homeowners. "This is one of the largest single investments a person will make," says Tracy, "and it deserves careful consideration."

- **Your real estate agent:** An agent can help ensure that you're getting the design and home that best fits your needs. Most times, for example, a buyer's agent has specific information and knowledge about builders and their homes. Most builders are up front about what percentage they pay in commission to a buyer's agents. Because some agents specialize in particular home types or markets, if you are intent on buying only a newly constructed property, you should make sure your agent serves this market. (See chapter 4 for a detailed discussion of buyer's agents.)

- **The inspection process:** Think a new home doesn't need an inspection? Think again. "A newly built home needs an inspection just like any other home in the buying process," says Tracy. "Many times, the new-home owner may be left holding the bag if something is overlooked (such as bad framing, or incorrect dimensions, for example) until after the typical one-year warranty period expires."

- **Energy efficiency:** Some homes come with energy-saving features, such as passive solar energy (via large windows that face the afternoon sun as a way of keeping heating bills at bay). Other examples may include solar panels and even trees planted in such a way as to prevent the summer sunshine from heating certain areas of the home. Check with your builder to see what energy saving options are available for your home.

No home is perfect; in addition to the considerations specified above, a new home may present the homeowner with the same challenges and rewards that an existing home does. Even a brand new home will have kinks that may need to be worked out before you are completely happy living there.

How to Focus Your Choices

Which type of home is right for you? When you buy a home for personal use, you're not only purchasing a worthwhile investment, you're also buying a lifestyle, a neighborhood, and any and all surroundings in the immediate vicinity. You're buying into the neighborhood schools, houses of worship, entertainment venues, parks, recreational facilities, police and emergency facilities, cultural amenities, and other elements that make up a community. So start ranking these factors in order of importance to you.

Next, you should begin to research the variety of available homes that meet your preferences. Try driving around neighborhoods that appeal to you and attending a few open houses—opportunities to walk through homes that are for sale—to get a sense of the houses in those in neighborhoods. Certain features that are typical for the area where you are interested in living will stand out, and you will begin to understand which characteristics you want in a home.

In chapter 8, we'll discuss specific criteria to look for in neighborhoods and homes as you work with your real estate agent to view homes, narrow down your choices, and eventually make your home purchase. However, as you begin your initial research, it's important to figure out which characteristics in a home and community are most important to you. This will help you to better focus your search and work with your agent.

Key Factors to Consider

Because buying a home is such a personal decision, only you know what's most important for you and your family in a home or neighborhood. Here are a few key factors to consider before starting your home search:

1. Are you looking to buy a home surrounded by lots of land, one in the suburbs, or one in a city? Your preferences regarding population density may be influenced by the availability of land where you'd like to live, home prices in your target area, and other issues of concern to prospective homeowners (schools, parks, cultural life, etc.).

2. Do you want to live in an area where the population is growing, stabilized, or decreasing? Areas where new homes are being built and new businesses are coming in tend to attract high population growth, and could look very different five years from now.

3. What kinds of environmental features spell *home* to you—forests, hills, lakes, ponds, or oceans? Natural elements can mean all the difference between being happy in a home or pining for one that's situated in your favorite setting. Keep this in mind as you look at homes.

4. What are your educational needs now, and for the next five to ten years? Consider whether you will need a home in close proximity to elementary schools, high schools, and colleges, and factor this into your home-buying decision.

5. What kinds of entertainment do you enjoy? Make a list of your most enjoyable recreation spots—anything from parks and lakes to movie theaters, opera houses, live theater, professional sports arenas, or bike paths, and look for a home that's within close driving (or walking) distance to these amenities.

6. How important to you is a family-friendly neighborhood, or proximity to senior-oriented activities? These features and amenities will go a long way toward creating a home life where your favorite activities are accessible and enjoyable.

With this information in hand, you won't go into the home search blindly, hoping that the right dwelling comes along. Instead, you'll be taking a proactive, educated approach to the process.

Transportation Considerations

In many places around the country, housing is being built in once-dormant urban areas to accommodate people who want to live close to their workplace. These urban dwellers reason that the time they used to spend commuting could be better spent doing something else, such as engaging in family activities or enjoying cultural events. In exchange for this convenience, they are willing to accept a smaller home size in some urban areas.

If you fall into this category, then you should take your commute into consideration when shopping for a home. Not only should you look at the number of miles from your front door to the workplace, but you should also check out traffic patterns and congestion, in order to select a home that's situated at or below your own maximum "drive time." If you'll be using public transportation to get to work and/or to travel throughout the community, be sure to consider the home's proximity to bus stops, train stations, or other such forms of mass transit.

Take this short quiz to figure out what key commuting issues to factor into your house hunt:

1. How will I commute to work?

☐ walk   ☐ drive   ☐ taxi
☐ train   ☐ carpool   ☐ bus

2. What's the maximum amount of time I'm willing to spend on my morning and afternoon commute?

☐ 15 minutes   ☐ 30 minutes   ☐ 1 hour or longer

3. Based on the neighborhoods I'm interested in, what's the commuting distance to my workplace?

☐ 0–10 miles   ☐ 11–20 miles   ☐ 21–30 miles or more)

4. Would I like to live near public transportation?

☐ Yes   ☐ No

5. Would I use public transportation when making short trips to the store, the mall, and/or nearby communities?

☐ Yes   ☐ No

Here are some other important transportation-related considerations to think about:

- How close are the nearest public and private schools?
- How do the children from the neighborhood get to school? Do they take buses or do their parents drive them?
- Is public transportation available for commuting or shopping?
- How far away is my church, synagogue, or other house of worship?
- Are amenities like restaurants and malls easily accessible by car?
- Are airports, freeways, or railroads within driving distance, if I'm traveling for business or pleasure?
- Or, is the home far away from the hustle and bustle (if that's your preference)? (Keep in mind that, if you're shopping for a retirement home, the commute time to work will be inconsequential.)

These and other issues should be factored into your home-buying decision. To find the answers to any questions that you may not have considered, you may want to visit a local school and/or attend a school board meeting (see below), drop in on a government or other community meeting, eat out a few times in a local restaurant, read local newspapers in your target areas, or talk to your real estate agent. Use the information you gather to find a home that's situated conveniently close to the amenities, schools, recreational facilities, and businesses that you need to get to on a regular basis.

School Systems

If you have children, or if you're planning a family in the near future, be sure to do some homework on the area school systems. In many areas, where your child goes to school depends on where you live. In other areas, there are "choice" programs, which allow you to select from various options within a certain geographical area.

"Good" schools can mean higher property values and better home appreciation, since future buyers will also be on the lookout for the best school districts. If your home is situated within the jurisdiction or in close proximity to

Survival Toolkit

At Your Fingertips

In August 2005, RE/MAX International announced a new strategy for making all current MLS real estate listings available to consumers in most parts of the country. Visitors to www.remax.com are able to access a collection of properties listed by all real estate companies from across the nation through this single Web site. A home buyer first narrows his search by geographic area and price range. When the property search results are delivered, he can then narrow his search further by entering a "wish list" of home features; this yields a list of properties better suited to him. Best of all, the home buyer can save this refined search by clicking on the "Dream Home Request" button. From that point on, whenever new properties are added that fit the wish list criteria, an e-mail notification will be sent to the home buyer.

The streamlined site also includes added resources, such as past home sales data, a state-of-the-art neighborhood comparison tool, a mortgage calculator, school report cards, moving tips, and maps. Home buyers can also contact the agents listed for further information or to schedule a showing. "We've designed the site to put information at consumers' fingertips," says Kristi Graning, RE/MAX International senior vice president of IT and eBusiness. "We know consumers want immediate satisfaction, and through this system they are able to receive better property information, as well as a quick response, when they want one, from real estate professionals."

a well-regarded elementary school, middle school, high school, or institution of higher learning, then the odds that it will sell at the right price—and in a shorter amount of time—could be higher.

Be sure to consider the public school system, as well as private and parochial options, as you conduct your research. The Web is a good place to start: Many school districts post information online about their educational options, key test scores, awards, and student accolades. Real estate agents are typically well versed in this area, so they can provide valuable information and guidance. If it's feasible, you may also want to talk to parents in your target neighborhoods to get some firsthand advice and feedback on the area schools. We'll discuss more resources for research and specific questions regarding local schools in chapter 8.

Beginning Your Research: The Power of the Web

Changes in technology—the Internet, the widespread use of e-mail and cell phones, and the increasing popularity of personal media devices—have made the flow of information cheaper and easier than ever before, including information on real estate. For example, in years past, real estate brokers cooperated to publish their available real estate listings in looseleaf binders, which were updated periodically. These published listings might or might not contain a picture of the home. Now, consumers can access information online through Web sites like www.remax.com that gather many real estate listings on one site. Properties can be sorted by price, location, number of bedrooms, and other criteria.

However, while the Internet provides a large volume of information, it can't tell consumers which information is reliable and which is not. Some sites that appear to provide useful resources or information may, at best, simply forward you to another truly informative site; at worst, the site operator may angle to collect personal information from visitors for improper uses, such as identity theft. Investigate the Web sites that you plan to use and try to know who you're dealing with online.

Viewing Properties Online

It's no secret that more and more consumers are finding that there are many benefits to searching the Internet as a first step in their house hunt. This allows them to preview many properties and their specifications quickly. So where do you start? You should first look at Web sites of reliable companies that offer searchable listings online.

Although large real estate networks may establish Web sites, such as www.remax.com, that provide access to a broad range of U.S. and international properties, at the local level most brokers also have their own Web sites where consumers can search through MLS information to preview homes before viewing them in person. Visitors to such local brokerage Web sites select a property type (the categories typically include residential, commercial, farms, and vacant land). Often, buyers can further specify a price range and whether they require a certain number of bedrooms. Many individual agents also have Web sites, where home buyers can obtain background information on prospective agents before they retain their services.

After entering home feature preferences, a list of local properties will be displayed. If a property looks promising, clicking a link will provide more detailed information about the property, allowing for fairly extensive home searches (either locally, regionally, statewide, or even nationwide) before seeing the homes in person. In addition, buyers can see what types of features are typical in their target homes and adjust their home feature wish lists.

Through a mix of still photos, virtual tours (room-by-room, panoramic, 360-degree views of a home's interior and exterior features), and data such as asking price, size, number of rooms, neighborhood, and related information, consumers can quickly whittle down their options before actually visiting a property. Figure 1.1 is an example of a typical RE/MAX home listing.

In the listing shown in Figure 1.1, general property details are provided, such as the home's price, its size (in square feet), and lot size. If you click on the "Map Property" feature on the right side of the listing, you can immediately see whether the property is located in an area that you find desirable. For example, is it close to a park or near a highway that you would use to get to work? These factors will allow you to quickly narrow down your list of prospective properties.

Next, you might click on "Recent Nearby Home Sales." Not every MLS area nationwide makes this information available, but where it is available, you can see if the asking price for the home you are interested is in line with the price of other recent sales. Keep in mind that a comparison of prices between a house you're considering and other homes nearby that have recently been sold is more useful if the homes are similar in size, location, and features.

Next, you can see a description designed to give you a few details—and,

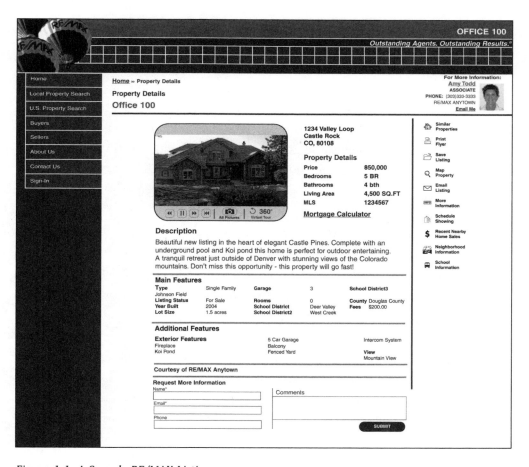

Figure 1.1: A Sample RE/MAX Listing

frankly, to get you excited enough to look further. Under "Main Features" you'll find the basic information that most buyers want to know right away. For example, the home may be listed as single family, a condo or townhouse, a multifamily (other than a condo or a townhouse), or a rental. Its listing status may say "For Sale" or "For Rent." Be sure to look at the fees listed, which should include the amount of any monthly homeowners' association fees.

The "Additional Features" section gives you greater detail about the home itself. This is where the type of appliances, the garage size, and outdoor extras such as hot tubs or pools are described. Compare this against your developing wish list. If the home's features aren't exactly what you want, try clicking on the "Similar Properties" link at the right of the listing to see what else is available. When you find a home that interests you enough to investigate further, click on the links that provide you with neighborhood facts (see Figure 1.2) and school statistics (see Figure 1.3).

Knowing this kind of information in advance of the showing (when a real estate agent walks you through the home for the first time; see chapter 8) can help you eliminate a high number of properties and neighborhoods that might be less well suited to your needs and tastes. You can concentrate instead on the best prospects and take those prospective choices to an agent.

At Your Fingertips

For home buyers, the Internet goes beyond just providing home-search data and virtual tours. The industrious buyer can also perform detailed research into schools and neighborhoods, estimate the differences in cost of living for various areas, get prequalified for a mortgage (which is an initial step toward the more thorough **preapproval** process to be discussed in chapter 7), and prepare and submit loan applications.

On the Web, you can also figure out new home costs, including monthly payments, insurance expenses, and property taxes, as discussed in chapter 2; get your hands on the latest interest rate information; and find a good real estate agent and/or title company. Once your search becomes more targeted, you can use the Internet to take virtual tours of possible homes, read up on the basics of

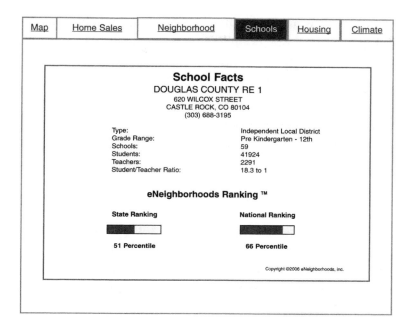

Figure 1.2: A Neighborhood Facts Snapshot on www.remax.com

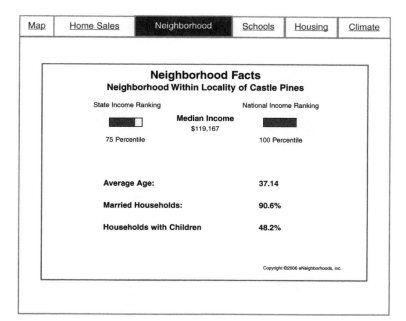

Figure 1.3: School Facts for Douglas County, Colorodo

financing, or browse through a few articles about the market and neighborhoods that interest you. As your purchase process nears its final stages, you can use closing-cost estimators to help you figure out how much you need to bring to the closing table in order to complete the deal, access moving-cost calculators (often available at national movers' sites) to plan for your move, and find change of address forms, offered by the U.S. Post Office, at www.usps.gov.

In addition to searching for real estate and mortgage information, buyers may want to search online for the latest financial and real estate industry trends. For example, the U.S. Department of Housing and Urban Development (www.hud.gov) sponsors a Web site that includes a wide range of information on real estate–related issues (including a document called "100 Questions & Answers About Buying a New Home"). Mortgage giants **Fannie Mae** (www.fanniemae.gov) and **Freddie Mac** (www.freddiemac.com) also provide Web-based information that home buyers can use to make the most informed decisions possible.

Remember to pay attention to the sources of information you're gathering and be sure to double-check everything you learn on the Web against a couple of other reliable sources, rather than taking the information at face value.

Survival Toolkit

Know Who You're Dealing With

For reliable information, you may want to consider visiting the Web site of the National Association of REALTORS® (www.realtor.org). Known throughout the industry as NAR, this organization is comprised of real estate professionals who agree to abide by a code of ethics. NAR provides consumer information and conducts surveys to better understand the real estate industry and real estate markets. While this site is geared toward NAR's members, you can find up-to-date news and research that may help you in your home search. Note that not all real estate agents are NAR members, who are properly referred to as **REALTORS®**. (From here on, we will use the term *Realtors* to refer to NAR members). See chapter 4 for more on NAR and Realtors.

Caught in the Web

If the Web entices you to search around "without obligation to buy," you're certainly not alone. NAR has noted that, while only 2 percent of buyers used the Internet to buy a home in 1995, this proportion rose to 71 percent in 2003 and 74 percent in 2005, according to David Lereah, NAR's chief economist, in a recent press release. Clearly, the Web is fast becoming one of the most popular research tools for home buyers when conducting a home search. And savvy consumers are increasingly realizing the value of preparing in advance for their search: The latest trends, according to NAR, indicate that home buyers spend over seven months "pre-researching" their purchase, reviewing homes, neighborhoods, financing, and real estate agents. The World Wide Web serves as a convenient and valuable tool in this process.

But just how effective is the Web in ultimately finding that dream home? NAR's "2005 Profile of Home Buyers and Sellers" showed that 38 percent of buyers first learned about the home they ultimately purchased through a real estate agent; 16 percent through a yard sign; 15 percent through the Internet; 7 percent from a friend, neighbor, or relative; 7 percent from a home builder; 5 percent from a newspaper advertisement; and 5 percent from a seller they knew. The Internet is one useful resource, but there are lots of tools available for finding that perfect home. We will explore all of them in this book.

Making Your Choice

Today's home buyers face an array of choices when it comes to selecting a home. Take the time to review all your options before whittling them down to the select few that you would enjoy coming "home" to every day. In the next chapter, we'll delve into the pros and cons of homeownership, and the various costs involved in purchasing a home.

CHAPTER TWO

Are You Ready to Buy?

How do you know when it's time to consider buying your first home—or moving to a different home? Renters should consider whether they are ready for the commitment involved in maintaining a home, whether they can benefit from home-mortgage tax deductions, whether they plan to stay in one location long enough to recoup the benefits of homeownership, and whether their income will permit them to buy a property that they want. In this chapter, we'll explore the various considerations involved in deciding if you're ready to purchase a new home, and in determining what you can afford, based on your current savings and household income.

Renting Versus Buying: Tipping Factors

When renters decide to make the move into homeownership, the main driving force is usually "to build **equity,**" says Amy Marsico, real estate agent and owner of RE/MAX Real Estate Advocate in Chicago, referring to a homeowner's financial interest in a property. "They feel that they're paying so much in monthly rent, and that it's going nowhere."

The same payment could be going toward a mortgage, allowing you to build up equity over the long term. When you buy a home, you make an investment in the house itself and in the community where you will live. Like any investment, you should look at your home purchase as an important part of your overall plan for a sound financial future. However, unlike other investments, your home is an investment that you can enjoy while you increase its value.

Advantages of Homeownership

Owning a home has many benefits. For one, it can provide a sense of stability for you and your family. In addition, your new home may offer you more space and (depending on the type of home you purchase) may fulfill some of your personal aspirations, such as having a yard for your kids and pets. As a homeowner, you'll experience a greater amount of control over your surroundings. You will be able to make repairs as quickly as you deem necessary—rather than waiting until your landlord or super has an opening in his schedule—and you can make sure all repairs are done to your satisfaction. In addition, you can remodel to create the home you've always wanted (based on your budget, of course); you're not limited by your landlord's rules and restrictions.

Where homeowners also differ from their renting counterparts is in the "pride of ownership" that comes from owning a property, rather than simply "borrowing it" in exchange for a fee. When you rent, that monthly check goes into someone else's pocket. When you own, you are making an investment, deducting mortgage interest and property taxes, and enjoying a home that's truly yours. So, while owning a home provides stability and personal satisfaction, it's also an investment that should reflect your overall savings and investment strategies, such as your retirement account(s), college savings account(s), money market account(s), or stock portfolio. This may be the biggest investment you ever make, so you may even want to consider seeking the guidance of a certified financial planner to evaluate how your home purchase fits into your overall financial plans.

Home buyers who are currently renting should also factor in the tax advantages of homeownership when evaluating what they can afford. Jeff Scislow, broker associate with RE/MAX Results in Eden Prairie, Minneapolis, notes that if someone is paying $1,500 a month in rent and a lender qualifies him for a $2,000 monthly mortgage payment, this buyer may think he is going to have to find another $500 a month to own a home.

"In many cases the buyer may not feel that he can spend an extra $500 a month to buy a house," says Scislow. "The tax break that homeowners receive as a result of the mortgage-interest and property deductions, however, may be enough to make the home affordable."

The mortgage-interest deduction allows property owners in most cases to deduct the total amount of mortgage interest paid to a lender in a calendar year. This deduction is recorded on the Schedule A—Itemized Deductions tax form, and is based on a Form 1098 sent to you annually by your lender. The mortgage-interest deduction can be fairly substantial for homeowners, particularly during the first few years of loan payback, when a significant portion of their monthly payment is used to pay off the interest on the loan.

Making these calculations and other financial decisions well in advance of the house hunt can help buyers determine if they are truly ready and able to buy, and can give them a realistic idea of what they can—and are willing to—spend on a home.

Advantages of Renting

In certain markets and under certain conditions, you may want to rent—at least for a while—instead of buying. If, for example, property prices in a particular region have peaked and are leveling off, then it may be prudent to rent until market conditions change. Perhaps national mortgage-interest rates are high, or if they are relatively low but you still can't afford the mortgage loan for the home you are determined to have, then it may be better wait until interest rates fall before buying. Prospective buyers who are determined to live in a specific area that's currently out of their financial reach may also want to wait. For example, a couple with young children may want to live near their extended family or in a town with a particular school system. If their desired neighborhood is beyond their means, the couple may consider renting in the area while continuing to save.

Also, someone who plans to move again in the very near future may want to reevaluate the decision to buy a home right away. When you're buying and selling, you incur costs beyond the home's purchase price. Moving costs, closing costs, and the cost to market the home for sale are just a few of these added expenses. Assuming that you buy a home relatively near its market price, its value is unlikely to increase so rapidly in just a few years that you'll be able to sell it for enough to cover these additional costs. In addition, a mortgage is typically paid off over a period of fifteen or twenty years, with the majority of the mortgage payment being allocated to paying off loan interest during the first few years of the loan. Therefore, your mortgage payments early on don't contribute as much to paying off the purchase price of your home (known as building equity in your home) in the early stages. For these reasons, it generally doesn't make good fiscal sense to purchase a home if you're planning to move again within a few months.

Finally, if you're a former homeowner who has been renting for a while but not quite long enough to qualify for "first-time" home buyer loan programs (discussed in chapter 3), you may want to continue to rent until you do qualify.

How to Compare

Chicago real estate agent Amy Marsico says that renters should understand first that there are hidden costs of homeownership. "Buying a home involves property taxes, assessments, homeowners insurance, closing fees and attorney fees, and homeowners' association fees," says Marsico. She notes that renters and home-owners alike have utility bills and phone bills, but renters should understand how these costs may change when they buy a home.

Indeed, the financial considerations in the rent-versus-buy decision are numerous. How will your homeownership costs—such as home repairs, utilities, insurance and property taxes—compare to your rental costs, including utilities, the inability to claim a mortgage deduction, and apartment upkeep expenses that you bear? How does the prospect of an increase in property taxes or mortgage payments stack up against the possibility that your landlord will raise your rent?

For a simple comparison, you can turn to online tools that compare renting to owning. Ginnie Mae (the Government National Mortgage Association, a wholly owned corporation within HUD that provides financial assistance to low-to-moderate-income home buyers), for example, has a calculator on its Web site at www.ginniemae.gov, under "Homeownership." You can enter information such as your current rent, home-purchase price, percentage of down payment, length of the loan (in years), interest rate, and the number of years you plan to stay in the home, in order to come up with a side-by-side comparison of renting versus buying. RE/MAX Relocation also has a calculator at www.remax-relocation.com, where you can enter similar information to come up with an accurate comparison.

Whether you opt to rent or buy is a personal choice that should be based on financial, living, family, work, and related factors, all of which can have a significant impact on the decision. In terms of dollars and cents, Marsico says buyers ultimately need to look at the total affordability of buying a home, past the initial down payment and closing costs, before deciding whether to purchase or continue renting. "The initial down payment may be difficult for some to come up with," she says, "but after you move in you may find out that your monthly obligations are lower than they would be if you were renting."

Getting Down to Business: The Costs of Homeownership

Let's face facts: For most people, the primary consideration in determining if they're ready to buy a home is cost. If you're thinking about buying a home, you've (hopefully) already started saving toward one aspect of the cost—the down payment. But what are the other costs involved in purchasing a home? Let's take a moment to explore the various expenses you will face as a home buyer.

The Down Payment

Home buyers are usually expected to contribute some cash up front toward the purchase of the home; this is called the **down payment**. A down payment is paid at the closing, in addition to all other closing costs incurred during the transaction. (See chapter 10 for a detailed discussion of how closing works.) For most loans, you will be expected to contribute 20 percent of the purchase price in the form of a down payment. There are less common mortgage options that permit between 5 percent and 20 percent down, and even a zero down (100 percent financing) option, but in general, the higher your down payment, the lower your monthly mortgage payments and closing costs are likely to be.

In addition, a substantial down payment may make you appear to be less of a risk to lenders. Lenders often view a homeowner who is willing to put a substantial sum of money as a down payment as more likely to pay her monthly mortgage commitment on time and avoid loan defaults. A **loan default** is the failure to pay a loan amount when it's due, and can lead to loan **foreclosure**, when a lender legally repossesses the home due to nonpayment of the mortgage debt. As a result, if the buyer is putting down less than 20 percent of the home's anticipated purchase price, an additional $100 or so usually will be added onto the monthly payment for **private mortgage insurance** (PMI), a type of insurance that protects the lender against loss, should the borrower become unable to make payments on the mortgage loan. (See pages 37-38 for more on this type of insurance.) This means that the more you contribute to a down payment, the more likely you are to save money by avoiding extra mortgage insurance costs.

The Mortgage

When you purchase a home using a mortgage, the loan is paid back in monthly installments over time, and you pledge the title to the home to the lender as part of the loan arrangements. If you fail to keep up with loan repayments, the lender then has the right to take the property and sell it in order to recover the lender's costs and as much of the outstanding home loan as the sale proceeds allow. The buyer's pledge of the property title is called a mortgage.

Your monthly mortgage payment will typically include a repayment of both the **principal** and the **interest** on the loan. Principal is the amount you owe for the actual purchase price of the house; principal payments build up your equity, or your investment, in the home. Interest payments go to the lender as payment for providing the mortgage. Usually you can expect that during the first several years of owning your home a lower percentage of your monthly payment will go toward the principal and a higher percentage toward the interest owed.

With a **conventional mortgage** (one that is not obtained through a government program such as the **Federal Housing Administration** or the Veterans Administration), a borrower has equal monthly payments, a set period of time in which to repay the loan (the **term,** usually thirty years), and a fixed interest rate that is established when the mortgage is created and does not change. Conventional mortgages typically limit a loan to an amount that is 80 percent of the home's value. This **loan-to-value percentage,** or ratio, is sometimes abbreviated as LTV. So, if a house is valued at $200,000, then the lender will provide $160,000 (80 percent of the home's value), and the borrower will be asked to provide a down payment of $40,000 to buy the house, which represents 20 percent of the home's value.

In addition to principal and interest, your mortgage may also include taxes and insurance payments. (In fact, you'll often hear the term *mortgage* associated with the acronym **PITI,** which stands for "principal, interest, taxes, and insurance.") We'll discuss each of these components of a typical mortgage in detail later in this chapter.

The Interest-Rate Factor

The interest rate that you pay on a mortgage can greatly affect your monthly payments, as well as the amount you'll pay over the life of the loan. As such, you should factor it into your calculations when determining how much home you can afford. Using a mortgage calculator, a $205,000 home loan at 6.5 percent interest, for example, translates into a $1,300 monthly payment. The same $205,000 home loan at 7.5 percent interest would require $1,400 in monthly payments. If you wanted to make a $1,300 monthly payment at 7.5 percent interest, you would only be able to borrow $185,923. This shows how just one percentage point can mean a $20,000 difference in the loan amount that you can afford. (Note that to arrive at these calculations, you'll need to use a special mortgage calculator, available on sites such as www.remax.com or www.ginniemae.gov. We discuss mortgage calculators later in this chapter.)

To get the best interest rate, you should brush up on what's currently being offered on the market. Check out the business or homes section of your local paper (or the local paper that covers the area where you'd like to move) to determine the going rate. You'll likely be shown two different interest rates: the actual interest rate for the loan, and the **annual percentage rate** (the "APR"), which reflects the cost of the mortgage expressed as a yearly rate. The APR usually includes various negotiable amounts, such as prepaid interest, loan-processing fees, underwriting fees, credit life insurance, points, and more. All of these are discussed in detail on pages 141–142.

As a buyer, you should consider both the basic interest rate and the APR when comparing loans. The APR is generally higher than the "straight" interest rate for the mortgage because it includes up-front costs paid to obtain the loan. The APR reflects both the interest rate and other fees as one figure, which means it reflects the actual cost of the loan. The APR can be useful when you're comparing the loans being offered by different lenders, because a buyer can compare cost and services for each loan. In other words, the APR allows home buyers to compare apples to apples when considering various loan options, and helps them become better informed consumers. Understanding the basics of interest rates—and how they affect your monthly payments, can give you a better idea of just how much home you can afford to buy.

Taxes

As a homeowner, you pay the property taxes on your new home. The bills are generally paid on a yearly, quarterly, or monthly basis, and cover such community and government services as schools, fire and police departments, parks, garbage pickup, and recreation facilities, among others. You can have your mortgage lender fold these tax bills into your monthly mortgage payment, or you can have your local tax assessor bill you directly and pay them on your own. If your loan amount is more than 80 percent of the home's appraised value, your lender may require that your monthly payment include not only principal and interest on the loan, but a monthly **escrow** for property taxes and insurance. (An escrow refers to money held in trust by a third party, payable upon certain conditions being met. We'll discuss escrows further in chapter 10). In such cases, the lender will pay from these escrowed funds all property taxes and insurance premiums when due. Note that you can deduct the amount of property taxes that you have paid from your income tax, if you itemize your return. For more information on what can be deducted, read the Internal Revenue Service's Publication 530, "Tax Information for First-Time Homeowners," available online at http://www.irs.gov/publications/index.html.

Insurance

The purpose of insurance has typically been described as protection against loss, theft, or damage. Much as you would insure an automobile or boat against such hazards, a homeowner must protect his property in case a problem occurs. When you're buying a home, you generally need to purchase several types of insurance. Below is a breakdown to help you sort through them.

Homeowner's Insurance

Homeowner's insurance is required for all homeowners who have financed their homes, and is *highly recommened* for those who pay for their homes outright as well. Should fire or another type of disaster (such as a hurricane or tornado) damage your property, homeowner's insurance will kick in and cover the home's replacement cost. This insurance coverage also protects you against personal liability, in case someone falls and hurts himself/herself on your property, and then sues you for damages. In addition, homeowner's insurance includes theft coverage, should someone break into your home and steal your valuables.

Homeowner's insurance is broken down into three categories:

- Dwelling: Protection for the home itself
- Contents: Insurance for assets inside the home
- Liability: Protection in the event that someone gets hurt on the property

In addition to the basic policy, your insurance agent can also include riders, or additional coverage, for items such as expensive equipment and jewelry. See chapter 9 for more on homeowner's insurance.

Private Mortgage Insurance (PMI)

When a borrower's down payment on a home is less than 20 percent of the total loan value on a conventional loan, she must take out private mortgage insurance (PMI) to cover the lender's investment should the borrower default on the loan.

The cost of this coverage varies. The typical buyer of a $200,000 home who makes a $10,000 down payment shells out about $500 a year for PMI coverage. Once the 20 percent threshold is met, either as a result of the loan being paid down or the home's value increasing to a point where the total mortgage is less than 80 percent of the value, PMI is no longer required.

Flood or Earthquake Insurance

Flood or earthquake insurance is additional hazard insurance that goes above and beyond the coverage provided by a typical homeowner's insurance policy. It's required on homes that are located in designated hazard or "flood" zones, as established by the Federal Emergency Management Agency (FEMA). Homeowners obtain the coverage through FEMA's National Flood Insurance Program. Note that while floods are covered through this program, earthquakes are not (nor are they covered by standard homeowner's policies). However, earthquake insurance is usually obtainable through what is known as an **endorsement** to a homeowner's insurance policy. To find out about adding earthquake insurance to your policy, consult your insurance agent or broker.

Title Insurance

This is a policy that protects both buyer and lender by assuring them that the person who is passing on the title—typically the seller—has the legal right to do so. **Title insurance** kicks in if the title is "clouded" by someone else's claim to some or all of the value of the home. A past debt burden that was legally filed as a lien, for example, can obscure the title on a home and create issues for the person trying to pass that title along to the buyer. (See chapter 10 for more on this subject.)

Closing Costs

Buyers will incur certain costs, beyond the home's sale price, as part of the home purchase itself. These closing costs may affect how much home a buyer can afford. Closing costs are comprised of various fees we'll be discussing throughout this book, including home inspection fees, appraisal fees, loan-origination fees, discount points, title-search expenses, purchase of a home warranty, tax service fees, wire transfer fees, and (if it's required in your area) attorney's fees or other professional service costs.

The borrower may negotiate to share some or all of these costs with the seller, as agreed upon in the purchase agreement. We cover closing in detail in chapter 10.

The "Other" Home-Buying Costs

It's all too tempting to think that once your down payment has been made, escrow closed, and settlement completed, that you're done with out-of-pocket expenses associated with homeownership. But there are other expenses that should be factored into the equation, including utility hookup and/or transfer costs, deposit(s) for new telephone service, and other fees that you may not have considered.

The cost of keeping up a home can be substantial as well, depending on the condition and age of the property and just how many updates or remodeling projects you intend to undertake. Such costs include everything from replacing worn-out carpets and updating kitchens, to replacing furnaces, water softeners, circuit breakers, and other systems. In addition to the value of your time when you search for and move into a new home, there are short-term costs associated with relocating.

Utility Service Connection Fees

Water, electricity, cable, and phone companies generally charge between $25 and $100 to hook up service to your new home, depending on the company itself and the going rate in the area. These fees are often included in your first bill—or, pro-rated over your first few invoices—and should be taken into consideration when purchasing a home.

Deposits

The same utility companies that charge hookup fees will sometimes ask for up-front deposits to establish service. These charges will often be waived if you have favorable credit, or if you've already been doing business with the company in question. Don't forget to ask for free installation deals, which many of today's telecommunications companies (cable, telephone, Internet service, and so forth) are offering as a result of increased competition for customers.

Commuting

Perhaps you'll no longer be taking mass transit to get work once you move. If that's the case, you may need to consider buying a car—and then, of course, you'll need to factor in the cost of fuel and car insurance. Or, you may need to purchase a rail pass for your daily commute to work, which may cost more than what you're currently paying to get to the office. Take all these expenses into account when determining how much you can—and want to—spend each month on your mortgage.

Changing the Locks

You don't want to move into a home knowing that the previous owner—or anyone else, for that matter—may have the keys to your new abode. To get the locks changed, you'll need to hire a locksmith, who will charge about $12 to $30 per lock to change the pins in your lock cylinders. Or, if you find that it's cheaper, change the locks on your own by installing new doorknobs and dead bolts.

Licenses and Registration

If you're moving to a new state, don't forget to consider the costs of new motor vehicle licenses and registrations after the move. Here are a few things to think about:

- Most states require residents to register their automobiles within ten to thirty days of moving. You'll need to pay for new license plates ($12 and up) plus vehicle registration fees, which are tied to the weight or price of the car (generally $20 to $80, depending on location).

- You'll also have to get a new driver's license, which will probably set you back about $20 to $70, plus time spent at the Department of Motor Vehicles getting your photo taken.

- If you have any business or professional licenses (such as an engineering license or a medical license), you'll also have to get those transferred to your new state and/or county. The costs of doing so vary greatly, depending on your profession, and you may need to take qualifying exams in your new state to practice there as well. The cost of these exams varies from state to state.

Decorating Expenses

It's not uncommon for a new homeowner to pay an initial lump sum for important items like window treatments, shower curtains, furniture, and appliances. If you were previously renting a smaller residence, for example, then your new home may look empty once you move your belongings into it.

Food and Supplies

Depending on how far you're moving, you may need to throw out a great deal of food and related items, such as perishable goods that may spill or spoil during transit. This means restocking these goods when you get to your new home. Expect to pay at least the cost of your typical grocery order to stock the refrigerator, plus the cost of spices, condiments, and other necessities that you may not transport.

Depending on your individual situation, there may be other costs associated with moving as well. If you have a child in preschool, for example, then you'll need to pay any initiation fees and up-front costs associated with getting her into a new school. If you're going to join a workout center or gym, then you'll need to pay the initial membership fees. The list of extra costs can be kept manageable by listing the expenses in order of importance and tackling them one by one as they come due.

How Much Can You Afford?

Just how much house can you afford? Answering this question early in the home-buying process will help you make the right housing choice for your lifestyle and financial situation. A sensible home-buying strategy takes into account how much of your savings you will put toward a down payment, what percentage of your income you want to devote to a mortgage, how quickly you want to pay off a mortgage, and what additional costs you will pay regularly to own the home. These factors also determine the amount you may be eligible to borrow for a mortgage.

And just how big will that monthly mortgage payment be? Here's a basic—although by no means definitive—way to estimate your mortgage payment: First consider the size of the loan you will need. If you're unsure of the range you should be using, read the section in chapter 1 on researching properties in different neighborhoods. Or, you can consult a real estate agent to get an idea of what your "dream home" will cost you.

Next, figure out how large a down payment you can make, and subtract that from the total price. For example, for a $200,000 home, a 20 percent down payment will be $40,000, requiring you to finance $160,000. Finally, decide on a term for your mortgage (thirty years is a standard term) and research the going interest rate in your newspaper or through a reputable online source, such as www.freddiemac.com. With these numbers in hand, consult the Monthly Mortgage Calculator found in Table 2.1. Multiply your desired loan amount by the corresponding figure on the chart, and then divide by 1,000. So, in this example, a $160,000 loan at 7 percent interest over thirty years will cost $1,064 a month in principal and interest payments. And then, of course, you will need to add in taxes and insurance costs.

Table 2.1: Source: Bank of America. This table provided for illustration purposes only; the monthly payment on your loan may differ. The monthly payment is an estimate of the principal and interest per $1,000 of your loan, and does not include other charges. We assumed a 20% down payment was made; if less than 20%, mortgage insurance is required and an additional monthly fee would apply. Estimated payments are rounded, and are not intended to offer any advice or assure your eligibility for any product offered by Bank of America, its affiliates or any other financial institution. The mortgage amount that you may qualify for will depend on your credit history and debt-to-income and loan-to-value ratios.

TABLE 2.1 MONTHLY MORTGAGE CALCULATOR

Rate	Term (in years)					
	5	10	15	20	25	30
	per $1000	per $1000	per $1000	per $1000	per $1000	per $1000
5.000%	$18.87	$10.61	$7.91	$6.60	$5.85	$5.37
5.250%	$18.99	$10.73	$8.04	$6.74	$5.99	$5.52
5.500%	$19.10	$10.85	$8.17	$6.88	$6.14	$5.68
5.750%	$19.22	$10.98	$8.30	$7.02	$6.29	$5.84
6.000%	$19.33	$11.10	$8.44	$7.16	$6.44	$6.00
6.250%	$19.45	$11.23	$8.57	$7.31	$6.60	$6.16
6.500%	$19.57	$11.35	$8.71	$7.46	$6.75	$6.32
6.750%	$19.68	$11.48	$8.85	$7.60	$6.91	$6.49
7.000%	$19.80	$11.61	$8.99	$7.75	$7.07	$6.65
7.250%	$19.92	$11.74	$9.13	$7.90	$7.23	$6.82
7.500%	$20.04	$11.87	$9.27	$8.06	$7.39	$6.99
7.750%	$20.16	$12.00	$9.41	$8.21	$7.55	$7.16
8.000%	$20.28	$12.13	$9.56	$8.36	$7.72	$7.34
8.250%	$20.40	$12.27	$9.70	$8.52	$7.88	$7.51
8.500%	$20.52	$12.40	$9.85	$8.68	$8.05	$7.69
8.750%	$20.64	$12.53	$9.99	$8.84	$8.22	$7.87
9.000%	$20.76	$12.67	$10.14	$9.00	$8.39	$8.05
9.250%	$20.88	$12.80	$10.29	$9.16	$8.56	$8.23
9.500%	$21.00	$12.94	$10.44	$9.32	$8.74	$8.41
9.750%	$21.12	$13.08	$10.59	$9.49	$8.91	$8.59
10.000%	$21.25	$13.22	$10.75	$9.65	$9.09	$8.78
10.250%	$21.37	$13.35	$10.90	$9.82	$9.26	$8.96
10.500%	$21.49	$13.49	$11.05	$9.98	$9.44	$9.15
10.750%	$21.62	$13.63	$11.21	$10.15	$9.62	$9.33
11.000%	$21.74	$13.78	$11.37	$10.32	$9.80	$9.52
11.250%	$21.87	$13.92	$11.52	$10.49	$9.98	$9.71
11.500%	$21.99	$14.06	$11.68	$10.66	$10.16	$9.90
11.750%	$22.12	$14.20	$11.84	$10.84	$10.35	$10.09
12.000%	$22.24	$14.35	$12.00	$11.01	$10.53	$10.29

Will You Qualify?

As we've discussed, when buying a house, you will be faced with several new expenses, which you should take into account when determining how much house you can afford. These costs may include your monthly mortgage payment; annual property tax obligations; annual, quarterly, or monthly insurance payments; and home maintenance costs, both in the form of regular upkeep and isolated repairs. Lenders are aware of these additional expenses and typically will take them into account when deciding how much to offer you as a mortgage amount.

Most lenders will only lend a part of the price of the home to the buyer. Mortgage lenders commonly use what are known as **qualifying ratios** to figure out just how large a mortgage you can afford. Qualifying ratios compare a buyer's income against a combination of certain financial elements of a mortgage, including mortgage principal, interest, taxes, and insurance. Not every lender uses the same qualifying ratios.

Although the rules for mortgage companies and their underwriters may vary slightly regarding how they qualify a borrower, for the purposes of this book, we will use a conservative approach. Two ratios are computed and analyzed for each loan application—a ratio for housing expenses and a ratio for debt. The first ratio is derived by dividing the anticipated monthly payment (including principal, interest, taxes, and insurance [PITI]) by the borrower's **gross monthly income** (GMI). The resulting ratio should not be greater than 28 percent if the down payment is less than 20 percent. For down payments of 20 percent or more, the ratio should not exceed 30 percent. For example, if a buyer's annual household income is $55,000, then his gross monthly income is approximately $4,583, and his maximum conventional loan housing expense (at 30 percent) would be about $1,375. In this case, the lender will likely be willing to make a loan for $1,375 or less a month.

Ready for some more number-crunching? In addition to limiting the percentage of your income that can be paid exclusively toward housing expenses, most lenders restrict your total housing and *non-housing* debts as well. The second ratio is found by dividing the borrower's total monthly debt obligations by the applicant's gross monthly income. That includes credit card payments, student loans, and so forth. This ratio should not be more than 36 percent regardless of the down payment. So, taking the case of the buyer mentioned above, whose gross monthly income is $4,583, his total allowable debt would be approximately $1,650.

Here's one example of how qualifying ratios work:

Gross monthly income (GMI):	$4,583
Total allowable housing costs (GMI x 30 percent) =	$1,375
Total allowable monthly debt (GMI x 36 percent) =	$1,650
Home purchase price:	$100,000
Down payment: (20 percent of home's sales price)	$20,000
Mortgage amount needed:	$80,000
Monthly loan principal and interest payment: (Based on 7 percent interest on a thirty-year loan)	$532
Monthly property tax and insurance payments:	$200
Other monthly debt (car payments, credit card payments, etc.):	$600
Total monthly debt:	**$1,332**

In this example, the borrower would qualify for the loan he is seeking, based on qualifying ratios. This is because his total monthly debt ($1,332) is less than 36 percent of his GMI ($1,650), as required by this lender. See the worksheet on page 47 to evaluate your own financial situation using these formulas.

Be aware that this is just a hypothetical estimate of how lenders will balance your debts and income to come up with a feasible answer to the question of how much you can afford to borrow. The above ratios are intended as guidelines and can vary slightly from lender to lender and are sometimes influenced by market conditions. In some areas of the country, for example, property taxes on a $100,000 home may be much higher (or much lower) than the amount estimated above. Homeowner's insurance may be higher in some areas where extreme weather, such as hurricanes or tornadoes, has cost the insurance company money to make home repairs following a natural disaster. Speak to your real estate agent, lender, insurance provider, and property tax assessor before plugging any of these numbers into your own equation.

Mortgages come in many different shapes and sizes, and these variations can affect mortgage affordability. For example, if a property has a high appraised

Now try plugging in your own financial data to see what your monthly housing payments might be (based on what you would like to borrow) and to assess if you might be likely to qualify for a conventional loan:

Monthly Income: _____

Total allowable housing costs (GMI X 28 percent): _____

Total allowable monthly debt (GMI X 36 percent): _____

Estimated Monthly Expenses:

Mortgage payment (principal and interest): _____

Property taxes: _____

Insurance: _____

Total housing expenses: _____

Other monthly debt: _____

Total monthly expenses: _____

Worried that you won't qualify for the loan you'd like? In the next chapter, we'll discuss ways to reduce your debt and improve your financial picture.

value, compared to the mortgage amount that the buyer is seeking, the mortgage interest on that property may be lower—because the mortgage lender's risk in making the loan is relatively low. A buyer with a mortgage that is paid off in a shorter period of time (for example, over fifteen years rather than thirty years) may have a higher monthly payment, while paying less interest over the life of the mortgage.

Doing the Math

As you can see, the mortgage-lending process is a real numbers game. It involves salary numbers, credit scores, savings account balances, investment account statements, and other financial factors. If you enjoy working with numbers and would like to figure out some of the basic mortgage calculations on your own, then you're in luck. Mortgage lenders use a few fundamental equations to figure out where their customers stand, and you can use them, too. Here are the most popular:

- **Cash Required:** This is how much your closing costs and down payment come to when added together. It's the funds needed for you to close on your home.

  Cash Required = Total Closing Costs + Down Payment

- **Debt Ratio:** This is the portion of your monthly income that can be applied toward monthly long-term debt obligations, such as a mortgage. Different lenders use different debt-ratio guidelines, depending on the loans they offer, but most determine your debt ratio by dividing your principal, interest, property tax, insurance payments, and other non-housing-related costs **(PITIO)** by your monthly income. Government home-loan programs tend to have higher debt-ratio percentages (thus allowing more home buyers to qualify for loans).

  Debt Ratio = PITIO ÷ by Total Monthly Income

- **Down Payment:** This is the difference between the home's sale price and the total loan amount. It's the up-front cash that's required at closing (for example, a 10 percent down payment on a $150,000 home would be $15,000 down at closing).

  Down Payment = Home Sale Price − Loan Amount

- **Front-End Ratio:** This is the percentage of your monthly income that can be applied to your monthly housing payments. Lenders have different ways of determining this ratio, but, in general, they divide the PITI amount of the property by your monthly income. As with debt ratios, government home-loan programs tend to have higher front-end ratios, which allow more home buyers to qualify for homes.

  Front-End Ratio = PITI ÷ Total Monthly Income

- **Maximum Loan Amount:** This figure represents the total loan amount that a lender offers a buyer, based on factors such as income, debt, and cash available for a down payment. For example, a lender offering to finance a $200,000 home may approve a maximum loan amount of $160,000—or 80 percent of the property's value. That means the buyer must pay the remaining 20 percent ($40,000) as a down payment. It's even possible, although less common, for a lender to approve a maximum amount as high as 98 percent of the home's value. (Remember that just because a lender approves a higher maximum loan amount doesn't mean that you should necessarily borrow that much. You should still opt for a loan amount that makes sense for you.)

  Maximum Loan Amount = Lesser of Home Sale Price or Appraised Value x Loan-to-Value (LTV) Percentage

- **PITI:** This is the sum of principal, interest, property taxes, and insurance payments. For homeowners who have taken out a "PITI" mortgage, all these fees are included in the monthly mortgage payment (as opposed to having to pay insurance and taxes out of pocket, when the bills come in).

  PITI = Principal + Interest + Property Tax + Insurance

- **PITIO:** This figure represents the sum of principal, interest, taxes, insurance, and other monthly non-housing costs.

  PITIO = Principal + Interest + Property Tax + Insurance + Total Other Costs

Online Loan Calculators

As part of your research, you can use certain Web sites to plug in your own numbers and quickly come up with a rough estimate of how much you'll be able to borrow. There are a number of financial calculators available online that can help you evaluate how much home you can afford, what your monthly mortgage payments may look like, and other important factors. The Web sites of many banking institutions include pages where you can quickly and easily enter loan information to determine how much you'd be able to borrow. RE/MAX provides loan calculation tools online at www.remax.com, in its "Residential" section. Fannie Mae, a private, shareholder-owned company that works to make sure mortgage money is available for people in communities nationwide, also provides online calculators.

Here are Web addresses for a few specific online loan calculators:

- **RE/MAX**

  http://www.remax.com/residential/mortgage_tools/index.htm

- **Ginnie Mae**

  www.ginniemae.gov/2_prequal/intro_questions.asp?Section=YPTH

- **Fannie Mae**

  www.mortgagecontent.net/scApplication/fanniemae/affordability.do

- **Freddie Mac**

  http://www.freddiemac.com/corporate/buyown/english/calcs_tools/

You may want to add the above URLs to your Web browser's list of Favorites and consult them as you begin searching for affordable homes in your target area(s).

Dollars and Sense

Sure you qualify for that $500,000 home, but do you really need it or want it? That's a question that Rosalie Daniels, broker-owner at Hamilton, New Jersey–based RE/MAX Tri County, often asks her buyers, particularly those whose financial situations qualify them for high-end homes.

"Buyers really need to look at what they can afford versus what they'll be comfortable in, and what they can reasonably maintain," says Daniels. If, for example, a family shells out thousands of dollars to take three or four ski vacations to Colorado every year, would it be worth it to give that up in order to purchase a higher-priced home?

"These questions go beyond the basic calculation; it's about looking at your lifestyle and comfort level to figure out what price ranges truly fit what you're looking for," says Daniels. "Just because someone qualifies for a certain home, that doesn't mean it's going to be comfortable for them."

Where Daniels also sees buyers facing challenges is in producing accurate pictures of their financial futures. The young couple who want to start raising a family in the near future, for example, should consider what kind of income they'll be living on should one parent stop working to care for the child(ren). As Daniels notes, "They should plan for the fact that they might have to make house payments from one income, instead of two."

It's important to take these and other lifestyle factors into consideration when poring over your calculations, since mere numbers themselves don't paint an accurate picture of exactly what you can afford to pay—or should pay—for a home. In deciding how much you want to spend on housing each month, don't forget to take into account these expenses you may want to plan for:

- Vacations
- Contingency money in case you or your partner lose your job
- Dining out and entertainment (and money for the baby-sitter!)
- The possibility of you or your partner returning to school
- Money for other financial investments
- A cash reserve to handle any home maintenance or repair bills that might come up
- Funds for your children's education

While you want to purchase your ideal home, you don't want to sacrifice the things you most enjoy, or the things that add to your security, to afford it. Always remember to look at the complete picture as you plan to buy your home.

Calculating Moves

To get the best idea of what you can afford when buying a home, work through some of the calculations discussed in this chapter—either online or off—before filling out a loan application or spending time looking at homes that are outside your price range. Doing your homework first will give you a good feel for exactly where you stand, and help ward off any surprises down the road. Take some time with these basic calculations, and tap one or more of the Internet's user-friendly calculation tools. As a result, you'll find that you're much better prepared when it comes time to apply for your mortgage loan.

Next, we'll examine your financial house to see if it's in order and reveal steps you can take right now to get closer to that down payment, resolve any existing credit blemishes, and improve your chances of qualifying for a loan when you're eventually ready to obtain financing.

CHAPTER THREE

The Fiscal Fitness Challenge

Now that you've seen all the costs involved in buying a home, you may be feeling slightly intimidated. Don't be! According to the U.S. Census Bureau, by the end of 2005 Americans owned more than 75 million homes. Like the millions of Americans who are already homeowners, you too will work through the process and reach your dreams of homeownership.

As you begin the home-buying process, it's important to realize that there are plenty of actions you can take now to reach your down payment goals by the time you're ready to buy. In this chapter, we'll discuss various options open to you as you strive for the financial targets you started setting in chapter 2. Likewise, we'll explore the many proactive steps you can take to clean up your credit and improve the likelihood that you'll qualify for the loan you'll need to move into that dream home. Also in this chapter, we'll examine the paperwork you should have in order—and you should review beforehand—to put you on the fast track to getting a loan.

Ideally, you should start this process about six months before applying for a home mortgage, to give yourself time to improve your financial situation before a **mortgage broker** or bank reviews your application. Inaccurate credit reports can take time to clear up, for example, as can any arrangements that need to be made with current debtors or other lien holders. You may also need some time to save for a down payment, or arrange for resources (with family, for example) that you'll be tapping for your down payment. The earlier you start getting your financial house in order, the better shape you'll be in when you're ready to search for a home. It's time to get fiscally fit.

A Penny Saved . . .

One way to convince a mortgage lender that your credit and finances are stable enough to qualify for a loan is by establishing and sticking to a household budget based on your monthly income, your investment portfolio, and your current and anticipated future expenditures. A budget also can help you plan and control your month-to-month cash flow as well as keep you on track to buy your new home.

There are a number of software programs available on the market today to help you manage your finances. Or, if you prefer, you can use the sample budget worksheet on page 55 as a model. In this example, you first make projections for the upcoming month, and then compare those projections to the "actual" amounts received or spent.

By taking the time to create this estimate of income and expenses, or by using a software program that does this for you automatically, you'll get a good handle on how much you can afford to spend in mortgage payments and see clearly what price home you can realistically afford.

Alternative Sources of Funding

Not all homeowners can come up with hefty down payments for their homes, but that doesn't stop them from getting the properties they want. If you're having difficulty putting together that initial down payment, you may want to consider some of the following helpful resources.

WORKSHEET   YOUR MONTHLY BUDGET

Category	Budgeted Amount	Actual Amount	Difference
Income			
Wages/salary			
Interest income			
Income Subtotal			
Expenses:			
Housing payment			
Taxes			
Food			
Utilities			
Transportation			
Educational expenses			
Entertainment			
Miscellaneous/Other			
Total Expenses			
Net Income (Income minus Expenses)			

Friends and Family

One of the first options to explore is getting financial help from friends or family, who may be allowed to contribute a certain percentage toward your down payment, if your lender permits it. (Note that some lenders don't allow buyers to use "gift" money towards a down payment; others may require buyers to disclose just how much of the money has been gifted to them.) Check with your lender for specifics on amassing your down payment this way. Getting a loan from a loved one comes with certain benefits: It's easy to qualify for, and will typically be either low-interest or interest-free. While this prospect sounds tempting, only you can decide whether you're comfortable being in debt to your father-in-law, or hearing endless stories at family gatherings about how your sister helped you get your first home. Be sure to weigh the pros and cons of this option, and always approach the situation in a professional, respectful manner, regardless of how close you are to the relative or friend who is doling out the money. It's generally advisable to work out the loan terms in writing, even if you're borrowing from friends or family. That way, everyone involved knows what they're getting into, and what their respective roles are. You may also want to consult with an attorney on this issue, to help clearly spell out the financial terms of the deal.

Your IRA

Tapping into your Individual Retirement Account (IRA) is another way to secure the funds you need. As a first-time home buyer, you may be able to withdraw up to $10,000 from a traditional IRA for a down payment on a primary residence without having to pay a penalty fee for early withdrawal (which is generally imposed whenever you take money designated for retirement prior to age 59½). This $10,000 limit is a lifetime limit, so if you have withdrawn money from your IRA in the past, the amount you can withdraw now without penalty may be lower. (Note that for holders of Roth IRAs, the rules for qualified distributions are slightly different.) Once you exceed this $10,000 ceiling, penalty fees will apply.

These allowances are made for first-time homeowners only, and the IRS has strict rules about who qualifies for this status. In addition, there may be certain tax implications involved in withdrawing money from your traditional IRA. To learn more about the IRS rules governing these transactions, visit www.irs.gov. As always, consult a qualified professional before making any important financial decisions.

Special Programs for Home Buyers

Down payment assistance and advice, as well as alternative loan options, may also be available for first-time home buyers and home buyers with certain backgrounds, such as veterans of the U.S. armed services. Here are some resources you can use to find such information:

- **Department of Veterans Affairs Loans (VA Home Loans):** Available to veterans of the U.S. armed forces, these loans are made by private lenders, such as banks, savings and loans, or mortgage companies to eligible veterans for the purchase of a home. Applicable for homes purchased for the veteran's personal occupancy, these loans are sometimes made without any down payment at all and generally feature lower interest rates than those ordinarily available with other kinds of loans.

- **Housing Counseling:** Contact your local Housing and Urban Development (HUD) office for information on housing counseling, down-payment assistance, grant programs, and other tools available to home buyers. You can call HUD's national office at 800–569–4287 for more information, or visit www.hud.gov/offices/hsg/sfh/hcc/hccprof14.cfm for a state-by-state list of contacts.

- **Community Home-Buyer Programs:** Contact your local city, county, and state housing bureaus for information about first-time home-buyer programs in your area. Some of these groups offer programs that require just 3 percent down if the primary buyer is a first-time home buyer. Check with these programs to determine how a "first-time" home buyer is defined. For example, an individual or family who has owned a home in the past, but not within the last three years, may also qualify as a first-time home buyer.

Opportunities are also available at the state and local level. In Florida, for example, the State Housing Initiatives Partnership (SHIP) program provides funds directly to local governments to increase affordable housing opportunities in their communities. SHIP lends money to buyers at no interest for thirty years, and with a very low down payment. Buyers must attend a home-buyer education class, meet specific income guidelines, contribute a small percentage of the sales price (usually 1 percent) to the transaction in the form of a down payment, and purchase a home priced at or below SHIP's current guidelines.

As an example of a local program, consider the Chicago Department of Housing's New Homes for Chicago Program. With an eye toward creating home-ownership opportunities for city residents, the program encourages developers to construct new homes for purchase by moderate-income, working individuals and families. The city offers business incentives that reduce developers' costs, in addition to providing purchase-price assistance to eligible families up to a certain, predetermined amount. Qualified buyers can obtain mortgages for these properties through the City Mortgage Assistance Program.

Consult your local real estate agent, city or state office that handles homeownership programs, or the Internet (search for *first time home buyer*) for more information on these programs or other similar opportunities.

Using One Home to Fund Another

A homeowner looking to purchase a new property often uses some or all of the equity in his current home as a down payment. This "rolling over" of money from one home to the next is a common practice, and it can help minimize the financial impact of "moving up" into a larger home. For example, say you purchased a $150,000 home in 1998 and sold it in 2006 for a $75,000 profit (after paying off the mortgage). You may opt to reinvest that money in real estate by putting that $75,000 toward the down payment for your new home.

Luckily for homeowners, the tax laws relating to home-sale profits are fairly generous. When selling a primary residence, single owners can realize up to $250,000 in profit—the cap is $500,000 for married homeowners—before owing any capital gains taxes. (The capital gains tax is a federal levy on the difference between your investment in your property [or any other investment asset] and the amount you receive upon its sale.) Consult your financial advisor or attorney on how best to handle this rollover from a tax standpoint.

Keep in mind that this strategy requires you first to sell your current home, receive the profit check from that house, and then use some or all of it to pay for your new home. It's a fairly seamless process, except for one sticking point: The original home sale must be closed before that money becomes liquid, and ready to use toward the new purchase (this can be done at closing). Talk to your real estate agent about how appropriate this approach would be in your own situation.

Another option for current homeowners is the **bridge loan,** which homeowners often use to cover both mortgages during that "in between" period when one home is being sold and another is being purchased. Terms for these loans can vary, with some designed to pay off the original home's mortgage and others simply mixing the old debt with the new. Because these loans often fetch high fees and interest rates, you'll want to weigh all of your options (such as borrowing against a 401[k]), before taking one out.

Through the Lender's Eyes

In chapter 2 we covered qualifying ratios, which allow lenders to assess how much they are willing to lend a loan applicant. However, there are other factors that lenders consider when determining if you qualify for a loan. Depending on your individual situation, a lender may review your overall financial picture (and that of anyone else who will be listed as a cosigner on the mortgage papers), focusing on the following items:

- Job history, including the length of time and salary you earned at each job
- Current employment information
- Credit history, including both accurate and inaccurate credit "blemishes" that appear on your credit report
- Savings or other resources you may be able to tap for down-payment funds
- Your total liabilities (or money that you regularly owe), including monthly credit card obligations, car payments, contractual cell phone bills, student loan(s), and alimony and/or child-support payments
- Your history of making payments on outstanding debts, such as other mortgages, monthly rent, credit card balances, and automobile loans

- A household budget that correctly reflects how your money is earned, spent, and saved
- Any other important financial information that could affect your ability to purchase a home and pay back the mortgage

All these factors are important to lenders because they illustrate an applicant's ability to establish good credit, hold down a job, and pay bills—all representative, in theory, of a person's ability to pay off a mortgage over a period of time.

If you're currently renting, lenders will likely ask your landlord about your reliability. Be prepared for this thorough look into your payment history and know where you stand before the process begins. Whether you've been paying rent to a landlord, writing monthly checks to a roommate, or paying off a mortgage on another home, the **home-loan underwriter** (the person who accepts and rejects mortgage applications) will want to know just how well you've done at paying those monthly obligations. Since housing payments are generally thought to be the largest monthly payment shelled out by an individual or family, they serve as a good gauge of your future ability (and willingness) to pay off your mortgage, as agreed. Remember that lenders want to issue you a loan in exchange for as little risk as possible. As such, when they examine your payment history, ideally they are looking for no late payments within the last twelve months, the maximum of one late payment within the last twenty-four months, and an overall history of making housing payments a priority.

Painting Your Financial Picture

Oftentimes, people become so excited about buying a home that they want to pick up the phone, call a real estate agent, and start lining up showings at homes currently for sale. While this part of the process is fun, that's not the best way to go about house hunting. First, you should gather information on your finances and put all your paperwork in order. By getting a handle on your income, expenses, and debts, you'll have a much better idea of what you can afford and how much you'll need to borrow before you fall in love with that front-hall colonial that's way out of your reach.

Tracking Your Progress

When you buy a home, lenders expect you to have completed your personal financial review before coming to them for a preapproval letter, which basically states that—based on the information you've provided—you can indeed afford that $250,000 beauty you've had your eye on for the last few months. Now—not later, when you're in the middle of negotiating a purchase contract—is the time to take a deep breath, gather the documentation you'll need, spread it out on the kitchen table, and get a good grasp of your own financial picture.

As you (and whoever else will be listed on the mortgage papers) review the last ten or so years' worth of your financial data, pay particular attention to the following documents, which the lender will likely require you to present in order to obtain a mortgage:

- **Paycheck stubs:** Lenders are most concerned with average income, so that means not only this week's paycheck, but also the pay stubs accumulated over the last two years. And while steady employment is an attractive quality in a candidate for a mortgage, it's not the be-all and end-all. If you've changed jobs on a frequent basis, just be ready to explain why.

- **Tax returns:** A lender might ask to see past income tax forms that you have filed. If you haven't retained copies of your tax returns for those years, you can request them from your local IRS office. If you're self-employed, especially, you should have tax returns handy for lender review to substantiate any salary information you provide. Lenders will pay special attention to the adjusted gross income on which taxes were paid over the last one to two years (not just the gross income of the business itself).

- **Credit report:** Like it or not, much of the decision making that goes into the lending process revolves around your credit report (and that of anyone else who will be listed on the mortgage papers along with you). The lender will charge about $50 to pull your credit report, although the three large credit reporting agencies have created a site at www.annualcreditreport.com where consumers can access their own reports online once every twelve months for free. (See pages 68–72 for more information on credit reports.)

- **Bank statements:** When reviewing your loan application, lenders will probably ask for copies of your most recent bank statements. What are they looking for?

They want to see a steady history of savings and a bank balance that reflects well-managed finances. They're looking to make sure that bouncing checks is a rare or nonexistent occurrence in your financial life.

- **Alimony, child support, or other income:** If you receive monthly payments for child support or as part of a divorce settlement, you'll likely be able to include these figures as part of your gross income. Dig out that court settlement (or divorce decree) as proof of this income. Likewise, the lender will want to review any 1099s or other proof of freelance or part-time income that you include on your loan application. Lenders generally want to see verification of these payment or income amounts before incorporating them into your overall financial picture.

- **Dividends and investments:** When evaluating income level, lenders typically consider your investment portfolio, plus any long-term investment dividends, as part of your income. Keep year-end statements (typically issued every January) handy, as well as your latest monthly or quarterly statement.

- **Liabilities:** As we discussed in chapter 2, to qualify for the best possible mortgage rates, your liabilities (which include car payments, credit card payments, mortgage loans, student loans, and alimony and child support that you're obligated to pay) shouldn't exceed a certain percentage of your income, typically around 36 percent. Pull out your monthly bills, add them up, and then compare the total to your monthly income. If you filled out the worksheet on page 55, you've already completed this step.

- **Assets and reserves:** Lenders like to see that you have at least two months' worth of PITI payments on hand (three months' worth is even better). Other assets, such as IRAs and CDs, can be included in this total, but only at 60 to 70 percent of their value—factoring in liquidation costs and early withdrawal penalties.

With these documents and other pertinent information at your fingertips, you'll bewell equipped to discuss the home-buying process with your real estate agent, lender, or other professional who will be helping you through the process. Better yet, you'll have a good idea of exactly where you stand financially before getting into the buying process.

Reviewing Your Records

Now that you've collected all the documents you'll need, what do you do with this mass of paperwork? Being surrounded by tax returns, credit reports, and pay stubs can be downright daunting for most of us, but there are a few steps you can take to break this review down into a more manageable process.

Start by reviewing your salary history, asking yourself the following questions. Be sure to include answers for any co-borrowers as well:

- Are there any gaps in my employment history? If so, can I explain them in a way that a lender would (a) believe and (b) understand?

- Has my salary remained steady over the last five to ten years? If it has fluctuated, can I explain why? (If you were working for a dot-com firm in the late '90s, for example, then a lender who knows market trends would understand a gap in employment and/or a salary decrease between 2000 and the present.)

- Over the last five to ten years, have I demonstrated my ability to hold down a job and make a respectable wage?

- What are my prospects of keeping this present job (or beginning a new job) at my current salary level or higher over the next two to five years? The answer to this one will help you personally; the lender won't ask you to predict your employability. However, for your own peace of mind you'll want to know that you'll indeed be able to afford the home you're buying.

If you're self-employed, lenders will likely also ask for a current profit-and-loss statement, and will compare year-over-year figures to establish your ability to pay off the mortgage. Again, if your profits and losses have fluctuated over the last few years, be sure to have a believable and understandable explanation as to why that has happened and how you expect to maintain profitability going forward.

Next, you'll want to assemble a set of your past pay stubs, tax returns, and/or bank statements for lender review. Since you've done the work to put the documents together, be sure to make a copy to protect against any of them being misplaced. And, while there's not much you can do at this point to change your past tax or job situation, it's helpful if you at least have these documents ready to go when the lender asks for them.

Finally, keep in mind that you should only hand over those documents that the lender actually requests (unless, for some reason, you feel it would help your case to provide additional paperwork). Inundating lenders with papers that may or may not be relevant to your application opens the way for them to find something to disqualify you. And be ready to promptly answer any inquiries that the mortgage company might have.

Survival Toolkit

Preparation Is Key

It is important to have your financial ducks all in a row before going into the home-buying process. Pat Murphy, manager of RE/MAX Town and Country in Rutland, Vermont, says that not all buyers are ready to take on the task. Some are unsure of their credit scores; others don't have a firm grip on their personal financial affairs. These kinds of uncertainties can lead to more significant challenges down the line, says Murphy, who adds that the buyer who is unsure of his financial picture also won't be well equipped to negotiate when the time comes.

"Too many buyers say, 'Well, I'll make an offer on the house, and then I'll come back later to see if the financing comes through,'" Murphy explains, noting that this is the wrong way to go about house hunting.

Instead, a buyer should research his credit score and financing options, including finding lenders who can provide him with a prequalification and/or preapproval letter. (See chapter 7 for more information on these letters.)

In areas where desirable homes sell within just a few days (or even less), being able to act—and react—quickly is critical. Having a solid, organized financial plan makes the task all that much easier. "Being financially prepared means transactions can go forward quickly, making the offer more appealing to the seller and increasing the buyer's chance of getting the home that she really wants," Murphy notes.

Lack of Credit or Payment History

You may be wondering, "What if I don't have a financial history?" If you've always lived with your parents, just graduated from college, and/or never had a credit card of your own, for example, then your financial house isn't just empty, it's non-existent. While you might think that lenders would find this "clean slate" status appealing, the reality is that it's difficult to make a large loan like a mortgage to someone who hasn't at least established credit and payment histories. Since lenders tend to be "historical" in nature (looking more closely at what you've done financially over the last five to ten years than at your potential earnings or ability to pay), the borrower without a track record poses special challenges.

If you don't have a credit history, consider yourself a "non-traditional" borrower. If you're looking to buy within the next month or two, your best bet may be to speak with a real estate agent about the possibilities. He or she can point you in the direction of a good mortgage broker. Mortgage brokers specialize in matching people with unusual credit situations with lenders who are willing to make loans to those who don't fit the parameters of the "typical home buyer." Remember to be realistic during this process, and realize that a lack of job and/or housing payment history will need to be offset by a large down payment (of 20 percent or more).

The good news is that a plethora of creative financing options has emerged over the last few years. In an effort to grow their loan portfolios and expand homeownership opportunities, lenders have developed a number of programs targeting first-time buyers or those with questionable credit histories.

The Bankruptcy Challenge

Individuals who have filed for bankruptcy face special challenges when they want to buy a home. On the one hand, they are operating with a clean slate, in that much of their debt was wiped clean. On the other hand, there's a perception that someone who declared bankruptcy once may be compelled to do so again, thus increasing the lender's risk when issuing a mortgage loan. With that in mind, lenders considering loans to those with a history of bankruptcy will be looking for:

- Positive income verification. Put simply: You make more than enough money to cover your bills, including your new mortgage.

- A history of paying off your debts since the bankruptcy was finalized. If the bankruptcy was discharged five years ago, for example, lenders will want to see a clean bill of health financially from that point on.

- In some cases, a two-year waiting period following the date of your bankruptcy discharge. For example, the Department of Veterans Affairs (VA) allows buyers who file for bankruptcy to apply for a VA home loan if they are eligible; however, applicants must wait two years after the discharge date of their bankruptcy to purchase another home.

- In certain instances, a larger-than-usual down payment. This is to compensate for your credit history, especially if it's been less than two years since the bankruptcy discharge.

If you're concerned that a past bankruptcy filing will place homeownership outside your reach, take heart: A wide range of creative financing options can be tapped in today's mortgage market. It may take a little more elbow grease, but the patience and diligence will pay off when you find the right lender.

Changing Life Situations

Certain life situations, such as divorce or unexpected illness, can have a negative impact on a person's financial picture. Here's a look at how these issues may affect the home-buying experience.

Divorce

While divorce was once thought of as a significant financial black eye, it is so commonplace in today's society that lenders have rewritten their rules on working with such buyers.

A recent divorce can pose challenges for a home buyer who suddenly finds that her financial situation has changed dramatically overnight. Divorce can mean a significant loss of income, particularly if she has gone from a dual-income to a single-income situation (or, if one spouse relied on the other for income). Added expenses, such as the payment of child and/or spousal support, debt that was previously shared by two people, and the cost of starting over, also come into play.

The good news is that if you already owned a home before your divorce, you may be in a favorable position for two reasons. First, you already have an established track record of mortgage payments that a lender can use when reviewing your new loan application. Second, you may have received money from the sale of the marital home, and, as a result, likely have access to sale proceeds for use as a down payment.

But even if you don't have a track record of mortgage payments on a previous home or proceeds from the sale of a home, you may still qualify for one of the many loan options available on the market today. Lenders will take into account income from all sources (including support payments, under most conditions), and will then calculate the payment that your new financial situation will allow. By way of documentation, you'll have to pull out those divorce settlement papers that you filed away, and have them ready for the lender to review, if requested. From there, the lender will come up with an interest rate and term that best suit your needs, based on a mortgage you can afford.

In Sickness and in Health

Illness and accidents are two life situations that can send your finances into a tailspin, particularly if they have prevented you (or any cosigners) from earning a living or paying bills. Mortgage lenders will factor any such gaps into the equation, and you'll likely be asked to explain why they occurred. Such questions will focus on your financial, residential, and credit history.

You may also want to consider providing proof of any prior health-related issues that affected your financial situation. Hospital bills, insurance paperwork, and accident documentation (from, say, your workplace) may help you make your case as a credit-worthy mortgage candidate, as will any other supporting documentation that you may possess concerning any past, health-related issues. Of course, you should carefully consider any privacy concerns you may have before sharing medical information with third parties.

Your Credit Report: Get Your Copy First

Credit scores play an important role in the home-buying process. Many factors contribute to your credit score, including your credit-payment history, the number of years of established credit you have, the number of inquiries the credit-reporting companies have recently received about your credit history, the total number of open revolving-credit accounts you have, and your overall credit mix. Ideally, your credit mix should show a variety of credit sources, such as bank loans, auto loans, student loans, and department store and major credit cards. These sources should preferably carry low (or zero) balances and reflect a history of timely payments.

To determine your credit score, lenders pull reports from the three major credit-reporting agencies: TransUnion, Equifax, and Experian (formerly TRW). They generally use the median score when assessing your loan application. Those scores generally take into account the following:

- Late payments on any open accounts
- The length of time since you established credit

- How long you've resided at your current home
- Your employment history
- The level of credit you've tapped versus how much available credit you have
- Any negative credit issues, such as bankruptcies or debts sent for collection.

The credit-reporting agencies generate what is known as a FICO score, which is a three-digit number representing the relative risk that a lender would assume if the lender loaned you money to purchase a home. The results range from 300 to 850. The higher the score, the more attractive a buyer appears to lenders, who

Survival Toolkit

VantageScore

In March 2006, the nation's three consumer credit reporting companies introduced a new way of reporting credit scores that they hope will make the process easier for consumers and creditors to understand and use. Known as VantageScore, it provides consumers and businesses with a score that's consistent across all of the reporting companies (whereas in the past, each used its own methodology and the scores often differed from one to the next). The system is based on the following score ranges (out of a possible 501–990):

    901–990: A
    801–900: B
    701–800: C
    601–700: D
    501–600: F

You can learn more about VantageScore online at www.vantagescore.com. The system is being marketed and sold by the three national credit reporting companies, TransUnion, Experian and Equifax.

perceive buyers with higher credit scores as less likely to default on mortgage payments. Lenders generally offer the best interest rates and mortgage products to borrowers whose credit scores are at the high end of the scale. For a FICO score to be generated, your credit report must include at least one credit account that's been open for six months or more and one credit account that has been updated (meaning that a creditor reported your payment history to the reporting agencies) within the last six months.

The term *FICO* is taken from the name of a company called Fair, Isaac and Co., which provides the credit-score formulas to the credit-reporting agencies. According to Fair, Isaac and Co., the median FICO score in the United States is 723. Borrowers with a score of 700 or more generally have a better chance of getting a loan with the best possible terms.

A FICO score below 620 is considered unfavorable, according to the nation's two largest mortgage providers, Fannie Mae and Freddie Mac. The borrower whose score falls under this threshold may still be able to obtain a mortgage but may have a hard time finding one with the best available mortgage interest rates. In some cases, the borrower may need to work with a **subprime lender**. A subprime lender is one who specializes in working with borrowers who have a history of late or missed payments and are considered by lenders to be high risk. Subprime lenders often charge more in closing costs and interest to offset the increased risk they incur with these less-than-ideal borrowers.

Historically, FICO scores were largely kept under wraps by both the credit bureaus and by the lenders who based crucial loan decisions on this data. Credit bureaus recently made the information available to the public. As a result, home buyers can find out where they stand before shopping around for loans and can take simple steps to boost their credit scores enough to make a marked difference in the loan rates and terms being offered.

To improve your credit score, you must first know where you stand. Obtain current copies of your credit reports—complete with FICO scores—from the three major credit bureaus. Contact information for each of them is provided on page 72:

Get Your Free Credit Report Here

A recent amendment to the federal Fair Credit Reporting Act (FCRA) requires that, at your request, each of the national credit bureaus provide you with a complimentary copy of your credit report once a year. In the interest of promoting accuracy and privacy of information in your file, the FCRA is strictly enforced by the Federal Trade Commission (FTC), the nation's consumer protection agency.

This is good news for consumers, who at one time had to jump through hoops to obtain this important information. Free reports became available at the end of 2004, with all states rolling out the service over the following ten months.

To make it easy for consumers, the three credit bureaus have established a central Web site, toll-free number, and mailing address where you can obtain your free reports. Here's the information you'll need to get started:

- To order online, visit www.annualcreditreport.com and fill in the information online, or complete the Annual Credit Report Request Form (available at www.ftc.gov/credit) and mail it to:
  Annual Credit Report Request Service
  P.O. Box 105281
  Atlanta, GA 30348-5281

- To order by phone call 1-877-322-8228

Through this service, you can order your credit report from each of the three nationwide credit-reporting companies at the same time, or select only one or two, if you so desire. In order to obtain your report(s), you'll be asked to provide your name, your address (and previous address, if you've moved within the last two years), your Social Security number, and your date of birth.

To ensure that your personal data is kept private, you may also be asked to provide one or two pieces of information that the agencies assume only you will know. Once you've entered the accurate information, you'll get a copy of your credit report online immediately. If you order your report through the toll-free number, the request will be processed and mailed to you within fifteen days, according to the Annual Credit Report Web site. Should you choose to download the form and send in a printed copy, be sure to factor in extra time for mailing.

Equifax Credit Information Services, Inc
P.O. Box 740241
Atlanta, GA 30374
1-888-766-0008
Web site: www.equifax.com

Experian (formerly TRW)
P.O. Box 2002
Allen, TX 75013
1-888-397-3742
Web site: www.experian.com

TransUnion LLC
P.O. Box 1000
Chester, PA 19022
1-800-888-4213
Web site: www.tuc.com

Take a look at each bureau's Web site to understand how to request a copy of your credit report and score.

Between the Lines

Once you've pored over your credit report and reviewed your credit score, it's helpful to understand how your credit score is figured. While the calculations that go into FICO scores aren't public knowledge, there are some fundamental dynamics that come into play to create your three-digit score:

- **Payment history:** The way you've handled past purchases you've financed (auto loans, mortgages, credit cards, and so forth) comprises about 35 percent of your FICO score. These calculations place greater emphasis on recent credit history than on actions from the distant past.

- **Your current debt level:** The amount of money currently outstanding on your credit cards, bank loans, or other debt makes up about 30 percent of your FICO score.

Don't Be Tempted by Quick Fixes

As you work to improve your chances of receiving a loan and a favorable interest rate, avoid companies that claim to be able to magically fix your credit score. In most cases, these companies charge a lot of money to do very little for consumers and may actually do more harm than good. Some may ask for a substantial up-front payment of fees to do the work, then "disappear" without having made any progress in fixing your credit score. Others will neglect to inform you of your legal rights or how you can address many of the problems on your own at no charge.

Steer clear of these "quick fix" promises, and focus instead on improving your credit by following the advice in this chapter. The Federal Trade Commission provides some facts for consumers on credit repair scams through its Web site at http://www.ftc.gov/bcp/conline/pubs/credit/repair.htm. The information offered at the site includes a warning to consumers about credit-repair services that claim to be able to create a new credit identity or charge you in advance for services to be provided at a later time. You should also know that, by law, every credit-repair service must give you a copy of a document called "Consumer Credit File Rights Under State and Federal Law" before you sign a contract for its services. Be sure to read the document carefully and understand what it says before signing anything.

- **How long you've been on the books:** The length of time you've been using credit affects about 15 percent of your FICO score. The longer your credit history—and the more timely your payments—the better.

- **Credit analysis:** The mix of credit that you hold (credit cards, mortgages, leases, auto loans, etc.) makes up about 20 percent of your FICO score. Newly opened credit accounts are also analyzed when determining your score.

Based on these facts, there are certain steps you can take to start improving your credit score right now. You can't change how long you've been on the books, nor can you feasibly figure out exactly what kind of mix the credit analysis is shooting for, but you can certainly bolster the factors that comprise 65 percent of the process: your payment history and your current debt level.

You can also control your recent credit history by not overextending yourself financially in the months leading up to a home purchase. Here are more specific tips that you can begin following immediately to improve your chances of getting a higher FICO score the next time your report is pulled:

- **Pay bills on time.** The longer you can maintain this habit, the better your score will be.

- **Maintain low balances.** A surefire way to lower a FICO score is by maxing out all your credit balances. Try to pay down revolving credit in amounts larger than just the "amount due" every month and, if possible, pay off all unpaid balances within thirty days.

- **Leave open accounts open.** A closed account is a red flag when it comes to FICO calculations. That's because lenders see the closing of accounts as a way to cover up the fact that you're overburdened by debt. So even if you're carrying a zero balance, leave the account open.

- **Pay off outstanding loans.** Even a $100 outstanding balance on an account you thought was out of your hair five years ago can come back to haunt your FICO score. Be sure to pay off any of these lingering debts in the months leading up to your home purchase.

- **Avoid credit that you don't need.** Don't take on any new, unnecessary credit or increase your credit limits. These actions could have an adverse affect on your credit score.

- **Stay on top of things.** Obtain copies of your credit report and credit score regularly, and keep an eye out for any inaccuracies. If you do find errors, contact the creditor associated with the account or the credit reporting agencies immediately to correct the mistakes.

- **Avoid excessive inquiries.** Too many inquiries (generated when an existing or new creditor pulls your credit report) during a short period of time (say, twelve months) can bring your credit score down. That's because such activity could signal that either you're opening more credit accounts due to financial difficulties, or you're overextending yourself by taking on excessive debt that you may not be able to repay easily.

- **Avoid large purchases, if possible.** Buyers should be careful to limit major purchases—such as boats, cars, or other high-end items—prior to applying for a home loan. Such acquisitions can throw a buyer's debt ratio (the sum of your monthly debt payments divided by your total monthly income) into an unfavorable balance, making a desired home that much less attainable.

Keep in mind that potential home buyers should think several months ahead when making financial decisions, since any or all of these decisions can affect their ability to obtain the right mortgage at a good interest rate.

Resolving Credit Disputes

If that blemish on your credit report is inaccurate, then, according to the Fair Credit Reporting Act, both the reporting company (the credit bureau) and the information provider (the individual or company that provided the information to the credit bureau) are responsible for correcting the mistakes. If, upon inspecting your credit report, you notice any of the following, contact both parties immediately to get the error resolved:

- A payment that was recorded as "late" when it wasn't

- An old account that was paid off but still shows an open, overdue balance

- The name of a creditor with whom you've never done business

- Any credit inquiries that you didn't authorize (these are usually listed at the bottom of the report, and can make a difference when it comes time for a loan underwriter to review your report)

- Any other inaccuracies or mistakes that may have found their way onto your report

While it was difficult, at best, to get credit bureaus to remove erroneous information from reports in the past, consumer advocates and new federal laws have forced major changes in the industry. Today, credit bureaus must investigate the items in question (usually within thirty days), as long as the queries are legitimate (and not "frivolous" by their standards). The credit bureaus also have to share all the data you provide to support the inaccuracy claim with the individual or company that initially provided the information.

Once the information provider receives notice of the dispute, that organization or individual must investigate the issue, review the case, and report the results back to the credit bureau. If the information is found to be inaccurate, then the information provider must notify all three national credit bureaus, which in turn must correct the information contained in your file. Upon completion of the investigation, the credit bureau must provide you with the written results and a complimentary copy of your corrected report.

Not all credit issues can be resolved smoothly, so if an investigation doesn't resolve your dispute with the consumer reporting company, request that a statement of the dispute be retained in your credit file and in future reports. That way, when lenders review your file, they can see that you've taken the time to try to solve the problem, even though a clear resolution wasn't reached. For a fee, you can also ask the reporting agency to hand out this documentation to anyone who has recently reviewed your credit history.

Final Steps

In addition to reviewing your financial history, pulling your credit reports, and compiling documentation for your home-loan underwriter, there are certain steps you can take to improve your chances of getting the loan and interest rate you want. Although this process is best started at least six months before you want to buy a home, every consumer can benefit from the actions listed below.

Pay Down Your Debt

Ideally, your total debt should be no more than 36 percent of your income, based on the debt-to-income ratios used by mortgage lenders. So if your monthly income is $2,000, for example, then your total debt should be $667 or less per month. If your own ratios are tilting in the wrong direction, now is the time to pay down some of that debt well in advance of your mortgage application review to improve your chances of getting a loan. Put an emphasis on high-interest debt (such as credit cards) rather than low-interest instruments like student loans. Do not close out existing credit card accounts. They provide a history of credit, and, as we mentioned earlier, closing a long-held account could be a red flag to a loan reviewer.

Get a Cosigner, If You Need One

If your own financial picture is less-than-ideal, and if a mortgage loan is out of reach, one option is to ask a family member or another individual with good credit to cosign the loan with you. Think about this option very carefully before jumping in. The loan will be yours, and you'll be responsible for paying it. However, if you don't fulfill these obligations, the cosigner will be on the hook for the payments. However, if the cosigner has good credit, it may make the difference between getting and not getting the loan. If you're a young adult, and if your parents have good credit and a desire to help you "get out on your own," asking them to cosign a mortgage can be a particularly useful strategy. Just remember: If for any reason you don't fulfill your commitment, the lender will look to the cosigner for payment, and any goodwill between you and the cosigner could be soured.

Educate Yourself about the Home-Buying Process

While you're assembling your paperwork, credit reports, and other pieces of your financial life, you'll also want to take some time to familiarize yourself with the general home-buying process. Talk to real estate agents about this process and discuss past home-buying experiences with family, friends, and coworkers who have recently purchased homes. Information gathered from these sources will help you become better prepared for the road ahead and also may provide you with the names of reliable mortgage brokers, real estate agents, inspectors, real estate attorneys, and the like.

Know Your Options

Maintaining your high credit score should be a lifelong goal, and not just something that you rush to do when it comes time to hand over the completed mortgage application to a home-loan underwriter. Understand that it takes time (sometimes thirty days) to resolve disputed items, and that it can take sixty days or more for the changes to be reflected on your credit report—and, inevitably, in your FICO score.

Now that you understand how your credit history and FICO score can affect your loan application, you may be wondering if a poor score means that you won't be able to get a mortgage. Fortunately, there are more loan products on the market today than ever before, and many of them are targeted at buyers with less-than-perfect financial histories. However, you should take any steps you can to improve your credit score, not just for your immediate interest in buying a home, but to establish a financially sound future.

CHAPTER FOUR

Introducing the Real Estate Agent

Now that consumers have greater access to information—such as home-listing details, neighborhood demographics, and crime statistics—the collaboration between a home buyer and a real estate agent can be more effective than ever before. Compared to a decade ago, many more real estate resources are publicly available. The Internet and the myriad "do it yourself" real estate seminars promise lots of advice. But it's useful to remember that anyone can create a Web site that offers "real estate information," and real estate seminars are all too often given by motivational speakers who don't actually buy and sell real estate themselves. Even real estate books can be self-published and distributed. Home buyers face the challenge of sorting through all this information. How do you know which information to trust?

A real estate professional who knows her market, keeps on top of current issues in the real estate field, and listens to her clients can be a great resource in cutting through all this information clutter. You can conduct initial research, narrow your choices, and then turn to the real estate agent to help decipher this information, understand what's not being said about the property, negotiate the best price, and then shepherd the transaction to completion. This allows you to focus on areas where you are the expert—your own tastes and needs—while the real estate agent provides services based on her areas of knowledge, including the local market, purchase negotiations, the home due-diligence process, and closings.

In this chapter, we'll explore the different types of real estate agents, and what you can expect from these professionals. A professional, of course, is someone who is paid for his services. Real estate agents usually get paid a commission based on a percentage of the home-sale price. Later in this chapter we'll cover commissions and other forms of payment in detail. Finally, we'll discuss how to best work with your agent as you search for your next home.

Know Your ABCs—Agents, Brokers, and Commissions

You've no doubt heard the terms **real estate agent** and **real estate broker**. What's the difference? Technically speaking, the real estate broker is the person who handles (or "brokers") the transaction between buyers and sellers. Brokers usually operate through their agents (sometimes called sales associates), who represent the broker in assisting clients. An agent licensed with a brokerage might also hold a broker's license; in this case, the agent may be referred to as a broker-associate. Typically, the licensed agent or **broker-associate** is the person who works directly with home buyers and sellers.

A real estate broker often operates an independent company (a brokerage) that is affiliated with an international, national, or regional franchise network such as RE/MAX. Such large franchisors often leave the operations and decisions regarding the brokerage up to the broker (who has better knowledge of the local real estate market). However, franchisors generally offer proprietary business strategies, branding, national advertising, education, and ongoing franchise development support. The more information and support the franchisor provides to its local brokerages, the better customer service the local brokerage is likely to give you.

In the United States, federal and state lawmakers view homeownership and real estate investment as crucial, not just to individual wealth, but to the economy as a whole. As a result, a variety of laws are designed to promote homeownership, to encourage investment in real estate, and—perhaps most important—to protect real estate buyers and sellers. Real estate brokers and agents must obtain a license from the state in which they practice in order to represent clients in real estate transactions. So, while individuals can represent themselves without a license when it comes to buying or selling real estate, they generally can't represent *someone else* without violating state law.

Most states require real estate brokers and agents to complete a set number of hours of education and successfully pass an exam in order to receive a real estate license. For example, in California agents must complete three semesters or four quarters of college credits. Texas mandates 150 hours of real estate–related courses, including courses on contracts, the law of agency, and real estate principles. In most states, agents have to pass a real estate exam by earning a score of 70 or higher (out of 100) to qualify for a license. Brokers must meet additional requirements to qualify for a broker's license, often including a specific number of years of experience.

States also exercise ongoing oversight of the real estate industry through branches of state government, often called **real estate commissions**. (The name is a little confusing. These state *commissions* refer to government entities, not the money paid to a real estate agent. See Appendix A for a complete list of state real estate commissions, along with contact information. State real estate commissions establish regulations for real estate agents and brokers that are designed to protect consumers. In addition, these commissions often create or approve standard forms, such as disclosure forms and purchase agreement forms, and they collect—and attempt to resolve—consumer complaints about real estate licensees.

Special Agents: The REALTOR®

Of the approximately 2.5 million licensed real estate agents in the United States, approximately 1.2 million (that is, roughly half of them) are entitled to call themselves *Realtors*. The term *Realtor* refers to a licensed real estate broker or salesperson who is also a member of the National Association of REALTORS® (NAR), a voluntary organization of real estate professionals. Members must subscribe to the organization's Code of Ethics and meet its standards regarding issues such as an agent's duties to clients, his representation of facts relating to properties and/or transactions, cooperation among agents, and acceptance of commissions and profits. NAR was founded in 1908 in Chicago. During its nearly one-hundred-year history, NAR has provided educational materials to brokers, agents, and the public, and supported the creation of Realtor organizations at the state and local level to promote ethical practices among real estate professionals.

Buyer's Agents, Seller's Agents, and Dual Agents

Now that you know what an agent or broker does, you should determine whether you want that agent or broker to work exclusively on your behalf. Real estate licensees typically have certain obligations (known as **fiduciary duties**) to their clients, including loyalty and confidentiality. Therefore, it's important to know whose interests the agent really represents—the buyer's, the seller's, or neither of the parties' interests—in order to understand where her loyalties lie.

Agents generally fall into one of three categories: **buyer's agents, seller's agents,** or **dual agents**. In the past, all real estate agents essentially functioned as seller's agents. They represented the seller's interests, either directly or indirectly through a concept called **subagency** (whereby an agent shows properties to a buyer, but ultimately owes her fiduciary duty to the seller). Today, while an agent will treat all parties courteously, he is more likely to represent the interests of either the buyer or the seller, but rarely both at the same time.

Because the real estate agent technically works for a broker, it's important for you to understand who puts your interests first and how the brokerage handles the information you give to its agents. As a home buyer, you should confirm that your agent represents your interests alone or you should understand the impact of the agent's representation of both you and the seller.

Buyer's Agents

When you're buying a home, retaining a buyer's agent is usually best. A buyer's agent is a professional who has agreed to represent only the buyer, and places that buyer's interests first. This means that if the buyer's agent receives information about the seller that can help your negotiating position (such as the seller's lowest acceptable price), the buyer's agent may disclose that to you or otherwise use it to your advantage. The buyer's agent also will generally avoid disclosing confidential information about you and your financial position to the seller, or to the seller's agent, unless the agent believes it will further your purchase goals. If, for example, you have the financial means to pay cash for a home (and thus avoid the mortgage-lending process), the agent may use that fact as a bargaining point

The buyer's agent also helps you analyze comparable sales (sales in and around the neighborhood that have closed in the last twelve months), also known as **market comps,** to help you get a good grasp of typical home values in the area. This can be part art form/part science in a market where home prices are changing rapidly. See chapter 8 for more information on how market comps are determined.

Buyer's agents also may protect their clients' interests by including certain advantageous provisions in the home **purchase and sale agreement**. Such provisions or contingencies may permit you to cancel the agreement if the home is appraised for less than the purchase price, if the home inspection reveals too many problems with the house, or if you don't receive an acceptable mortgage commitment. See chapter 9 for more about these agreements.

Buyer's agents may ask you to sign an agreement that permits your agent to have a short-term, exclusive right to represent you in the home-search process. Such contracts, often called buyer's agency agreements, are common in the real estate industry and are even required in some states. You can understand why. Real estate representation is a rather formal process. If you and an agent have a conversation and one of you walks away thinking that you've verbally agreed on the terms of representation—and the other one isn't under the same impression—it can lead to confusion or disputes. A buyer's agency agreement can also make your agent more dedicated to your home search, since your agent can invest her time and resources on your behalf, knowing that you will buy only through her for a specified period of time, and not through any other agent.

Remember that by signing a buyer's agency agreement, you are obligated to live by its terms. Before you sign, read the contract carefully and ask as many questions as you need to so that you understand your commitments. In particular, you should get answers to following questions:

- How long is the term of the agreement? If you are working with an agent who is new to you, you should keep your commitment relatively short until you are comfortable with your working relationship.

- How will the agent get paid? Generally, the seller pays a percentage of the home's purchase price to his agent at closing, and the seller's agent then splits this payment with the buyer's agent. (See pages 90–91 for more on how agents are compensated.) Be sure to ask about these arrangements before signing the agreement.

- What does the contract require of you? A typical caveat is that you notify your agent whenever you find an interesting property through another source. For example, if you visit an open house without your agent, and you want to make an offer on the home, you will still have to work through your agent to do so.

In addition, you may consider including in writing what you both mean by appropriate "follow up" by the agent and provide for termination of the agreement before the term is up if these goals aren't met.

What if you sign a buyer agency agreement, only to discover that you don't get along with the agent? Home buying is a very personal process and home searches are rarely stress-free. Occasionally, miscommunications or personality conflicts may arise. Limit this potential problem at the outset by interviewing a few potential agents before deciding on the right one for you. (See the next chapter for key questions to ask during this process.) If you are already working with the agent, ask yourself honestly why you aren't seeing eye to eye. Maybe your agent doesn't understand your search parameters. Your search styles may be vastly different. Sometimes, buyers are reluctant to commit to one property, fearing that, sometime down the road, they'll be unable to opt for a different property—one they actually prefer. This reluctance may be construed as a tug-of-war between buyer and agent. (If this sounds like what you're going through, you might consider looking for a lower-priced, more conservative home investment that gives you more flexibility.) Don't let these problems fester. Discuss them with your agent as directly and professionally as possible, try to find common ground, and, if you still feel that you are not working well together, sit down with her to examine your alternatives. The real goal, after all, is to find a home that's right for you. Your agent understands this and should put that goal first.

The Seller's Agent

A seller's agent, also known as the listing agent, agrees to work (on behalf of her broker) with a seller to set an appropriate selling price, market the home for sale, and negotiate and organize the home sale. The agent and the seller execute a contract giving the seller's agent the exclusive right to market the home for a specified period of time.

Because the seller's agent works for the seller, he will share information that he receives from potential buyers with the seller, if it benefits the seller. For example, if a seller's agent learns that you, as the prospective buyer, are determined to live in a particular school district, he may convey that information to his seller, to help the seller negotiate with you to the seller's best advantage. On the other hand, the seller's agent generally will not reveal information about the seller (such as the seller's lowest acceptable sales price) to a buyer, except to achieve a sale that is in the seller's best interests.

Dual Agency

A dual agent is one who facilitates a real estate transaction for the buyer and the seller at the same time. Many states define dual agency by law. In some states, dual agency occurs only if an individual agent personally works with both buyer and seller, with the express written permission of each one. (Such express written permission makes the agent a disclosed dual agent.) In other states, a real estate brokerage itself may be considered a dual agent when one agent within that brokerage represents the buyer and another in the same brokerage represents the seller. Some states use the term **transactional brokerage** to describe this multiparty relationship.

It would be possible for the real estate agent acting as a dual agent to know—or for two agents within the brokerage under a "dual agency" arrangement to share—strategies and confidential information about both buyer and seller. But, as a practical matter, such information is normally kept confidential where the parties have relationships with separate agents.

A dual agent doesn't profess absolute loyalty to either the buyer or the seller, which means that both buyer and seller may lose some strategic negotiating advantages in this situation. For example, state law often prohibits dual agents from advising the buyer of the seller's lowest acceptable price. Therefore, the buyer may end up paying a higher price than he would if he were represented by a buyer's agent, who might use tougher negotiating tactics than a dual agent would. Or, the dual agent may refrain from telling the seller whether the buyer is likely to make another, higher offer, so the seller accepts a lower price than she otherwise would. Buyers and sellers who use dual agency or transactional brokerage arrangements should be aware that the real estate agent involved in the transaction is first and foremost concerned with making the sale itself, rather than seeing the best outcome for either the buyer or the seller. As a result, buyers and sellers involved in dual-agency arrangements must look out for their own financial interests to a greater degree than if they were represented exclusively.

Despite these drawbacks, there are times when buyers and sellers may want to accept dual-agency representation. Perhaps both buyer and seller really want to work with a particular agent or brokerage. Or the buyer and seller may be experienced enough to look out for their own interests in the transaction and feel less need for exclusive representation. Maybe the geographic area where the property is located only has one real estate brokerage, in a state where representation by the same brokerage (but different agents) is considered dual agency.

Agency Disclosure Forms

Whether you are working with a buyer's agent, a seller's agent, or a dual agent, at the outset of your relationship, your agent should provide you with a disclosure form that outlines the agent's duties and responsibilities. You should read this form carefully and ask questions of your agent to ensure that you understand the relationship. Doing this up-front will help to avoid misunderstandings down the road. See Appendix B for sample agency disclosure forms.

States that permit dual agency require both the buyer and the seller to sign a disclosure form acknowledging that they understand and agree to such representation. (See Appendix B for a sample of a dual agency disclosure form). Some states specify the required disclosure form language by law; others may require that buyers and sellers be given written information (such as an agency disclosure brochure).

What's Your Type?

So which type of agent is right for you? Buyer's agents, seller's agents, and dual agents each have local knowledge about the area's housing trends, its schools, and taxes. Each can help buyers find available properties within their price range, provide **property disclosures** (which detail any defects or problems relating to the property, see chapter 9), let you know which legal forms you have to complete, arrange home inspections, and present offers to sellers. However, only the buyer's agent works exclusively in the buyer's interest; therefore, as a buyer, you may find the buyer's agent is a stronger ally when you're engaged in negotiations or house hunting in competitive markets.

Note that if you're buying a new home and selling the home where you currently live, there's a chance that you might use the same agent for both transactions (especially if you like the agent and get along well with her). In that case, one agent will ultimately serve in two different capacities (both presumably to your advantage).

The Open House Agent

Real estate has its very own spectator sport—open houses. You put together a list of houses to visit on a Sunday afternoon, then drive to the neighborhood, enter the home, sign in with the real estate agent on duty, and take a tour.

A visit to an open house is a great way to find out what you can expect from homes in your target neighborhood. You may even find that perfect home while attending an open house, and you may decide to move quickly to make an offer. You should be careful, however, about how much you disclose about your financial situation to the agent who is conducting the open house. This agent is generally the seller's agent.

A seller's agent often holds an open house or two as a way to market the home. Remember that the seller's agent is free to disclose to the seller any information that a buyer provides. So it's generally not wise to share any confidential information with the agent conducting the open house.

If you and the seller's agent at the open house hit it off, and you'd like to have that agent represent you as a buyer's agent in your home search, that often can be worked out. The agent may agree to represent your interests as a buyer first with respect to a number of other homes in the area, and he may even be able to represent you on a dual-agency basis for the open house property itself. You and the agent should discuss the agent's priorities to make sure that you clearly understand them and know exactly how the agent will proceed from that point on.

Commissions and Other Types of Compensation

The real estate profession is unique in one key respect: Its practitioners often only get paid for a job well done. Think about it—you have to pay your painter, your lawyer, your doctor, and your Web site designer, whether or not their efforts were successful or to your liking. In real estate, however, the most typical method of payment is one that takes place only after both sides have successfully concluded the transaction.

The most common way for your real estate professional to get paid is for her to receive a percentage of the purchase price of the home, known as a **commission**. Home sellers pay this commission to the seller's agent, and the seller's agent, in turn, offers part of this percentage—usually a 50/50 split—to the buyer's agent. The commission payment is generally made at the closing, where the money is transferred to the agents once all the paperwork is signed.

Commission percentages are negotiable and may differ greatly, depending on the experience or type of services that the real estate agents provide. Commission rates are typically set by arrangement between the seller and the seller's agent; the home buyer has no say in the matter. Occasionally, however, a home is sold by its current owner (known as **for sale by owner** or **FSBO** [pronounced FIZZ-bo], see pages 112–114) or by a limited-service real estate agent, and little or no compensation is offered to the buyer's agent. In this situation, you, as the buyer, may agree to pay your agent directly. You might then offer less money for the home to offset the direct compensation you'll be making to your agent—essentially splitting the savings that the seller expects to garner by selling the home himself.

A buyer may come across a home that is being sold under a fee-for-services payment arrangement, whereby the sellers choose the brokerage services they want and pay specifically for those services and no others. Sellers may view this option as a way to save money, because they don't have to pay a professional for a full range of services. Problems arise when the seller doesn't have the experience to complete the transaction with such limited support. The seller may even expect the buyer's agent to take on the extra work, which may mean that the buyer's agent is no longer working exclusively in the buyer's best interests (some agents will not agree to take on the extra liability this entails, with its potential for conflict of interest). Look carefully at these arrangements to understand when, as a practical matter, these costs will be shifted from the seller to the buyer.

Keep in mind that sometimes the transaction falls through after all the work has been done. Maybe the home inspection revealed too many defects, or the buyers were unable to sell their existing home in time. Perhaps the seller's employer decided not to move her overseas after all, and the sellers and buyer worked with their respective agents to agree to cancel their purchase agreement. In these situations, real estate agents working in a "commission only" arrangement can and do spend time and resources on potential sales for no compensation at all.

Services You Should Expect From Your Real Estate Agent

When you interview your real estate agent, you should ask him exactly what he can do for you. Some agents may have materials prepared for you, outlining the scope of their services; others will talk you through their services. At a minimum, real estate agents will generally search through the local Multiple Listing Service for prospective homes, show you properties within your price range, fill out standardized purchase agreements, suggest reputable local mortgage lenders, guide you through the inspection process, help you decipher home inspection reports, recommend an attorney specializing in real estate, and arrange a title search on the property you eventually choose. However, there are many other ways agents can help you in your home search as well.

Running the Gamut

Tim Maitski, a sales associate with RE/MAX Greater Atlanta, says agents will often create a personalized map of prospective properties, discuss various commuting alternatives, offer advice on schools and neighborhoods, and give you books, brochures, Internet links, and other information on the home-buying process. In addition, your agent can guide you in myriad ways as you navigate the home-buying process, including:

Create a Home-Buying Strategy

You and your agent should discuss and agree on a home-buying game plan. In doing so, you should answer the following questions:

- How much can you realistically afford to spend on a home, and how much would you prefer to spend?

- Are you interested in just one neighborhood or are there several in which you would be willing to buy?

- What is the maximum commute time you can tolerate—and what is your ideal commute time?

- What kind of recreational facilities do you want nearby?

- Are you flexible on home size?

- Are you willing (and able) to fix up a home, or do you need a place that requires little or no work?

- What kind of neighborhood is right for you, based on your interests and habits? How much space do you prefer between you home and your neighbors'? (Consider your own habits—if you're a night owl who practices on the drums in the wee hours, you should choose an area where you won't bother your neighbors.)

Evaluate What You Can Afford

Your agent can help you determine how much you can afford to spend on a home. In addition to working with you to analyze how much you should spend, she can also assist you in becoming prequalified to buy, and review with you the tax advantages of homeownership and other financial considerations.

Make Your Home Search Smoother and More Efficient

Your agent will target home markets that are best for you, then arrange home tours and establish an efficient tour schedule so that you can compare more homes in less time.

Maitski says you should expect your agent to identify any problems or issues relating to the property before you make an offer to buy it. In addition, your agent should check comparable prices of recent home sales in the area—information that is used to come up with a good initial offer. The agent will then present the offer to the seller's agent or the seller on the buyer's behalf, and handle negotiations, keeping the door open should current negotiations fail. "Sellers may reject an offer at first, but reconsider a few weeks later," says Maitski.

Walk You Through the Final Steps

Once the contract is signed, your agent will be on hand for the inspections, review the inspection reports, and negotiate and write up any amendments to the contract based on the inspections. She will also help you analyze which are significant problems that should be fixed and which aren't. She will assist you in securing appropriate financing for the home, attend the final walk-through prior to closing, ensure that all repairs were done, and look for additional problems that may have developed since the contract was originally signed.

Agents also network extensively with the local lending community, and are in a good position to match buyers with financing programs that best suit their needs. They may also recommend local service providers (such as attorneys, plumbers, insurance agents, and roofers) if they need such services.

The agent will review with you the **HUD-1 settlement statement** (also known as the "closing statement" or "settlement sheet," a standard form used in all home purchases that itemizes closing costs for the purchase of residential property). She will ensure that you know what to bring to the closing and how to get there. At closing, the agent will make sure that you receive all required documentation, including warranties from a pest-control company that the home is free of termites and other infestation, property disclosure forms, and any covenants or condominium association documents. "Then the agent will help the buyers celebrate the purchase of their new home," Maitski concludes.

Tracking the Hunt

One important role that a real estate agent should fulfill is keeping track of the progress of your home search. You need to maintain good records of which homes you've seen (and when), which ones you've been interested in, and which ones are likely purchase possibilities. Oftentimes during the process, you begin to pinpoint what you really want in a home, and, armed with this knowledge, your agent can help you conduct a more targeted and effective search.

In addition, once you have offered to buy a home, you can expect your agent

CHECKLIST CONTRACT PROGRESS

Property Address _____

Legal Description _____

Seller _____ Listed By _____

Buyer _____ Sold By _____

Mail Away _____ ? Seller _____ Buyer _____

Referral _____ Contract Date _____

Escrow Deposit _____

Telephone Acceptance Date _____

Date Buyer Notified _____

Signature Acceptance in File _____

Date Balance of Escrow Received _____

Date Mortgage Applied for _____

Where/When Mortgage Applied for _____

Address of Mortgage Company _____

Date Mortgage Commitment Received _____

Date Mortgage Approved _____

Date Title Insurance Ordered _____

Title Company Address _____

Date Contract Sent to Title Company _____

Date Survey Ordered _____

Date Survey Received _____

Date Termite Inspection Ordered _____

Date Termite Inspection Report Received _____

Date Home Inspection Ordered _____

Date Home Inspection Report Received _____

Date Percolation Test Ordered _____

Date Percolation Test Report Received _____

Contract Closing Date _____

Actual Closing Date _____

Walk-Through Date _____

Walk-Through Completed and Forms in File _____

Date Escrow Check Ordered _____

Date Escrow Check Received _____

Date Closing Statement Received from Title Company _____

Date Closing Statement Reviewed with Seller _____

Sign Removal _____

Lock Box Removed _____

Comments: _____

to carefully monitor timetables and details to ensure a smooth closing. Barbara Quist, broker-owner at RE/MAX Advantage Realty in Spring Hill, Florida, developed the "Contract Progress" checklist (see Figure 4.1 on pages 94–95) to keep close tabs on deals as they progress from initial purchase offer to closing (and a little bit beyond).

Talk to your real estate agent about how she tracks the progress of your deal, and ask to see any forms or other documentation being used to ensure that the road from contract to closing is a smooth one.

Around the Neighborhood

One of the biggest advantages of working with an experienced real estate agent is the vast knowledge that he can share with you about the surrounding areas, from statistics about local neighborhoods down to history and information about individual homes in the area. "Hone in on a community first, and connect with a real estate agent who is familiar with it," advises Linda O'Koniewski, broker-owner of RE/MAX Heritage in Melrose, Massachusetts.

The information agents share is complemented by their access to the Multiple Listing Service, which inventories all available properties by region. Agents augment this database—which, in most cases, features much more information than the "public" MLS sites that are available online—with their own experience in locating homes in neighborhoods that match your house-hunting "wish list." They become intimately familiar with the housing market, refer to their own history of transactions in those neighborhoods, and come up with a list of what's available and in what price ranges. Whether you're looking for a quality school system, nearby shopping, close access to highways and byways, or any other amenities, the real estate agent will likely be able to point you in the right direction.

Most agents farm specific areas, meaning that they market to these precise areas by knocking on doors, attending community events, and sending out direct-mail pieces. Agents do this either because they already know an area well and are able to effectively tell buyers about its attributes, or because they want to become intimately familiar with the homes in the area. Often, an experienced agent may have already visited many of the homes in her farming area. "Buyers should work with an agent who is able to rattle off facts and figures about various communities and neighborhoods that might be interesting to the buyer," says O'Koniewski. That knowledge can prove invaluable during the home-buying process, when variables and unexpected surprises are quite common.

Because they stay in close touch with the markets they serve, agents also have a wealth of knowledge about unpleasant factors that might affect your home purchase. For example, an agent may be aware of areas that are particularly prone to sinkholes (natural depressions in the land that can affect a property's structural integrity), or may have firsthand knowledge of reported faulty construction on a townhouse or condo complex.

Geoff Loughery, broker-associate with RE/MAX One of Las Vegas, Nevada, also believes that buyers should focus on the community first, then the home itself. "A buyer shouldn't choose a house only because it's the prettiest or has the best interior paint," he recommends. "Décor can be changed, but it's harder to change the community that the home is in." Parents of young children, for example, should check out the availability of sidewalks for family strolls, while senior buyers may want to find areas with social events targeted to their age group. An experienced local agent can help you evaluate a neighborhood for the facilities and qualities that are important to you.

Here are some key pieces of neighborhood information that your real estate agent should be able to share with you:

- School "report cards," detailing the strengths and weaknesses of the school districts in areas where you're considering buying a home
- Neighborhood demographics (number of young families, number of single adults, etc.)
- Crime reports
- A listing of nearby health facilities (such as hospitals and clinics)
- Key economic indicators (such as job and population growth)
- Community characteristics and cultural events
- Housing characteristics
- Climate information
- Information about local institutions such as civic or community organizations, houses of worship, the local library, and area colleges

- A visual tour of the community
- Township or county information (such as each home's proximity to municipal and county government offices)
- Local newspapers
- Information regarding utilities

These and other details can help you whittle down the many choices you'll be facing when it comes time to start looking for homes. If you have young children, for example, then school report cards and proximity to parks and family amenities will be important. If you're moving into a new area and looking for a job, then key economic indicators will be paramount. And, if you're pursuing an advanced degree, then a list of area higher-education institutions and libraries will be helpful.

Financial Assistance

If there's one area most real estate agents are well versed in, it's financing. After all, without adequate financing, the home-buying experience will never come to fruition. That's because finding the right home, the ideal neighborhood, the perfect amenities, an affordable price range, and your favorite housing style mean

Survival Toolkit

No Steering Allowed

When working with a real estate agent, you should understand that there are certain questions you should not ask your agent about the neighborhood, since your agent is prohibited by law from pointing you to properties based on any of these factors. Agents cannot steer you toward or away from particular neighborhoods based on their racial, ethnic, or religious makeup, for example.

The National Fair Housing Alliance is an organization that can provide you with more information about these restrictions. It can be reached at 202–898–1661, or locate your local office online at www.nationalfairhousing.org.

nothing if you can't obtain a mortgage to complete the deal.

Navigating through the wide array of mortgage options may be confusing, even for an experienced buyer, and real estate agents can provide valuable advice and guidance to help you find the most appropriate financing method for your situation. With this in mind, you can expect to discuss finances with your real estate agent early on in your relationship with him. One of the first questions he may ask is, "How do you plan to finance your home's purchase?" to which you will likely give one of the following answers:

- I expect to be able to pay cash (or pay in full, without a mortgage) for my home.
- I will put down 20 percent or more of the sales price, and will need the rest financed via a mortgage.
- I plan to put a substantial down payment on the house (say, 60 percent), based on proceeds from the sale of my current home.
- I have minimal cash for a down payment, and will need a mortgage and/or financing program that allows me to finance more than 80 percent of the home's purchase price.

Of course, there are other variables and answers, but these four are among the most common. Your answers will help your real estate agent point you in the direction of a financing source that meets your needs.

Real estate agents generally work with a wide range of banks, online lenders, and mortgage brokers. Equipped with a good idea of your financial capabilities and needs, the agent can help you find a mortgage that best suits your individual situation. Remember that agents are not miracle workers (they don't dole out legal advice, nor do they approve or reject mortgage applications), but they can help you find the financing you need to buy a home.

Agents usually know all about community events, seminars, and workshops designed for home buyers who need extra help arranging or understanding financing. For example, they can advise you about "home buyer helper" programs (such as those that offer grants to cover down payments on homes purchased in certain areas of a city or county) and share with you any books or materials that might improve your chances of getting a mortgage.

Working with Your Agent Effectively

A real estate purchase is a complex legal transaction and a major investment—perhaps the largest one you'll ever make. Your agent can help guide you through the entire process, making it smoother and less stressful than it might otherwise be. She can coordinate all aspects of the transaction for you, from setting up showings and getting you into homes to scheduling inspections and arranging for the final walk-through and closing. Your agent can also advise you on factors affecting the future resale of various homes, should you decide to sell the one you choose down the road; current market values; a realistic offer price; inspection concerns; and the various terms and conditions you may want to place in an offer. An agent can also handle multiple offer situations (also known as **bidding wars;** see chapter 9). The newest, hottest listings often receive multiple offers from prospective purchasers. An agent who is experienced with these situations can help make *your* offer the one the seller accepts.

Be sure to take advantage of your real estate agent's local market knowledge, including price trends, neighborhood characteristics, real estate law, zoning issues, homeowners' association issues, financing, taxes, and insurance. You and your agent should sit down and plan a negotiating strategy as well. If homes in a particular market are moving quickly, your agent should know your parameters when it comes to negotiations, so he can bid on your behalf if you are temporarily unavailable.

Tell your agent as much as you can about your wants and needs—especially those that are not obvious. It goes without saying that most buyers want to buy a terrific house in record time and for the least amount possible, but what can you tell your agent about what will make a house *terrific* in your eyes? What hobbies and sports do you and your family pursue? Do you have a large family who like to visit for extended periods? Do you want to be close to an airport because your work requires you to hop on an airplane on a regular basis? Remember that the real estate industry tends to attract—and reward—agents with a sixth sense about the right home that "fits" their clients. As agents build up experience working in the real estate field, they develop the ability to gather seemingly irrelevant details about a client's lifestyle and translate them into homes that could be a perfect match.

Finding the home of your dreams is all about being able to identify potential problems, spot promising opportunities, and choose from a good selection of options. Your real estate professionals should serve as trusted advisors in that quest, and should smooth the way for you to realize your own American dream.

CHAPTER FIVE

Choosing Your Real Estate Professionals

I n the real estate industry, professionals must engage in personal interaction to succeed. Real estate agents usually work closely with local bankers, mortgage brokers, builders, attorneys, and others involved in home sales to keep current on market conditions and neighborhood issues. And they rely on referrals from family, friends, colleagues, and past customers to generate new business. Because people tend to buy and sell homes several times throughout their lives, the best agents build a regular clientele through repeat and referral business.

For home buyers, this means that your agent has a vested interest in doing the best possible job for you, for reasons that go beyond the commission she may receive from your home purchase today. If she does a good job helping you buy your first home, you will probably want her to help you buy your next one— and your friends may ask her for help and advice as well. It is better for the agent—and better for you—to forge a long-term relationship, since it takes extra time and effort for an agent to seek out a new client and for a buyer to find a new, reliable agent.

Now that you understand how real estate agents work and what services they offer (all covered in chapter 4), how do you go about finding a reputable one who will work well with you and meet all your needs?

In this chapter, we'll explore how to locate real estate agents, what questions to ask when selecting your agent, and when you need to consult an attorney.

Where Can You Find an Agent of Your Own?

According to the 2005 National Association of REALTORS® Profile of Home Buyers and Sellers, 44 percent of buyers in search of a real estate agent were referred by a friend, neighbor, or relative; 11 percent used an agent from a previous transaction; 7 percent found an agent on the Internet; 7 percent met their agent at an open house; and 6 percent saw their agent's contact information on a "For Sale" sign. Six other categories accounted for the remaining 25 percent.

You may meet an agent at an open house, where real estate agents open their listings for public viewing on certain days. As we've mentioned, you should be aware that the agent conducting an open house usually represents the seller of that particular house (so don't give your bidding strategy away to him). However, your personal contact with that agent may lead you to believe that he would represent you well in your home search. If the agent is unable to work with you directly, for whatever reason, he can often point you in the direction of a professional who would be happy to work with you as a buyer's agent. (For example, the open house agent might be a seller's-only agent; that is, he only works with sellers and not buyers). If you are looking at a new home, the open house may be staffed by the builder's representative. While he may be unwilling or unable to represent you during the transaction, he is likely to know someone who can.

What Should You Look for
When Choosing an Agent?

According to the NAR Profile of Buyers and Sellers, 41 percent of home buyers feel that the most important factor in choosing an agent is reputation, followed by an agent's knowledge of the neighborhood (24 percent). In terms of desired qualities in an agent, three categories are rated as *very important* by more than nine out of ten buyers: knowledge of the purchase process, responsiveness, and familiarity with the market. Of buyers who use an agent, 63 percent choose a buyer's agent. Overall, according to the survey, satisfaction with real estate agents is very high, with 85 percent of buyers saying they were likely to use the same agent again.

So there are certain qualities that are consistently sought after in agents, and for which you, too, should be on the lookout. You need to find an agent who can tell if a home is under- or overpriced, one who is trustworthy, and one who will devote the necessary time and attention to your home search. These attributes may not be readily apparent during an initial interview or phone call—particularly for first-time buyers who haven't worked with an agent in the past—but you should be able to pick up on an agent's ability to provide professional service after a few conversations. Most important, you should interview more than one agent, even if one is a friend, before choosing the right one for you.

A hot national housing market, low interest rates, and displacement from other industries have prompted increasing numbers of people to become real estate agents over the last few years. There are currently 1.25 million Realtors in the United States, according to NAR's September 2005 numbers. How can you find one with whom you'll be compatible, and who will help you find, buy, and settle into your perfect home? NAR statistics show that between 60 and 70 percent of home buyers work with the first agent they interview, instead of shopping around for an agent they really feel comfortable working with. If you want to get the best representation possible, then you should look at what qualifications and qualities typify top-notch real estate agents.

The goods news is that there are a lot of professional, sophisticated agents in the field who are fully prepared to help buyers find good homes. Let's take a look at ways to narrow down your choices so you can choose the right agent for your particular home-buying needs.

Look for Certifications

One way real estate agents distinguish themselves from the growing ranks of their peers is through education. In many cases, these agents are permitted to display after their names designations that reflect the certifications they have earned. You, as the home buyer, are the beneficiary of all that advanced knowledge and expertise.

Here are a few of the most common acronyms reflecting certifications, and what they stand for:

- **ABR®:** The Accredited Buyer Representative designation is the benchmark of excellence in buyer representation. The Real Estate Buyer's Agent Council (REBAC) of the National Association of REALTORS® awards this coveted designation to real estate practitioners who meet specified educational criteria and gain a specified amount of practical experience. To earn the ABR designation, agents must complete a two-day ABR Designation Course and earn a grade of 80 percent or higher on the exam. They must also complete one approved, elective course (such as Successful Relocation Representation or The Resort and Second Home Market); earn a grade of 80 percent or higher on its exams; and complete five successful transactions on which they acted solely as the buyer's representative.

- **CBR®:** The first nationally recognized buyer agency designation is sponsored by real estate associations nationwide. Real estate agents who earn the Certified Buyer Representation designation have skills necessary to help buyers both find their desired properties and negotiate for those properties in the most beneficial and professional manner. Issued in 1993 by the U.S. Patent and Trademark Office, this mark allows consumers to identify a buyer's agent who has been fully trained and who possesses the skills necessary to represent purchasers in a legal, ethical, and non-adversarial fashion. CBRs must pass a course that covers agency ethics, verbiage and forms, negotiating, due diligence, risk reduction, and marketing skills.

- **CRS:** Nationally recognized, the Certified Residential Specialist acronym is used by real estate agents who have completed advanced study in listing, selling, investment, and taxes, and who have a proven record of experience in hands-on residential real estate marketing.

- **CIPS:** The Certified International Property Specialist Network (CIPS Network) is the specialty membership group, within the National Association of REALTORS®, for international practitioners. CIPS designees have hands-on experience in international real estate transactions. (An international transaction is one that involves a buyer or seller who is based outside the United States, such as a resident of Latin America who purchases a condominium in Miami, or an American seeking to buy a summer home in France.) Those with the CIPS designation are required to close three international transactions involving other countries including those transactions occurring in an agent's local market. Agents must also complete a program of study focusing on the critical aspects of transnational transactions, including a two-day "Essentials of International Real Estate" course and a series of classes pertaining to real estate issues in Europe, Asia and the Pacific Rim, the Americas, the Middle East,and other locations. A multiple-choice examination is given at the end of each course, and agents must earn a score of 70 percent or higher to pass.

- **CRB:** The Certified Real Estate Brokerage manager (CRB) designation is recognized industry-wide as the symbol of excellence in brokerage management. The most successful brokerages are owned or managed by professionals holding this designation. CRB designees recruit and train their associates to handle real estate transactions with professionalism, and they encourage their associates to utilize the most up-to-date information, techniques, and tools. In addition, they possess skills in designing effective marketing programs to promote and sell property for the highest price and in the shortest period of time, and assist their sales associates in helping to quickly find a property matching each buyer's needs and wants.

- **e-PRO:** An e-PRO is a real estate agent who has successfully completed the e-PRO training program for real estate professionals. The e-PRO course, sponsored by NAR, teaches professionals the nuts and bolts of working with real estate online, and includes modules on understanding the Internet, e-mail communication and marketing, computer fundamentals, and how to prospect via the Internet.

- **GRI:** The Graduate REALTORS® Institute designation acknowledges real estate agents who have completed a comprehensive education program focusing on the nuts and bolts of real estate. This program is looked upon as being above and beyond the education required to earn a real estate license.

- **SRES:** To qualify as a Seniors Real Estate Specialist, real estate agents must complete an education program that provides real estate training for the client who is fifty-five years of age or older. SRES identifies individuals who have successfully completed its education program, along with other prerequisites.

- **CCIM:** A Certified Commercial Investment Member is a recognized expert in the disciplines of commercial and investment real estate. The CCIM curriculum offers essential knowledge for all commercial investment practitioners. The CCIM curriculum consists of four core courses that incorporate the essential CCIM skill sets: financial analysis, market analysis, and investment analysis for commercial investment real estate. The CCIM Institute estimates that a scant 6 percent of the 125,000 commercial real estate practitioners nationwide hold the coveted CCIM designation.

While researching agents, check out their Web sites, marketing materials, and/or business cards to find out which designations they hold. Then, refer to the list above to figure out which agents' areas of expertise would best suit your needs. It's important to realize that not all successful agents put the time and money into earning these designations. So the lack of acronyms after an agent's name doesn't necessarily mean the person isn't well equipped to help you through the home-buying process.

Do the Background Research

As a prospective homeowner, selecting the right real estate agent is critical. The most reliable way to retain a strong agent is to investigate and interview more than one and to look for certain traits that are common in agents who conduct professional, successful real estate transactions. Laura Byther, broker/owner of RE/MAX Absolute Realty in South Portland, Maine, notes, "A client should expect an agent to have effective negotiating abilities, broad market experience, and good communication skills. It's also important for the agent to provide a client with a market analysis and discuss the strategy for negotiating prior to making the offer."

Barbara Quist, broker/owner at RE/MAX Advantage Realty in Spring Hill, Florida, adds, "When searching for a real estate agent, put industry experience at the top of your list." Quist says that industry experience can shorten the search process, especially for first-time home buyers, since an agent who has been through many successful transactions can walk clients through the process with more speed and confidence than a novice agent.

RE/MAX International offers these ten suggestions that can help you identify the right agent for you:

1. Interview at least three real estate professionals before choosing one to represent you. Having a conversation with the person is a good way to find out if your personalities and goals match. Take notes as you're chatting. (See pages 110–111 for some key questions to ask.) Review your interview notes and think about each agent. An agent who is a good match will not make you feel anxious or pressured, but will inspire confidence that she can handle the transaction well for you.

2. Consider the agent's earned designations, check with the Better Business Bureau for any negative reports about him, and confirm the agent's current license status with the state's real estate commission. You want someone who is both experienced and in good professional standing.

3. Look around the neighborhood where you would like to live. Do all the "For Sale" signs have the same agent's name on them? Call that agent and arrange for an interview; even if she can't represent you as the buyer, she probably knows the neighborhood well enough to refer you to someone reputable who can.

4. Use the Internet. It's easy to search for a local agent using online tools like the "Find an Agent" feature available at www.remax.com.

5. Ask a neighbor or friend. Who helped them buy their home? Who would they retain if they decided to move?

6. Find an agent who understands how to use technology effectively in order to help you more quickly make an offer on and close the purchase of the home that you really want.

7. Ask for—and check—the agent's references (such as the agent's former clients, or service providers, such as attorneys, with whom the agent has done business). This shouldn't be a big deal. Checking references could confirm or undermine your impression of the agent.

8. Before signing a contract, be aware that the term *disclosed dual agent* often means that the real estate agent does not represent your interests 100 percent.

9. Select a strong negotiator. Ask your agent whether he has ever been in a tough negotiation and how he negotiated a fair price.

10. Talk money. Although the seller often foots the bill for the real estate professional's commission, it is the buyer who ultimately supplies the funds from which the seller pays that bill. Don't assume anything—ask point-blank what your financial obligations are throughout the process.

Ask the Tough Questions

The more research and due diligence you do at the outset, the better your home-search partnership will be. So be sure to ask the following questions during the interviewing process:

- **"How often will you notify me of new listings?"** Ideally, you would like to know as soon as a new home that matches your criteria hits the market. Buyers need to be especially well informed in seller's markets, where houses sell quickly and buyers must often make offer decisions within a short period.

- **"How often can I expect to hear from you?"** Just because your dream house isn't on the market yet doesn't mean you won't have questions. Be sure to work out an arrangement from the beginning about how often you can expect the agent to contact you. If the agent doesn't have a callback policy ("You'll hear back from me within two hours/thirty minutes/before the day ends"), you may not get the service you expect.

- **"Are you a full-time agent?"** A full-time agent will generally be able to devote more time and energy to your home-buying venture than a part-time profes- sional, who may not be as accessible, or as willing to drop everything to show you a new home.

- **"Who will you represent in my transaction?"** Know who your agent thinks she's representing—you, the seller, or both of you. Find an agent who represents your interests in the way that you deem best.

- **"How long have you actively worked in the area?"** An agent who has worked in the area a long time is more likely to be aware of properties that match your wish list. See page TK for a discussion of the advantages of working with a local real estate agent.

- **"Are you a Realtor?"** As discussed, Realtors are members of NAR and are generally full-time agents who have committed financially, educationally, and professionally to honing their skills as experts in the real estate industry.

- **"How do you work with your clients?"** It's important to understand the process by which you and agent will work together. Here are some questions that relate to this issue:

  Do you have a written plan for finding a home for me, and, if so, can I have a copy of it?

  Will you be dealing with me directly, or do you have assistants who call me with information and answer my questions?

  Do you personally take me to look at homes or does someone else take care of this?

  Will you be there when contracts are presented and handle all the negotiations?

  Do you have enough time in your schedule to take on my business?

  Do you offer any guarantees and, if so, what are they?

  Is there a provision in your agreement to represent me that permits me to terminate the agreement if I'm dissatisfied with your services? Please show me that provision and explain it.

- **"What other qualifications do you possess?"** An agent's personal or professional background may enable her to quickly and easily understand what it is you hope to find in a home. For example, an agent might have experience in restoring vintage homes, may ride or keep horses, may have lived in the geographic area that you are relocating from, or may have juggled the same school runs that you will.

By taking the time to ask the right questions and checking an agent's references, you will improve your chances of finding an agent with whom you feel comfortable and who will represent your best interests throughout the home-buying experience.

Can a Home Buyer Go It Alone?

You may have heard of home sellers who sell their homes without an agent (commonly known as homes For Sale by Owner [FSBO]). Can you do the same thing as a home buyer (that is, buy a home without an agent)? As noted earlier, home sellers and home buyers can represent themselves—but not anyone else—when they sell or buy their own homes. Many of these unrepresented transactions are between family members or other close parties. However, NAR statistics show that nine out of ten home buyers use an agent when completing a sale. Here may be a few reasons why.

Trend Spotting, Market Watching

One difference between using a professional and going it alone is the level of expertise that you have available to you during the transaction. Most people simply don't have the time to research and stay abreast of market conditions, recent home sales, neighborhood statistics, local school performance, surrounding amenities and development, and other similarly important criteria. However, your agent earns a living precisely by investigating and understanding these issues. Someone who represents home buyers and sellers for a living has an incentive to search out both obvious and non-obvious sources of market information. The agent has also most likely taken part in a number of home-buying transactions, each of which teaches him something about the process; a typical home buyer has not. Because agents stay on top of market and industry trends and tend to be intuitive about home pricing, they can usually spot "overpriced" home listings quickly and strategize with their customers in order to structure a reasonable transaction and save the customer time and money. In addition, the agent will often be affiliated with a franchise organization that provides targeted resources and support.

Professional License

State laws limit buyer and seller representation to licensed real estate brokers or attorneys to give buyers and sellers a measure of protection in the home-buying process. A licensed broker or attorney has an incentive to maintain high professional standards, since he is regulated by the state and can have his license revoked in certain circumstances. The broker, agent, or attorney must have taken dedicated educational courses and passed an examination before getting a license; this is designed to ensure that he has a certain degree of background knowledge. In certain areas, licensees are required to take additional classes (continuing education) to maintain their licenses, which helps them stay current on legal developments and market issues.

Going Solo

Even if you—or the seller—choose to not to pay for representation in the home-buying and home-selling process, you still need to follow most of the same steps to complete the transaction. This means that if you opt for limited or no representation, you are responsible for handling these steps yourself.

You will need to negotiate a purchase price, write up the contract, arrange inspections, decide how the inspection reports affect your offer to buy, review purchase agreements and make sure your obligations (to obtain a **mortgage commitment**—a written promise by a lender to make a loan—for example) are met on a timely basis. If you decide to go it alone, it's wise to learn as much you can about such steps and to stay abreast of any market changes (such as a steep drop in interest rates), financial issues, or legal developments that could affect your home purchase.

In addition, you need to recognize that a full-service real estate professional acting on behalf of one side of a transaction (say, the seller) is unlikely to be able to step in and provide additional services to you, as the buyer, if you choose limited or no representation. For the real estate agent, this could present ethical or legal conflicts, as well as time-management issues that militate against working for both you and the seller.

Pay to Play

Remember that the seller typically pays the commission on a home-sale transaction. If the seller is representing himself or opts for limited service, and doesn't offer a commission to your agent, you may have to make arrangements to pay your agent directly. This may make financial sense in situations where you are purchasing the home at a lower price; otherwise, it's an added expense that you should take into consideration.

When it comes to representation, investigate your options thoroughly, and know whom you're doing business with on both sides of the transaction. Working with an experienced professional is no substitute for becoming as thoroughly informed as possible. The more you understand about the home-buying process, the more effectively you'll be able to work with your real estate agent—and the more likely you are to find the home that you really want.

The Real Estate Attorney

In most states, attorneys are not required to participate in real estate transactions. However, in the United States, only attorneys—not agents—can practice law, which includes giving legal advice to clients and drafting documents that transfer legal rights. Most states permit a real estate agent to complete, but not create, purchase contracts, and to conduct closings on behalf of a home buyer.

When must you use a lawyer? First, if your state requires you to. A few states, such as Georgia, Massachusetts, and North Carolina, require a real estate attorney to be involved in the home-buying transaction. Second, you should consult an attorney any time your real estate professional recommends it. Third, you should use a lawyer whenever you are involved in an international transaction. Every country has its own set of laws and regulations concerning real estate, and navigating the process can be confusing for someone who doesn't know the "lay of the land." Finally, you enlist an attorney's assistance any time you feel that the transaction involves thorny legal issues. If the home is being sold as part of a "divorce sale," for example, and one spouse appears to be reluctant to move out and/or sell, then having an attorney in your corner can help to ward off any issues that arise.

When you consult an attorney for advice regarding a home purchase, that attorney becomes another member of your support team. Your lawyer may handle the title search, the contract, and the closing, ensuring that everything goes smoothly and by the book, but his role is generally much less wide-ranging in scope that that of your real estate agent when it comes to finding you a home and guiding you through the overall purchase process.

You should also consult an attorney whenever you need legal advice. Your agent can't give you a legal opinion. For example, your agent can't tell you if the homeowners' association really has the legal power to stop you from putting a six-foot-high bronze lion statue in your front yard. If the transaction includes any unusual provisions, if there are property line disputes, or if the home or its homeowners' association is involved in litigation, you may want to consult an attorney.

An attorney, like a real estate agent, should be chosen with care. Make sure you retain an attorney who's experienced and has a solid track record. If you have a good friend who has worked successfully with a lawyer in the past, you should consider contacting that lawyer. You can also get a referral from your real estate agent, coworkers, or through the Web site of the American Bar Association (ABA), at www.abanet.org. On the ABA's Web site, look for a link to the association's Lawyer Locator, where you can then narrow your search.

In selecting an attorney, you should take the following steps:

- Look for someone who is licensed to practice law in your state.
- Seek out someone who lists real estate as a practice area specialty.
- Check with your state to make sure that the attorney's license is in good standing; look carefully to see whether she has been charged with any infractions.
- Remember that you don't have to choose the first attorney you find. Ask about his experience in representing home buyers.
- Request references—and call them.
- Make sure you understand exactly how much and in what manner she gets paid. Most attorneys charge clients by the hour.

Now that you know the value that real estate agents and other reputable professionals can bring to the table, it's time to jump into the financing aspect of the home-buying process. In the next chapter, you'll learn about mortgage and interest rate basics, how to figure out what you can afford, and which financing sources will produce the best results for your individual situation.

CHAPTER SIX

All About Mortgages

Today's home buyer has more financing choices and options than her predecessors ever did. While the plethora of options now available is usually considered a benefit to consumers, all these options can make an already complicated process seem overwhelming. Choosing between two attractive options is one thing, but having to choose from among dozens of different programs and hundreds of lenders can confuse even the seasoned home buyer. In this chapter, you'll learn the nuts and bolts of mortgages and how to get the right one to finance your new home.

What Is a Mortgage?

A mortgage is a lien on a property representing a loan that must be paid back over a specified period. A mortgage is your personal guarantee to repay the sum that you've borrowed (and used to purchase your home) during that time frame. You can get a mortgage loan directly from lenders such as banks, organizations that represent home builders, and specialized mortgage lenders. Mortgages come in many different shapes and sizes, each of which has its own pros and cons. A thirty-year mortgage, for example, may be beneficial for someone looking to live in the home for a number of years, while a fifteen-year option may be more appropriate for a buyer who will be moving to a new home within a few years. It's important to select a mortgage loan that suits your financial situation, your future plans, and your lifestyle. Keep in mind that products, terms, and other details often change in the financial industry, so it's best to confer with a real estate agent and/or mortgage broker about the options available when you're ready to buy.

How Does Mortgage Repayment Work?

Mortgages are usually repaid in monthly installments. These monthly payments equal the total amount of the loan plus interest (and any other additional charges such as property taxes or maintenance fees) spread out over the term of the loan. Typically, in the early part of the repayment term, your monthly mortgage payments primarily go toward interest owed, as opposed to the house purchase price (the principal amount). For example, for several years, 95 percent of your mortgage payment might be credited toward interest and a mere 5 percent toward principal.

Banks structure the payments this way so that they get repaid for the "service" of lending money (the interest) before they get repaid for the home loan itself. This is because the home loan is usually secured by the home—if mortgage payments stop, the bank normally has the right to take possession of and sell the property to cover its interest cost and the remaining loan amount. If the sale of the house doesn't cover these costs, the homeowner who obtained the mortgage may be held liable to repay the remaining amount. Your lender should give you an **amortization schedule.** This document specifies what percentage of your principal is paid off each month (increasing with every payment), while the remaining interest owed decreases.

Types of Mortgages

There are many different types of mortgages, but most of them fall into one of three categories: *fixed rate, adjustable rate,* and *balloon.* In addition, there is the home equity loan, which is less useful for new homeowners but worth exploring so that you get a complete picture of what's available.

Fixed-Rate Mortgages

Fixed-rate mortgages carry an interest rate that is set at or before the time the loan is made. The interest rate remains constant throughout the term of the mortgage. That means if you have a thirty-year mortgage, payable in monthly installments, you'll be paying the same rate and the same amount each month for the entire length of the loan. At the close of the thirtieth year—if payments have been made on time over the last three decades—then the loan will be fully paid off. The predictability of the fixed-rate loan is its biggest draw: Borrowers can depend on their mortgage payment remaining constant over the life of the loan, knowing that it won't fluctuate with the going interest rates. This type of mortgage may appeal to borrowers who would rather not take the risk of seeing their interest rates rise during the course of the loan, but it may be undesirable for those who would prefer to take advantage of an economic environment in which interest rates are falling. When interest rates fall, borrowers seeking a lower rate will often **refinance** their mortgages to the lower, market rates. Lenders tend to demand a higher interest rate on a fixed-rate loan than they do when establishing the initial rate and payments for adjustable or balloon mortgages.

Adjustable-Rate Mortgages

Known simply as ARMs, **adjustable-rate mortgages** offer a fixed initial interest rate and a fixed initial monthly payment, neither of which is permanent for the life of the loan. The fixed initial period may extend from six months to five years, and once the initial period ends, both the interest rate and the monthly payment fluctuate—on a regular basis, as determined and disclosed by the lender in advance—to reflect the current market interest rates, based on **an index.**

Lenders use their own individual indexes and formulas, some of which may be more or less favorable for borrowers, so do your homework before signing on the dotted line. Lenders also use different adjustment periods. For example, some ARMs may be subject to adjustment every twelve months, while others may fluctuate every three to six months. Additionally, the amount that the interest rate can actually increase (or decrease) at any given point may also be limited—for example, it may not rise or fall by more than one-half of 1 percent.

ARMs tend to offer lower initial interest rates and monthly payments, in exchange for the borrower shouldering the risk that interest rates may rise in the future, after the initial, fixed period has expired. Lenders often keep introductory rates low on adjustable-rate mortgages as a way to entice borrowers to take ARMs, which—due to their fluctuating nature and ability to stay in line with the going mortgage interest rates—offer less risk to the lenders themselves. Lenders may, for example, set a very low rate for the first twelve months of the loan, and then boost the interest charged to the actual loan rate (your monthly payments rise along with the interest rate). Many ARMs also include a cap, setting an upper limit on the rate that may be charged to the borrower. For example, say the initial rate of your loan is 7 percent, with a cap of 12 percent. Even if the index rates jump to 16 percent, the maximum interest rate charged on your loan will be 12 percent. This holds true for the remaining life of the loan.

Balloon Mortgages

With a **balloon mortgage,** you pay a fixed interest rate and make a fixed monthly payment. After a predetermined period of time, however (such as five or seven years), the entire balance of the loan comes due all at once. This type of loan is neither feasible nor practical for most home buyers, but it can be a useful tool in certain situations. Sometimes the borrower who lacks the cash to pay off the entire loan balance when it's due will arrange for a new mortgage. Balloon mortgages are often thought of as a last resort for borrowers who cannot qualify for fixed-rate or adjustable-rate mortgages. They can also be useful for buyers who are expecting to remain in their homes for a relatively short period, since they carry lower interest rates than conventional thirty-year mortgages while still providing a fixed payment schedule for five or more years. The risk, of course, is what happens after the initial fixed period is over and you have to pay off the loan. Having a large payment due all at once can put tremendous pressure on a homeowner to either refinance, or risk losing her home because of nonpayment.

The most popular terms for balloon mortgages are 5/25 and 7/23. With a 5/25 balloon mortgage, the rate is fixed for a period of five years. While monthly payments are amortized over thirty years, after five years the entire balance of the loan is due at once. A 7/23 balloon mortgage employs the same concept, with the balance of the mortgage due after seven years. As discussed, you may wish to refinance your loan at this point; however, the lender is under no obligation to do so.

Home Equity Loans

Another type of mortgage is known as the home equity loan. (Home equity is the difference between the amount for which you could sell your home and the amount that you still owe.) Sometimes referred to as a second mortgage (or "borrowing against your home"), these loans allow borrowers to tap into their home's equity. Today's homeowners often turn to home equity loans to finance home improvements, their children's education, or large purchases, such as a new car.

This type of loan probably isn't going to be useful for you as a homeowner until you've been in your home for a few years and have accumulated some equity against which you can borrow funds. Home equity loans usually involve a floating or adjustable rate of interest and are amortized over a predetermined number of years.

Repayment Versus Interest-Only Mortgages

In determining what type of loan is best for you, you'll also need to choose between what is known as a repayment mortgage and an interest-only mortgage. Here's the difference between the two:

Repayment Mortgages

Repayment mortgages require you to pay back both interest and loan capital on a regular, predetermined basis—usually monthly. Provided you make all the agreed-upon payments, the loan will be fully paid off by the end of the mortgage term. With these types of loans, you'll pay mostly interest during the first few years of the mortgage, but, as time goes on, you'll begin to see the principal whittled down as you continue to make timely payments. Also called capital and interest loans, repayment mortgages are the more common of the two options.

Interest-Only Mortgages

Interest-only mortgages allow you to repay nothing but the interest on your loan, in monthly installments and for a fixed term. When that term expires (usually within five to seven years), you would either refinance the mortgage, pay off the entire balance in one lump sum, or begin paying off the principal. Historically targeted at the well-funded homeowner who could afford to either pay off the entire balance at the end of the term—or shell out more money for a higher principal payment when the term expires—these loans have lately been peddled to a wider audience.

If you're considering an interest-only loan, be sure to review your options and responsibilities carefully before signing any contracts. Interest-only loans may not always be the best choice, depending on your financial situation. Because you're paying off only the interest portion of the loan you're not building up any equity in your home. Should property values decrease at some point during the loan period, you could end up owing more than your home is actually worth.

Reverse Mortgages

Another mortgage that has garnered mixed reviews over the last few years is the **reverse mortgage.** Unlike a conventional mortgage, the reverse mortgage is an arrangement through which homeowners or buyers receive cash (typically in the form of monthly payments or a lump sum) in return for a mortgage on their home. The property is used as collateral for the loan, which is paid off when the owner either dies or sells the property and moves to another home. To be eligible, applicants must be at least sixty-two years old, and they must own and live in the home.

Reverse mortgages can be a welcome relief for senior citizens who have built up quite a bit of equity in their homes but have limited incomes. Recipients may use that lump-sum distribution to pay off bills that are in arrears, reinstate their homeowner's insurance, and/or pay for home repairs and maintenance.

When a homeowner opts for a reverse mortgage, he pays no monthly mortgage payments, but he is still responsible for property taxes, homeowner's insurance, and maintenance expenses. As long as he fulfills those responsibilities and resides in the property, he cannot lose his home. The amount of money available is based on the age of the youngest borrower, the current interest rate, the value of the home, and the specific mortgage selected. The borrower for the reverse mortgage must either be the owner or co-owner of the home.

Reverse mortgages may make the most sense for homeowners who have lived in and paid for their dwellings over a long period, and who are living on fixed incomes and in need of extra cash to cover bills, medical costs, and day-to-day living expenses. They're not a cure-all, so be sure to consult your lender or a financial advisor if you think a reverse mortgage may be right for you.

Other Mortgage Options

During the home-buying process, you're sure to come across variations of the mortgages we've discussed thus far. Let's take a look at some of the other mortgages currently on the market today.

Conforming Loans

Conforming loans are conventional loans that follow guidelines set up by Fannie Mae and Freddie Mac, two corporations that purchase mortgage loans from lenders and help to maintain a steady flow of affordable home-financing funds for Americans.

Fannie Mae and Freddie Mac establish maximum loan amounts, as well as specifying which properties qualify for these loans, the requisite down payments, and borrower credit and income requirements. Fannie Mae and Freddie Mac announce new loan limits each year. The 2006 conforming loan limit for a first mortgage is $417,000 for a single-family home.

Jumbo Loans

Jumbo loans exceed the limits set by Fannie Mae and Freddie Mac, and, as such, cannot be funded by these two corporations. They typically carry a higher interest rate than conforming, conventional loans. Because of this higher rate—and because these loans generally are used for higher-end homes—jumbo loans aren't for everyone. However, considered in the context of historically low U.S. mortgage rates, this product can provide some flexibility for the buyer who wants to finance a more expensive home.

Subprime Loans

Subprime loans do not meet the borrower credit requirements set forth by Fannie Mae and Freddie Mac. Such loans are generally made to borrowers who have less-than-perfect credit, due to missed payments or late payments. Lenders charge a higher interest rate for subprime loans to compensate for potential losses from customers who may run into financial trouble or default on their loan.

These loans are also offered to borrowers who may have recently filed for bankruptcy or have lost a home to foreclosure. Sometimes associated with **predatory lending practices** (see pages 150–153), these loans do serve a purpose, in

Two names will undoubtedly pop up at some point during the home-buying process: Fannie Mae and Freddie Mac. Here's a short description of each one:

The Mortgage Giants

Fannie Mae

Fannie Mae (Federal National Mortgage Association) was established by the federal government in 1938 (toward the end of the Great Depression), to help make mortgage funds more readily accessible to Americans. Authorized to purchase from lenders mortgages insured by the Federal Housing Administration (FHA), privately run Fannie Mae then "packages" those mortgages (which are made to low- and middle-income Americans) into securities that are subsequently sold to investors. In this way, Fannie Mae ensures that the supply of money available for home loans is replenished regularly. The corporation, which receives no government funding, operates under a congressional charter, and has its sights set on making homeownership more accessible for low-, moderate-, and middle-income Americans.

Freddie Mac

Created in 1970 by the U.S. Congress, **Freddie Mac (Federal Home Loan Mortgage Corporation)** does its part to boost homeownership by providing the mortgage industry with liquidity and stability. A stockholder-owned corporation that's traded under "FRE" on the New York and Pacific Stock Exchanges, Freddie Mac keeps money flowing to mortgage lenders in support of homeownership and rental housing, and in so doing helps lower housing costs and provide better access to home financing. Its portfolio of loans helps ensure a stable supply of money for lenders granting new home loans, while its financing for low- to moderate-income families helps people who might not otherwise be able to afford homes.

that they offer temporary financing to these applicants until they can qualify for a conforming loan (by, say, establishing a good track record of payments over a certain amount of time). A borrower may take out a 2/28 ARM subprime loan that allows him to prove over a two-year period that he is able to make on-time payments. When that period is up, he can reapply for a fixed-rate, conforming loan for the remaining twenty-eight years, based on that established track record.

Biweekly Mortgages

These mortgages allow you to pay half the monthly mortgage payment every two weeks. As a result, you'll wind up repaying the loan faster than you would if you were making monthly payments. A thirty-year loan, for example, can often be paid off within eighteen to nineteen years with a biweekly repayment schedule. How does it work? Well, instead of making twelve monthly payments throughout the course of the year, you make thirteen. That extra payment reduces the principal while reducing the time it takes to pay off a thirty-year mortgage.

No-Document ("No-doc") Loans

No-doc loans often are used by self-employed individuals who may have a hard time proving how much money they earn—or by loan applicants with poor or no credit history. No-doc mortgages involve a shorter application process, since you are not required to provide income, employment, or asset documentation. These loans, which tend to carry a higher interest rate and are not offered by all lenders, also feature a streamlined approval process because there is little subsequent verification.

Two-Step Mortgages

These loans combine the constancy of a fixed-rate mortgage with the lower rates of an ARM. Like balloon loans, they come in 5/25 and 7/23 variations. This means that for the first five or seven years of the thirty-year mortgage (depending on which option you choose), the interest rate remains fixed. Subsequently, the loan is either converted to a fixed-rate mortgage for the remainder of the term, or it becomes an ARM. Because there is a higher level of risk involved (since the interest rate will fluctuate after the five- or seven-year period expires) the opening interest rate for two-step mortgages is generally lower than that of a standard, thirty-year fixed loan.

Graduated Payment Mortgages (GPMs)

These loans start out with low monthly payments that gradually increase at pre-determined intervals. The lower initial payments allow borrowers to qualify for larger loan amounts, with the monthly payments growing steadily in order to make up the balance during the life of the loan.

Buydown Mortgages

A buydown mortgage carries an initially discounted interest rate that increases slowly (usually over a one- to three-year period) up to an agreed-upon fixed rate. This discounted rate allows borrowers to qualify for higher-priced homes. With buydown mortgages, borrowers pay an initial lump sum to the lender, which effectively reduces their monthly payments during the first few years of the mortgage. The 2-1 buydown, one of the more popular options, works like this: Suppose the interest rate on your mortgage is 9 percent. With a 2-1 buydown mortgage, your initial discounted rate is 7 percent. You pay this 7 percent interest rate the first year, and then pay 8 percent the second year, and 9 percent afterwards.

Forty-Year Mortgages

Fannie Mae recently began buying this type of mortgage; as a result, more lenders are offering them. With this loan, a borrower has forty years to pay off the debt, instead of the traditional thirty. Lengthening the term cuts the monthly payment slightly, but the trade-off comes in the form of a higher interest rate than you'd typically get for a thirty-year loan. Also, because you pay off the principal more slowly, it takes you longer to build equity and you end up paying more interest over the life of the loan.

Creative Financing

In addition to the loans discussed thus far, there are special options available to certain home buyers, such as veterans, immigrants, and members of certain professions, as well as government programs geared toward buyers with particular needs. If you're concerned about qualifying for a mortgage, work with your real estate agent or conduct you own research to learn more about the following mortgage programs and others for which you may be eligible.

FHA Loans

The Federal Housing Administration (FHA), which is part of the U.S. Deptartment of Housing and Urban Development (HUD), administers a number of mortgage loan programs. FHA loans have lower down payment requirements and are easier to qualify for than conventional loans. According to the FHA (www.fha.com), you don't need to meet a minimum income requirement to qualify for an FHA loan. However, debt ratios (determined through a thorough analysis of income and monthly expenses) keyed to the state in which the home will be purchased have been put in place to prevent borrowers from buying a home they cannot afford.

VA Loans

These loans, which are guaranteed by the U.S. Department of Veterans Affairs, allow veterans and service persons to obtain home loans with favorable loan terms, usually with no down payment. These loans are easier to qualify for than conventional loans, and are generally limited to a maximum amount established by the VA. Note that the VA doesn't actually make these loans; rather, it offers a guarantee of repayment to lenders. If the borrower fails to repay, then the VA is responsible for the covered amount. If you qualify, the VA will issue you a certificate of eligibility to be used in applying for a VA loan at a private lending institution.

In 2004, a federal law increased the amount of the maximum VA loan guaranty. This cap is now equal to 25 percent of the equivalent Freddie Mac–conforming loan limit for a single-family residence. For example, the maximum guaranty for 2006 would be $104,250—25 percent of $417,000, the 2006 Freddie Mac–conforming loan limit for a single-family residence. In most cases, the veteran can borrow up to this $417,000 with no down payment.

RHS Loan Programs

The Rural Housing Service (RHS) of the U.S. Department. of Agriculture (USDA) guarantees loans with minimal closing costs and no down payment for rural residents. The RHS offers two distinct loan programs:

- **Direct Loan Program:** This program is designed for individuals or families in need of financial assistance when purchasing a home. The funds are made available through the USDA's Housing and Community Facilities Programs (HCFP) in the form of home loans offered at affordable interest rates. According to the USDA, the majority of loans granted under this program are to families living below 80 percent of their communities' median income levels.

- **Loan Guarantee Program:** Through its Housing and Community Facilities Programs, the USDA also guarantees loans made by private-sector lenders. Should the homeowner default on the loan, then HCFP pays that private lender for the loan, thus ensuring that the lender receives adequate payback even in the event of a default. The borrower works directly with the lender, and makes payments to the lender. According to the USDA, an individual or family can borrow up to 100 percent of the appraised value of a home, thus eliminating the need for a down payment.

Other State and Local Housing Programs

To help put homeownership within reach of more people, many states, counties, and municipalities provide low- to moderate-income housing finance programs, down payment assistance, and/or special programs for first-time home buyers. Such programs tend to be more lenient when it comes to qualification guidelines and often call for lower up-front fees; in addition, grants may be available to help you come up with a down payment and closing costs.

Several loan assistance programs are offered at the local, state and federal levels, such as the Mortgage Credit Certificate (MCC). Authorized by Congress in 1984, the MCC provides financial assistance to first-time home buyers for the purchase of qualifying single-family homes, townhouses, and condominiums. Qualified borrowers receive a tax credit when purchasing their homes, thus reducing their federal income taxes; in effect, this amounts to a mortgage subsidy. The current tax credit rate is 20 percent or less. If you obtain a mortgage loan of $200,000 at 6 percent interest for thirty years, your monthly loan payment will be $1,199.10 per month. With an MCC credit rate of 20 percent, you'll receive a federal income tax credit for the year of $2,877.84. As long as your income tax liability exceeds that amount, you'll receive the full credit (with any unused portion carried forward for up to three years to offset future income tax liability).

To apply for the MCC, borrowers apply for a loan with a participating lender. The lender then determines if the borrower is eligible for an MCC, based on the preliminary indications of income, purchase price, prior homeownership, the location of the residence to be purchased, and potential tax liability.

Tom Wolfe, broker-associate with RE/MAX Properties in LaGrange, Illinois, guides buyers toward a down payment/closing cost assistance program offered by the Illinois Housing Development Authority (IHDA). The program targets first-time home buyers, and is available in certain communities that IHDA serves. Wolfe recently helped a single mother buy a $95,000, three-bedroom, ranch-style home in Chicago with just 2 percent down. She received a grant from IHDA for 4 percent of the purchase price to cover closing costs and other expenses.

On the state and local levels, creative new programs are continually emerging to assist home buyers who might not otherwise be able to fulfill the dream of homeownership. In weighing all your options, be sure to speak to your agent and your lender about any programs like these available in your community.

Special Programs from Fannie Mae

Real estate agents often use Fannie Mae as a resource when working with home buyers, mainly because the institution is very good at helping put the pieces together to make homeownership attainable. In 2003, for example, Fannie Mae set a record when it provided over $463 billion in financing for 4.2 million U.S. families to increase homeownership rates. Fannie Mae offers the following special programs to assist eligible home buyers:

- **Immigrant Initiative:** Fannie Mae's program called "A New Home in a New Country" is a comprehensive bilingual marketing campaign that helps lenders address the needs of immigrant borrowers nationwide. Through this effort, home buyers don't need to be permanent residents or citizens to buy a home in the United States. Flexible, low–down payment loans allow immigrant borrowers to apply for a home loan even if they are only in the process of obtaining a green card, or they do not have a complete history of income and credit in this country.

- **Timely Payment Rewards:** Just over a year old, this program matches Fannie Mae with lenders to make homeownership more affordable for borrowers with past credit difficulties. With this new mortgage option, eligible borrowers may finance their homes at an interest rate that is as much as 2 percent lower than what is typically paid for higher-rate alternative financing. (These rates are still higher than those designed for borrowers who are good credit risks.)

- **Community Solutions:** Introduced last year, Fannie Mae's Community Solutions mortgage is for America's firefighters, police officers, and teachers. The high loan-to-value mortgage options, available to Fannie Mae–approved lenders, are designed to assist eligible home buyers in purchasing one- or two-unit properties. The product offers flexible credit guidelines and qualifying ratios, as well as lower down payments with minimum contributions of 1 percent or $500 (whichever is less) from the borrowers' own funds.

For further information about these programs, or to learn more about Fannie Mae, visit the organization's Web site at www.fanniemae.org.

Choosing the Right Mortgage

In light of all these mortgage options, how do you determine which one is right for you? Consider these key factors:

- Your current financial picture

- Any changes you anticipate in your finances (one spouse planning to stay home with the children, one spouse going back to school, etc.)

- How long you plan to own your home

- How well equipped you are to deal with mortgage-payment changes that may result from interest-rate fluctuations

For example, while a fifteen-year, adjustable-rate mortgage may save you money in interest payments over the life of the loan, your monthly payments will be higher and interest-rate increases could cause your payments to rise higher still. On the other hand, a thirty-year, fixed-rate mortgage may be less desirable if interest rates are falling or if you only plan to stay put for three years. If interest rates are on a downtrend, for example, you may not want to "lock in" for thirty years (although there is always the option of refinancing at a later date, should

TABLE 6.1 FIXED-RATE VERSUS ARM MORTGAGES

	Pros	Cons
Fixed Rate	Budgeting is easier because you'll always know what your monthly payment is for the life of the loan, unless you refinance at a later date. Your loan's interest rate won't change, so increases and decreases in market rates do not affect you. Your payments will not become "suddenly unaffordable" due to higher interest rates.	The higher interest rates (compared to ARMs) could require a higher income in order to qualify. Should interest rates recede significantly, you'll need to refinance your mortgage in order to take advantage of them. Bear in mind that refinancing is often a costly and time-consuming process in itself.
ARM	Your initial interest rate will most likely be lower than the interest charged for a fixed-rate mortgage. Your initial payments should therefore be lower. ARMs can be easier to qualify for, since you bear more of the risk than the lender does. Payments will go down if market interest rates decline.	If interest rates increase, so will your monthly mortgage payments. A substantial interest-rate increase and a subsequent rise in your mortgage payments could make your monthly payments unaffordable, putting you at risk of losing your home and all the money you've put into it.

you choose to do so). Also, if you only plan to stay in your home for a short period, it might be advantageous for you to take a shorter-term loan, which has you pay off more of your principal balance earlier than you would with a thirty-year loan.

Fixed or ARM?

One of the first steps to take during this mortgage-research process is deciding whether to go with a fixed-rate mortgage or an ARM. Table 6.1 spells out the pros and cons of each option.

As you can see from Table 6.1, with a fixed-rate mortgage, your risk is lower but the cost is higher; with an ARM, by contrast, your risk is higher (because if interest rates rise, so do your mortgage payments), but your cost is initially lower (and it's easier to qualify for one).

As noted earlier, the interest rates on ARMs fluctuate according to movements in a specified index. Commonly used indexes include the national average mortgage rate or the Treasury bill rate. When using an ARM to finance your home, you can expect to see the monthly payment change along with the interest rates. As a consumer, you'll need to determine whether a lower initial interest rate on the ARM is worth the uncertainty about possible future increases in your mortgage payments.

Here are some key questions to ask your lender before agreeing to an ARM:

- What is my starting mortgage interest rate?

- How long will that starting rate be in effect?

- How often will my mortgage be adjusted? (Once a year? Every three years? Every five years?) Keep in mind that—unless interest rates are on a downward swing—the longer the span between adjustments, the better.

- Which index will be used to adjust my mortgage rate? Ask your lender for a chart that shows how that index has fluctuated over the last five to fifteen years, and use it as a guide when selecting your own mortgage. By reviewing rate activity over the last decade or so, you'll get a good idea of how rates tend to fluctuate. Talk to your real estate agent or mortgage professional to gain further insights in this area.

- What is the **margin** on my mortgage rate? The margin is the percentage that the lender adds to the index rate in order to come up with your mortgage rate. If the index rate is 8 percent, for example, and the margin is 3 percent, then your interest rate is 11 percent. The margin is basically the lender's markup and represents the company's cost of doing business and the profit that it will earn on the loan.

- Does my initial mortgage rate include a special discount? If it does, be prepared for a significant increase in your monthly payments when that initial rate is adjusted for the first time. To entice customers to sign up for a particular ARM, lenders sometimes offer "teaser rates" that are lower than the loan's actual interest rate.

- Does the ARM offer loan convertibility? If so, then you will be allowed to switch over to a fixed-rate loan at a designated time in the future.

- What limits or caps have been placed on the adjustments? You definitely need to know the maximum amount that your mortgage rate can increase, both in any single adjustment period and over the life of the loan.

- Is there a possibility of **negative amortization?** Negative amortization occurs when your monthly mortgage payments do not cover all the interest due on your loan. See the box on page 135 for more information on negative amortization and how it may affect the amount you ultimately owe.

- Is my ARM **assumable?** If so, you may be able to pass your loan on to a credit-worthy individual who would like to purchase your home. (See page 137 for more details on this practice.)

- What happens if the mortgage lender sells my loan? In most cases, the terms of the loan do not change when the loan changes hands.

- Is there a **prepayment penalty?** If there is, then you may be assessed a fee if you sell your home and pay off the loan earlier than the original loan term dictated. These penalties cover the interest that a lender loses due to prepayment of a loan. Some states prohibit lenders from imposing any prepayment penalty, so be sure to find out whether this is the case in the state where you want to buy a home.

As you weigh the pros and cons of each option, realize that there is no "right" answer. So ask your lender to carefully spell out your options before you make your final decision.

Beware of Negative Amortization

Amortization refers to the paying down of your mortgage through the gradual repayment of your mortgage loan in installments. It occurs when your monthly payments are large enough to cover the interest owed, plus a portion of the principal. *Negative amortization,* by contrast, is an increase in your total outstanding mortgage balance. This occurs when your monthly payments do *not* cover all the interest due on the loan (not to mention the principal). Some ARMs cap the amount your monthly payments can increase. You should be aware that if the interest rate increases and your payments do not keep pace, you run the risk of negative amortization (that is, rather than paying down your debt, you're actually increasing it). This "unpaid" amount (the difference between what you pay each month and the monthly interest due on the loan) is added to the balance of your loan and generates even more interest debt. At the end of the term, you could end up owing more than you did at closing! If you're getting an ARM, be sure to ask what limits there are on negative amortization.

Length of the Loan

When researching loans, be sure to consider the actual life of the loan itself (in years). How long you plan to reside in and/or own your home will figure prominently in your decision about which type of mortgage to select.

If your time line is five to seven years or less, for example, then an ARM, a balloon mortgage, or a two-step mortgage might be most appropriate because you are likely to sell your home and find a new home, with a new mortgage, before the balloon payment is due or before the interest rate and payments rise. (You should also factor into your thinking any prepayment penalties that the lender will hit you with if you pay off the loan before the end of the loan period.)

However, if you're looking to stay put for ten or more years, then a traditional fifteen-, twenty-, or thirty-year fixed-rate mortgage might be more desirable because these kinds of mortgages offer predictable payments over time.

A popular choice, due to the affordability of the payments associated with it, is the thirty-year, fixed-rate loan. You may also opt to repay these loans over fifteen, twenty, or forty years, depending on your circumstances. ARMs are generally available in increments of six months, one year, two years, three years, five years, seven years, and ten years. At the end of the initial term, the homeowner either pays off the remaining balance or refinances the loan. Normally, the shorter the payment period, the lower the interest rate. If you know you will only own a home for the first two to three years, a loan that is fixed for three to five years may suit you well and save you thousands of dollars compared to a thirty-year fixed-rate mortgage.

Size of the Loan

The actual amount of your loan can drive up your interest rate, particularly if the amount that's being financed exceeds the conforming loan limits, which are established by Fannie Mae and Freddie Mac. These limits are set annually. For 2006, Fannie Mae's single-family mortgage loan limits are:

First mortgages*

- One-family loans: $417,000
- Two-family loans: $533,850
- Three-family loans: $645,300
- Four-family loans: $801,950

Note: These limits do not apply to one- to four-family mortgages in Alaska, Hawaii, Guam, and the U.S. Virgin Islands, where conforming loan limits are 50 percent higher than the limits for the rest of the country.

Second mortgages

- $208,500
- In Alaska, Hawaii, Guam, and the U.S. Virgin Islands: $312,750

If the amount you're seeking to borrow for your home purchase exceeds these limits, you will not be eligible for a conforming loan.

When shopping for a mortgage, you're sure to run into a lot of jargon that the typical consumer doesn't understand (or generally care about, for that matter). Here are a couple of terms you may encounter—and that you should definitely understand when and if you do get a mortgage:

Know the Lingo

- **Assumability:** This applies to the loan that the home seller negotiated when she purchased the dwelling. Through this process, you would assume the obligations of the existing mortgage—a windfall if the terms and rates on the seller's mortgage are more favorable than those available in the current market. If you are selling a home and the buyer is assuming the existing mortgage, be sure to get a fully executed "release of liability" certificate from the lender; otherwise, you remain as the original mortgagor (borrower) and you could be held liable should the buyer (or future buyers) default. You may wish to involve a lawyer in this process.

- **Expandability:** An expandable loan allows you to increase the principal amount, should you require more funds down the road. The new loan amount would come with a new interest rate, which is generally based on both the initial mortgage rate and the prevailing rates. If you foresee high expenses (such as a child's education) in the future, be sure to discuss this option with your lender.

Other Mortgage Considerations

In addition to the factors addressed thus far, during the mortgage-shopping process you also need to look at the total cost of the loan, including fees, points, and any other items that might affect the affordability of the loan. Let's discuss some of these key items now, and what you should be on the lookout for.

Origination and Discount Points

When you take out a mortgage, you'll be introduced to two types of points: origination points and discount points. **Origination points** are the commission points charged by your lender, loan officers, and/or mortgage broker to cover the cost of making the loan. All lenders use origination points to evaluate, prepare, and submit your mortgage loan. Typically expressed as a percentage, one point equals 1 percent of the total loan amount.

Discount points are paid to the lender when a loan is originated, and they account for the difference between the current market-determined rate of interest and the actual lower interest rate of the loan. Put simply, they allow you to "buy down" the cost of the mortgage by paying a certain amount of money up front in lieu of paying interest over the life of the loan. Each point is equal to 1 percent of the original loan amount. So if you take out a $200,000 mortgage loan, then one point equals $2,000. In return for the points, you get a lower interest rate on your loan. Discount points may be paid by either the buyer or the seller at closing, and are available to borrowers using both fixed-rate mortgages and ARMs.

Here's an example of how discount points work: Let's say you want a thirty-year, fixed-rate mortgage loan. If a lender quotes an 8 percent interest rate on that $200,000 loan, then you can either:

1. Take the loan as offered, and pay no discount points; or,

2. Request from the lender an interest rate that reflects your payment of one, two, or three discount points.

For each discount point that you pay on a thirty-year loan, you can expect the interest rate to be reduced by 0.125, or one-eighth of a percentage point. Pay one discount point at closing on a $200,000 loan (or $2,000), for example, and you can lower your interest rate from 8 percent to 7 $^7/_8$ percent. Pay two discount points, and your interest rate will drop to 7 $^3/_4$ percent. Understand that these are hypothetical examples, used to help you grasp the concept of discount points. For actual numbers and quotes, please discuss your individual situation with your lender.

There are a few advantages to using discount points that go beyond just whittling down your interest rate. For starters, discount points can be tax deductible, which means you may be able to recoup on your tax return some of the up-front money paid to cover them. You should verify any tax deductions you plan to take with a tax advisor. Also, you may be able to negotiate with the seller to pick up some of the points on your loan. On the downside, you'll have to pay for your points all at one time (compared to interest payments, which you only pay for as long as you own your home), and paying points up front means you'll need more cash at the closing table.

When deciding whether to pay discount points, think about how long you plan to stay in the home and/or keep the loan. If you're going to hang onto your home for four years or longer, then chances are pretty good that you'll recoup the costs through lower monthly payments. However, if you're going to be moving and selling within the next four years—or if you think you might refinance the home during that period—then a traditional, no-points loan may be your best bet.

Lock-Ins

Another term you'll hear used often in home-lending circles is **interest rate lock-in**. When a lender agrees to an interest rate lock-in, that means the quoted interest rate is guaranteed for a specified period. Since interest rates can change frequently, most lenders offer an interest rate lock-in guaranteeing that interest rate if the loan is closed within a specific time frame, often thirty to sixty days. This can be particularly useful for home buyers when interest rates are rising.

Doing the Math

Getting the lowest possible interest rate is usually a key focus for home buyers. But buyers should also understand that the rate a lender offers and what the buyer actually ends up with may be two different things. In other words, the lender offering a 5.5 percent APR may not necessarily be giving you a better deal than the one serving up the 5.75 percent rate.

To make sure you're getting the best possible deal, speak with a variety of lenders and negotiate for the best possible terms, and at the same time, understand some simple concepts relating to interest rates and points.

Let's say you are presented with two different mortgages:

Lender #1 offers a $200,000 loan at a 5.5 percent interest rate with one point (added to the loan as $2,000 in additional principal).

Lender #2 offers a $200,000 loan at a 5.75 percent interest rate, but with no points.

Here's how to compare them:

- **Lender #1:** One point equals 1 percent of the mortgage, or $2,000. Using a mortgage calculator, you can determine that your monthly principal and interest payments (for a $200,000 loan + $2,000 for one point) will be $1,146.93. Your total payments over thirty years (interest plus principal) will add up to $412,894.

- **Lender #2:** Using a mortgage calculator, you find that this loan costs $1,167.15 per month over thirty years, or $420,174 in total payments over the life of the loan.

In the first scenario, the borrower uses the point to "buy down" the mortgage and get a lower interest rate, which translates into him paying less for the actual home over the life of the loan. When shopping for your loan, be sure to compare these fine points, and ask as many questions as necessary to ensure that you truly understand exactly how much you're paying, what you're paying for, and all the pesky terms and conditions that lurk within the mortgage papers.

Mortgage lenders may not automatically offer you the lock-in, so definitely ask for it if you want it. Be sure the time period of the lock-in covers the number of weeks or months before you expect to close on your home, and understand that if rates are falling, it may be best to wait until the last possible moment before locking in.

Annual Percentage Rates

As discussed in chapter 2, the annual percentage rate (APR) refers to the true cost of borrowing and includes any fees or prepaid interest involved in obtaining a loan. This amount is different from the note rate, or the interest rate that appears on the mortgage loan, or note. The federal Truth in Lending Act requires lenders to disclose the APR, which generally includes:

- **Points:** As discussed above, these are equal to 1 percent of the loan amount and are paid to your mortgage lender at closing.

- **Prepaid interest:** This is the interest you pay to the lender, based on the date the loan closes through the end of the month. Most mortgage companies assume fifteen days of interest in their calculations.

- **Loan-processing fee:** This fee is charged by some lenders for gathering information to enable the lender to process the loan.

- **Underwriting fee:** This fee covers the process of evaluating a loan application to determine the risk involved for the lender, and to prepare the file for closing.

- **Document-preparation fee:** This refers to the fee charged by the lender for drawing up loan documents.

- **Private mortgage insurance (PMI):** This insurance is required if your down payment is less than 20 percent of the total loan amount (see below).

- **Loan-application fee:** This is the fee you pay to a lender to review the formal document that's filled out when you apply for a mortgage.

- **Credit life insurance:** This refers to coverage that pays off the mortgage in the event of a borrower's death. Purchased by the lender, this insurance policy matches the loan balance at any given time, and, as such, will pay off the debt in full in the event of death. The payments for this coverage decrease as the mortgage balance decreases.

When you apply for a mortgage, the lender is expected to supply you with a good-faith estimate of closing costs and a truth-in-lending statement of financing terms within three business days. This estimate includes the note rate, along with the APR, which will be higher than that note rate because it includes the items specified above. The APR's purpose is to give borrowers a truer representation of the effective interest rate on their loan.

Private Mortgage Insurance

Lenders require this insurance if your down payment is less than 20 percent of the home's appraised value or sale price. Such insurance protects lenders should you default on your loan.

Costs for such coverage vary, but typically equal 0.5–1 percent of the total loan amount. The buyer who puts 15 percent down on a $300,000 home, for example, may pay an annual private mortgage insurance (PMI) rate of $1,275 to $2,550. This is typically divided into monthly payments.

The good news is that you are usually only required to pay PMI as long as your loan-to-value ratio exceeds 80 percent; in other words, until you have built up 20 percent or more equity in your home by paying down the principal loan amount (as opposed to the interest on the loan). At that point, you can notify the lender and request that the lender cease charging for PMI premiums. The Homeowners Protection Act of 1998 requires that, for mortgage transactions entered into on or after July 29, 1999, lenders must disclose in writing to buyers at closing how many years and months it will take for them to reach that 80 percent level, at which point they can cancel the PMI. In addition, lenders must automatically cancel PMI, even without notification from the homeowner, when the principal balance of the loan hits 78 percent of the property's original value.

Your mortgage will likely be the largest loan you will ever take out, so it is important to get one that suits you and your particular situation. This will depend on your personal circumstances and your plans for the future. Many mortgage options on today's market have hidden drawbacks, so be sure to get independent advice from a real estate or mortgage professional before making your final selection. By becoming an educated consumer, you'll have a much better chance of getting the financing that you want and need to buy the right home for you.

CHAPTER SEVEN

Lenders and the Lending Process

O nce you have a general idea of the type of mortgage that best suits your situation, the next step is to make comparisons among lenders. Prospective lenders include your local banks, credit unions, national mortgage lenders, and local, national, and online mortgage brokers, who search for and find loan options for consumers. Get frequent updates on possible rates and features. Your local newspaper (try the weekend real estate section) or the Web sites of reputable national lenders can be good resources. To get the specifics of each lender's rates and terms, contact the bank or mortgage company directly or ask a mortgage broker to give you this information.

In this chapter, you'll learn about the people and companies behind the mortgage-lending process, and how to work with them. We'll also explore how to narrow your choices, comparison-shop for the best rates and services, and work with a lender to get the all-important preapproval letter.

Mortgage Providers

Mortgages are ultimately provided to consumers as a result of cooperation between direct lenders (who lend money directly to consumers) and indirect funding sources. Direct lenders include banks, savings and loans, credit unions, and mortgage brokers (who work as independent agents for the mortgage lenders they represent). Let's take a more detailed look at the various participants in the mortgage-lending process.

Mortgage Bankers

These "direct" lenders are large enough to originate loans and create loan pools, or blocks of loans held in trust and pledged as security for the issuance of a **guarantee certificate** (a piece of paper that states that the buyer can purchase a home costing up to a certain amount). These loan pools are then packaged and sold directly to Fannie Mae, Freddie Mac, Ginnie Mae, and other investors. Mortgage bankers, which vary in size, include a number of national lenders such as Bank of America, Wachovia, Wells Fargo, and Chase. These lenders make money from the fees that you pay for the loan.

If you work with a mortgage banker, you'll probably deal with the same person (a loan officer) from the beginning to the end of the loan process. Once the loan closes, you may continue your relationship with the same company, or the lender may sell your loan to a secondary lender, like Fannie Mae or Freddie Mac. After you close on your loan, the company to which you make payments is known as the loan **servicer**. That firm will process payments, mail you monthly statements, and collect money for and make payments from any escrow accounts that were initiated at closing, such as those established for property taxes.

Local Financial Institutions

Local banks, trust companies, savings and loans, and other financial institutions are also in the mortgage business. Some have their own mortgage divisions, staffed with specialists who can help you with a home mortgage. If you already have a trusted relationship with a local financial institution, then you may want to make this your first stop in the mortgage-shopping process. It's estimated that about half the mortgage loans made in the United States today involve local savings and loans.

Portfolio Lenders

These institutions, which typically include larger banks and savings and loans, lend their own money and do not sell their mortgages on the secondary market to institutions like Freddie Mac and Fannie Mae. These lenders are typically savings and loans or banks that originate loans for their own portfolios, and, as a result, are not required to obey those institutions' guidelines. As such, they often develop their own rules for determining creditworthiness.

Credit Unions

Credit unions are financial cooperatives made up of individuals with a common affiliation, such as employment or place of residence. Credit unions accept member deposits, pay interest in the form of dividends, and provide installment loans to their members. If you do business with a credit union, be sure to check out its mortgage offerings. These institutions tend to offer very favorable rates and put a premium on customer service.

Mortgage Brokers

While they don't lend money themselves, mortgage brokers serve as intermediaries between home buyers in need of financing and lenders that want to make loans. They specialize in loan origination and receive a commission (usually paid for at closing, by the buyer) for matching borrowers with lenders. Brokers can be good at locating financing for buyers who don't meet the standards required by direct lenders, such as applicants with less-than-desirable credit scores. Mortgage brokers generally perform some or most loan-processing functions, such as taking loan applications and ordering credit reports, appraisals, and title reports. Like independent insurance brokers, mortgage brokers shop the market and arrange the most favorable rates and terms for buyers, relying on established relationships with lenders to help them do so. Due to the nature of their business, mortgage brokers generally know where the best deals are and which mortgage bankers are apt to grant loans to riskier borrowers.

For their services, mortgage brokers typically earn a certain percentage or commission on the total loan amount. On a $200,000 mortgage, for example, a

mortgage broker charging 1.5 percent would earn $3,000. These rates are nego-
tiable and vary widely from broker to broker and from area to area.

Online Mortgage Providers

A wide variety of mortgage providers are doing business online, and offer everything from basic services that will hook you up with a lender, to those that originate loans themselves. Make sure to research any online mortgage provider you're
considering using. It can be difficult to figure out whether or not an online source
is legitimate (as opposed to a bank or other institution with an office you can stop
by), and cyber-criminals have been known to pose as mortgage lenders to obtain
sensitive personal information, including bank account numbers and Social
Security numbers.

Narrowing Your Choices

Here's the good news: As a buyer, you can choose to work with any lender who's
willing to do business with you—even if it's your Aunt Sue. The not-so-good news
is that—family members aside—there are literally thousands of lenders to choose
from, and unless you've done business with any of them in the past, it's hard to
figure out which one is the best choice. If this is your first time out, be sure to
confer with any or all of the following sources to piece together a list of prospective lenders:

- Your home builder, if you're building a new home
- Your family and friends who have bought or refinanced a home recently
- Your real estate agent
- Your financial advisor, if you have one
- The newspaper's real estate or business section, where real estate agents and
  property owners often advertise homes for sale
- Your local phone book under mortgages, where local mortgage firms advertise
  their services
- The Internet, where you'll find a variety of tools at your disposal for locating
  and screening lenders. You could do a search for *mortgage lenders in* [your
  state] as a good way to start.

How can you sift through this information to find a good candidate? When selecting your mortgage lender, consider that lender's customer service record, rely on recommendations from trusted acquaintances or professionals, and seek out a lender that is experienced in the mortgage business. All these factors are important and should be considered before deciding on a lender.

Be wary of lenders that are advertising or offering rates that are much lower than the market rates: This discrepancy could be a red flag signaling problems down the road. Here's why: Most mortgage firms tap the same pool of investors who, in turn, "back" mortgages by purchasing them. Therefore, the firm offering substantially lower rates may be making up the difference by upping your closing costs, increasing junk fees (up-front charges by the lender that are not included in your points), and/or tacking on additional settlement fee. (See the section on "Avoiding Predatory Lendors" on pages 150–153.)

Realize that while finding a good lender is important, the loan officer who has been assigned to your case is even more critical, since you'll be working closely with that person as you work your way through the approval process. A loan officer should shepherd you through the process and serve as your advocate, while at the same time helping you obtain a quality loan (that is, a loan with the best possible terms). In doing so, he should be dependable, ethical, and trustworthy. While it's not always easy to spot these qualities on the phone—or even in person—keep your eyes and ears open for anything that might indicate that the loan officer isn't abiding by these standards. If someone tells you, for example, that he will fax you a copy of a certain document within a day—and then takes a week to deliver the document without a valid reason for the delay—then you may want to reconsider taking out a loan from his company.

Comparison-Shopping

It's important to confer with at least three mortgage lenders before choosing one. This can be done by telephone, in person, via e-mail or other online source, or by fax. The first two options are preferable because you will be talking to a "live" person, rather than having to rely on written information that could be rehearsed or sent from an unreliable source. As discussed, if you use online sources to compare mortgage lenders, be sure you know the person or business that is receiving your confidential, personal, financial information. Educate yourself about any lender you're considering for your mortgage. Your real estate agent is a good source when it comes to finding reputable lending sources.

When communicating with these lenders, take notes and then refer back to them to narrow down your choices. To make sure you're comparing apples to apples in an industry where interest rates and other terms change from day to day, it's best to do all your research on the same day. Here's a simple way to proceed: Make copies of the worksheet on page 149 and use it to record each lender's rates and other terms.

With this information in hand, you should be able to quickly determine which lender is offering the best deal.

Looking Beyond the Numbers

When choosing a mortgage lender, it's important to base your decision on several factors—not just on price alone. Here are some other important issues to consider:

- The lender's history, business record, and length of time in business. A good way to investigate this is by contacting the Better Business Bureau in the lender's home city or state, or by checking online resources such as Hoover's, Inc. (www.hoovers.com), which provides data about publicly traded companies.

- The lender's reputation, as determined by references from real estate professionals, referrals from associates, and basic research into the lender's practices. One way to find out if a lender is—or isn't—reputable is by doing an Internet search for recent news concerning the lender and/or its subsidiaries. If you come across too many negative news articles concerning a particular lender, then you might want to reconsider using that firm as your mortgage lender.

- The application and approval process. Ideally, this should be as uncomplicated as possible. Contact each lender and request a copy of the application and an overview of the process.

- Best customer service offerings. Ask yourself: Does the lender answer the phone, or are you routed through a series of annoying, automated messages? Does the lender respond to your requests quickly, or are you put off for days, wondering if your request is being processed?

WORKSHEET MORTGAGE COMPARISON CHART

Today's date: _____ Company name: _____

Phone number: _____ Web site: _____

Contact name: _____ Mortgage type: _____

Quoted interest rate: _____ Annual percentage rate (APR): _____

Points quoted: _____ Interest rate-lock ins? ☐ Yes   ☐ No

If so, interest rate effective for how long? _____

Minimum down payment:

With mortgage insurance: _____

Without mortgage insurance: _____

Prepayment penalties: _____

Is mortgage assumable? ☐ Yes   ☐ No   Is mortgage portable? ☐ Yes   ☐ No

Is mortgage expandable? ☐ Yes   ☐ No

Loan-processing time: _____

Closing-cost breakdown: _____

Application/origination fee: _____

Credit-report fee: _____

Transfer taxes: _____

Survey fee: _____

Appraisal fee: _____

Title fee: _____

Other closing costs: _____

- Breadth of product line. Does the lender offer home equity lines of credit, in addition to fixed-rate mortgages and ARMs, for example?

- Recommendations from others who have done business with the lender.

- Your real estate agent's feedback on the lender.

As you can see, when comparing lenders, you're looking for more than just a favorable rate quote. Be sure take into account all the factors specified above before proceeding with the application and borrowing process.

Avoiding Predatory Lenders

The issue of predatory lending has come to light in recent years, thanks to increased media attention spotlighting this abusive lending practice, which strips borrowers of their home equity, threatens them with foreclosure and ruined credit, and primarily impacts areas where homeownership rates are lower than usual. The U.S. Department of Housing and Urban Development (HUD) has taken an active stance against predatory lending, bringing to light many cases against lenders and other organizations that have victimized home buyers. Some lenders, for example, prey on consumers who can't afford homes by giving them loans that they can't possibly pay off. When the time comes to foreclose on such properties, the lender ultimately wins: Not only is the homeowner left without shelter, but she is also subject to poor credit ratings and other financial woes.

To avoid falling prey to these kinds of unscrupulous practices, particularly if your income is low or your credit is less than perfect, you should know the red flags to watch out for during the lending process. You also need to be able to distinguish the legitimate subprime market—which does charge higher fees to match nonconventional buyers (such as those who have low credit scores) with loans—from the predatory lending environment, which deliberately exploits buyers.

Here are some key predatory lending tactics to watch out for:

- **Unwarranted mortgage-broker compensation:** Good, reputable mortgage brokers take it upon themselves to arrange each loan with the best terms and at the lowest possible rate. For doing so, they charge a reasonable fee for their services. Be wary of brokers who attempt to sell you a loan with the most fees and the highest rate possible (as a way of pocketing more compensation for themselves). Talk to the broker about his commission rate before you begin

The Local Advantage

At RE/MAX Advantage Realty in Spring Hill, Florida, broker-owner Barbara Quist works with a large number of first-time and repeat buyers. Along the way, she's learned to recognize the key challenges that consumers face in their quest to become homeowners. One of these hurdles involves finding the right mortgage company or bank.

"I look for lenders who are reputable, who get the job done, and who are in our market area," says Quist, who feels the last point is especially critical. Working with a local banker allows for face-to-face interaction, and lets her buyers establish relationships with those lenders.

"If a buyer selects a lender who is out of the area—and winds up having problems with that lender—it can become complicated pretty quickly," says Quist. Just recently, she worked with a buyer who chose a lender based far away, and that lender was unfamiliar with the appraisal, home inspection, and survey standards in her local area. As a result, the appraiser the lender retained was unable to properly ascertain the property's value, since the lender could not provide the appraiser with the relevant local information and sales data.

Quist notes that buyers who are looking for loans on the Internet—or for loans from lenders based in far-off places—need to do extra homework to make sure they're working with a reputable, reliable firm that can deliver. Buyers with less-than-desirable credit might approach mortgage brokers for help, she says, while those who qualify for conventional mortgages should ask their professional and personal contacts for referrals.

"Rely on the advice of a real estate agent who is working in the area—someone who knows the market and is familiar with the various lenders operating there," Quist advises.

working with him, and be sure you're clear on exactly what fees he will charge at the closing table.

- **Flipping:** This is the repeated refinancing of your home loan, a practice encouraged by predatory lenders. Every time you refinance and "take a little cash off the top" for yourself, you not only end up paying a new set of fees, but you also place yourself further in debt to the lender for a longer period of time. Flipping also refers to the practice of buying homes at below-market rates and then selling them to unwary home buyers at inflated prices—a practice that may even involve collusion between appraisers, lenders, and others to the detriment of home buyers.

- **Extremely high points and fees:** When you take out a mortgage, it's common to pay a 1 percent origination fee and even another 1 percent of the total loan amount in points, along with the typical closing costs (which include appraisal fees, title search fees, and attorney fees). If, however, you see a high number of "junk fees"—such as a $150 credit check fee that should have cost $50—added onto your good-faith estimate, then you may be a victim of predatory lending practices.

- **Balloon payments:** As we've already discussed, balloon mortgages are a legitimate product available to buyers. However, they also provide an avenue through which a predatory lender can reduce your monthly payments and leave you paying only the accrued interest each month. Follow that up with a huge balloon payment that's due after a certain number of years, and it's easy to see how a homeowner might wind up losing her home as a result of such practices.

- **Equity stripping:** Buyers who have a significant amount of equity in their homes may be targets for this type of predatory lending. In this situation, lenders dole out an amount that is more than you can afford, knowing that you are likely to default. The lender can then foreclose and sell the house, effectively "stripping" you of any equity earned.

HUD also cautions buyers to be wary of predatory lenders, appraisers, mortgage brokers, and home improvement contractors (some of whom may actually be working together) who:

- Use false appraisals to sell properties for more than they are worth.

- Encourage borrowers to lie about their financial situation in order to obtain a loan.

- Purposely lend borrowers more money than they can afford to repay.

- Base interest rates on a borrower's race or national origin, rather than on his credit history.

- Charge fees for unnecessary or nonexistent products and services.

- Pressure borrowers to take out higher-risk loans, such as balloon or interest-only mortgages, or loans with unreasonable prepayment penalties.

- Prey on vulnerable borrowers in need of cash, due to debt, medical bills, or unemployment, by offering them **cash-out refinance** offers that burden them with additional debt and fees.

- Pressure you to purchase home improvements and then finance them at high interest rates.

- Insist that they are your only chance of getting a mortgage or a fair deal on a home improvement.

- Ask you to sign sales contracts or loan documents that are blank or inaccurate.

- Claim (falsely) that Federal Housing Administration insurance protects you against property defects or loan fraud.

- Add costs or loan terms at closing to which you never agreed.

These are all signs to watch out for when you're applying for a mortgage. If you suspect that predatory tactics are being used in your situation, contact the U.S. Department of Housing and Urban Development (www.hud.gov).

Other Steps That Make a Difference

So far in this chapter we have discussed what to look for in a mortgage lender and how to avoid becoming a victim of predatory lending. Shortly, we'll move on to the one of the most crucial steps in buying the home of your dreams—securing a preapproval letter from your lender of choice. However, before we explain how to begin this process, here are a few final tips to keep in mind as you shop around for the right lender. These steps can mean the difference between a pleasant experience and one fraught with complications:

- Never take anyone's "word for it." Instead, get information and commitments in writing and ask for a copy of every document that you sign. While a verbal agreement may seem fine at the time, you never know when someone may "forget" what was said. Having documented proof of all agreements will help you ward off problems down the road.

- Find out exactly how much you're expected to pay in finance fees, plus any other fees that may be charged separately at closing. Keep an eye out for hidden or "junk" fees. Check for certain miscellaneous fees, such as notary and document preparation fees. They can add up to hundreds of dollars in extra closing costs. If any fees stand out as unwarranted, speak up about them early in the process.

- Realize that the mortgage company that promises the lowest rates may not be the best choice. Find out how long those advertised rates are guaranteed for, and be sure to allow yourself enough time for closing, since even the smallest delays may void those early "teaser" rates.

In the lending world, there is no such thing as a "one size fits all" mortgage professional. Where one home buyer may have the best experience using his local bank as a lending source, another may have a better time using a mortgage broker. Your own individual situation will dictate whether a loan officer, a mortgage broker, or an online lending source is your best bet.

Your Secret Weapon:
The Preapproval Letter

A preapproval letter from a lender specifies the amount of money you can borrow from that lender to purchase a home. There's nothing like having this weapon in your arsenal as you approach the front door of that home you've had your eye on for the last month. With that in your corner, not only do you—as the buyer—know how much house you can afford, but the real estate agents and sellers that you're working with are equally confident that when a purchase offer is written up, financing issues aren't likely to hold up the transaction. Real estate agents know what price range to keep in mind for you when scouring the target area for prospects, and sellers know that you're not just out there testing the waters.

Note that there is a difference between getting preapproved and getting pre-qualified for a loan. The prequalification process is quick and easy, and provides an estimate (based on data you give the lender) of what you can afford. The preap-proval process, on the other hand, is much more intense. In getting preapproved, you basically go through the same motions that you would to get a loan, including providing necessary employment and financial documentation and authorizing the lender to run a credit report on you. A preapproval letter shows sellers that you've taken the time to go through the mortgage application process, thus cementing your position as a "legitimate" home buyer, and not just someone who is out there looking around at what's available. Note that a preapproval letter is not a guarantee of a loan; while the lender has vetted you as a buyer, the lender will still need to appraise the home you decide to purchase before making the loan.

Approval in Hand

Depending on the real estate market conditions in your area, a preapproval letter may help you in different ways. This tool can be particularly useful in hot real estate markets, where the best homes are bought and sold within days or even hours, depending on their desirability. Being able to prove that you can indeed purchase a home at a certain price, and that a lender is ready to loan you the money when the time comes, strengthens your negotiating position and makes your bid more likely to be accepted. On the other hand, you may be located in a real estate market where homes languish on the local MLS for months, waiting for the right buyer to come along. In those scenarios, a preapproval letter may be most useful as a way for you to rule out homes that you may not be able to afford and thus make your home search more efficient and practical.

Preapprovals also make the actual loan process that much easier and faster, since you've already turned over most of the information, data, and documentation needed to get mortgage approval. If you're approved through one major mortgage firm's preapproval program, for example, you can often anticipate a closing time frame of as little as three weeks after the purchase contract has been signed. However, keep in mind that, in most cases, forty-five to sixty days from application to closing is typical. Each lender's time frame will vary based on the transaction. If a loan-processing delay comes up, for example, then closing may need to be postponed until the issue is resolved. Or, if the home you're purchasing needs repairs that the seller doesn't have time to complete prior to the initial date set for closing, then the closing date may also be delayed.

If you're unsure about whether a preapproval is right for your situation, consider the following scenarios:

Home buyer #1 doesn't get a preapproval, and begins looking in his target area for homes priced between $150,000 and $500,000. He finds a $350,000 home that he likes, only to find out—after signing the purchase contract—that he can only afford a $250,000 home. Those weeks spent looking for homes are lost, as he and his agent are forced to start back at square one, this time looking for homes in his actual price range. The seller also loses out, since her home was taken off the market for two weeks while the buyer attempted to obtain financing. Would a preapproval letter have saved all parties valuable time? You bet.

Home buyer #2 obtains a preapproval letter, and soon finds herself up against dozens of other buyers who are looking for homes priced in the $200,000 range. At an open house, she makes a written offer of $195,000 for a great home, only to have her offer followed up by a $196,000 offer and a $197,000 offer from two potential buyers who haven't obtained preapproval letters. In a hurry to sell, which offer do you think the seller will pursue with a counteroffer? That's right: Home buyer #2 is sitting in a very good position.

For some, the preapproval process may also be an eye-opener. After going through the process, you may end up feeling as if now may not be the best time to purchase a home after all. Perhaps you need to clean up your credit, save additional funds for a down payment, or tap a local or state government program that helps first-time home buyers over the financing hurdles. Obtaining preapproval can help sort through those issues before you set out on your home search, making the entire process more manageable and your outcome more successful.

Getting Started with the Preapproval Process

The mortgage preapproval process should begin before you even start looking at homes. To get the ball rolling, first select a lender. As we've mentioned, a good starting point would be the local institution where you already have a relationship (say, the bank where you have a savings and a checking account, or where you've taken out car loans). You can also work with another local bank, a credit union, a mortgage lender, a mortgage broker, or an online lender. (Note that you're not obligated to do business with the lender that issues you the preapproval letter.) By providing these institutions with the documentation and information normally required on a loan application (and outlined in detail in the next section), you'll be able to get a handle on exactly what size loan you can afford, based on your income, credit score, and past payment history.

Once your application has been reviewed, the lender or broker will provide you with a mortgage preapproval letter, which you'll then show to the appropriate parties (home sellers, real estate agents, and so forth) as proof that you have the ability to qualify for a mortgage up to a specific dollar amount. When searching for homes, look for those with required financing at or below that number. When you find a home, the preapproval letter can also be updated to reflect details related to the home you're purchasing, such as the purchase price, thus giving your real estate agent a leg up when presenting your purchase offer.

A preapproval is generally good for a period specified by the lender. Once you find a home, you then officially apply for the mortgage, knowing that the lender already has much of the information needed to make the final decision. In most cases, you'll get a mortgage for up to the amount specified in the preapproval letter, unless, for example, you gave the lender inaccurate information during the preapproval process. Also keep in mind that before granting you a loan, the lender will appraise the home to ensure that it meets certain criteria. If the home you've contracted to buy is appraised significantly lower than the sale price, for example, the lender generally will not give you the loan (since the mortgage would be for an amount greater than the value of the house itself). Furthermore, if your situation changes—due to circumstances such as impending litigation or the loss of a job—the lender may withdraw its loan commitment.

The Paperwork

When applying for a preapproval letter, you need to fill out a loan application packet from the lender and provide all the necessary documentation (typically outlined in a checklist format). You may be charged an application fee of $20 to $40 to cover the cost of pulling credit reports for yourself and any co-borrowers.

It's a good idea to have all relevant paperwork and financial information on hand when you approach the lender, including the following:

- The numbers and balances of your checking and savings accounts, as well as your bank's address and your latest statements
- Your income tax forms for the last two years (particularly if you're self-employed)

- Retirement account numbers and balances

- Canceled checks or other proof of your monthly rent payments (or mortgage payments, if you currently own a home)

- Documentation of your debts and other financial obligations, such as alimony or child support

- A list of jobs you've held over the last ten years, including the employers' addresses and phone numbers, and the income you received from each one

- Your pay stubs and W-2s for the past two years, as well as any other proof of employment

In addition to the basic financial and employment information listed above, you may also be asked to produce the following:

- Car titles

- Statements specifying the value of securities that you own

- Copies of 1099 tax forms to show dividend, interest, and/or royalty income

- Proof of rental income (if you own rental real estate)

- Proof of alimony and/or child support that you are either paying or receiving (if any of the co-borrowers are divorced)

Please note that if you're working with an online lender, you should be wary of sending any sensitive information, like that specified above, over the Internet. Identity theft and other online threats are a fact of life in today's world. Always make sure you know with whom you are dealing with, and take proper precautions to ensure that your financial and other personal information does not fall into the wrong hands.

Having the necessary documentation on hand will not only help the lender verify your income and net worth, but it will also speed up the loan process. And speaking of speed, be sure to ask the lender just how long the preapproval process takes, and hold the company to that promise. Once the lender receives all necessary documentation, expect it to take up to twelve to fourteen business days to get preapproved—although it may take only a few hours or several days, depending on the lender and your financial situation. Stay on top of things, and remember to keep your real estate agent in the loop.

Don't Overdo It

Steve B. Anderson, sales associate with RE/MAX Elite in Las Vegas, sees too many borrowers attempting to get preapproved by multiple mortgage lenders when "shopping around" for the best mortgage terms. He warns those who take this approach to be careful, since too many prequalifications may adversely affect your ability to borrow money for your home mortgage in a timely manner.

That's because every time you apply for a credit card or any other type of loan, the lender always checks your credit history. Each and every credit check shows up as an inquiry on your credit report. Normally, inquiries are viewed as an indicator of credit risk. According to Fair Isaac (see chapter 3), the more inquiries on a borrower's credit file, the more likely it is that the borrower will not be able pay his bills (see http://www.myfico.com/CreditEducation for more on this subject). Potential home buyers who are shopping around for the best prequalification and/or preapproval terms for their mortgage are generating multiple inquiries on their credit reports, which inadvertently may compromise their ability to obtain a home mortgage or get the best rate available.

"Fortunately, these multiple inquiries don't count, but it may take precious time and effort by your loan officer to sort out these inquiries," says Anderson, citing Fair Isaac's new policy. This updated policy gives the benefit of the doubt to potential home buyers who rack up multiple credit inquiries while trying to find the best home mortgage by prequalifying with many lenders. According to Fair Isaac's new policy, all automobile- and mortgage-related inquiries that occur within a thirty-day period prior to the date the credit score is tabulated are ignored. For every fourteen days prior to this thirty-day period, only one inquiry is counted, no matter how many inquiries are made during a particular two-week period.

In the long run, inquiries have a relatively small impact on your credit score. Other financial factors, such as late credit payments and high debt, carry more weight in the equation. "Nevertheless, there is a possibility that home

(continued)

buyers who continue to shop around for the best home loan terms over a period of months could ultimately hurt their chances to obtain a mortgage," says Anderson. "So it's probably best not to get prequalified and/or preapproved by every lender, broker, or Web site that you visit."

Good-Faith Estimates

As we've discussed, there are numerous costs associated with purchasing a home, some of which are obvious (sale price, home inspection costs, appraisal costs, and so forth) and some of which crop up quietly (such as loan origination fees, tax service fees, and wire transfer fees). When you sit down with a lender to get approved for a loan, you'll usually receive what is known as a **good-faith estimate** that includes all these costs. Some lenders will give you the estimate right away, while others will send it to you via mail or fax within three days of loan application (as required by law, according to the Real Estate Settlement Procedures Act [RESPA]). Estimated costs generally correspond to the numbered lines contained in the HUD-1 or HUD-1A settlement statement that you will receive at the closing table. The HUD-1 or HUD-1A settlement statement will show you the actual cost for items paid at settlement.

The good-faith estimate serves as a reference tool for both lender and borrower, informing both of their financial obligations during the home-buying process. Keep in mind that this is only an estimate, and that the numbers and amounts may change before closing. Your lender should alert you to any changes that may ultimately impact the HUD-1 closing statement form or the HUD-1A (an optional settlement statement form used for transactions that do not involve sellers, such as those involving newly constructed homes.

While you're going through the lending process, consult with your real estate agent and other professionals you are working with for advice and guidance. Ask questions, and be sure that you completely understand and you're comfortable with the answers before proceeding. The financial aspect of the home purchase—which is absolutely crucial—may seem daunting; however, with the right dose of knowledge, education, and resources, you will be better prepared both for the cost of a home purchase itself and for the additional costs associated with owning a home.

CHAPTER EIGHT

Finding Your Dream Home

By now you've probably started doing some of the legwork necessary to get the home-buying process rolling. You're becoming familiar with credit scores, the different types of real estate agents available to you, how to steer clear of serious problems like predatory lending, and which mortgage may be a good fit for your particular needs.

Now comes the fun part: finding the right home. The good news is that the house hunt needn't be stressful or prolonged. According to the National Association of REALTORS® 2004 Profile of Home Buyers & Sellers, first-time buyers searched an average of nine weeks, and toured nine homes in that home-search period. The typical repeat buyer, that is, the buyer who already owned a home, looked for seven weeks and walked through ten homes before making her purchase. While this may sound like a long time, it's actually not considered "prolonged" by industry standards.

Depending on your own time frame, wants, and needs, the search could take longer and could find you looking at even more homes before making a decision. As you begin your search, bear in mind that the availability of homes for sale varies, depending on the time of year. Generally speaking, more homes are put up for sale during the summer months—particularly in areas where wintertime means snow and cold temperatures. Fewer homes are also on the market around the holidays, as families often take a break from the home-selling process at that time to gather for parties and other celebrations.

Earlier in this book, we encouraged you to consider your financial picture and to conduct some preliminary research—both with the help of your agent and on your own—into what neighborhoods and types of homes within those areas would be best for you. In this chapter, we'll explore how to narrow your choices to those neighborhoods that best suit your individual needs, and, eventually, to specific homes for which you may want to make a purchase offer.

Where to Begin

According to the National Association of REALTORS®, buyers use a wide range of resources when searching for a home:

- 90 percent retain a real estate agent
- 74 percent use the Internet
- 74 percent look for lawn signs
- 53 percent consult newspaper ads
- 51 percent visit open houses
- Fewer than 50 percent use "other" methods, such as hearing about a home from a friend or colleague, or by using corporate referral services.

These statistics show that most home buyers use more than one method to gain information on homes for sale. And while the search methods listed above are the most popular, less traditional ways to approach the house-hunting process are worth exploring as well. When looking for a home, be sure to tap all the resources available to you.

Smaller Markets

Obtaining information about homes for sale in large metropolitan areas like Los Angeles and Miami may be easy, but what about smaller markets, where newspaper coverage and data related to real estate is limited, at best? According to Frank Serio, broker-owner of RE/MAX by the Sea in the small market of Bethany Beach,

Delaware, buyers need to get targeted local knowledge about such areas. "It can be hard to tell whether a seller's asking price is too high for a particular smaller market, where buyers have less information to compare than they would in a big city," Serio says. He recommends that you begin by looking at recent home-sale prices for comparable homes. To effectively analyze the homes, you should look at each one's sale price per square foot, the relative age of the home, the size of the home and the lot, and its proximity to parks and busy streets. He notes that you may find additional information by talking to local real estate agents, by looking at maps of the area, and by consulting with local sources, such as the county tax assessor, the chamber of commerce, and local Realtor organizations.

Consider Unique or Unusual Properties

Certain homes have a special character or charm that distinguishes them from the typical home types discussed in this book, either due to their features, their location, or their historic value. Such homes only appeal to particular buyers. For example, Thomas L. Toole Jr., broker-owner of RE/MAX Main Line in Philadelphia, says, "An agent in our office recently sold the only home situated in Valley Forge National Historical Park. Built in the 1770s, the home wasn't easy to sell, based on its age, but it turned out to be a perfect match for one local buyer who was thrilled to find a historic property that came fully equipped with a rich, 200-plus-year history. It's a home that will never be duplicated."

First-time home buyers, in particular, need to make sure they understand what it takes to make an atypical home livable and comfortable. For the right buyer, however, finding that one-of-a-kind gem is worth the extra attention the property may require.

Foreclosures and Auctions

You've probably heard about foreclosure sales and real estate auctions as places to find a home—sometimes at a bargain price. **Foreclosures** take place when the current owner defaults on his mortgage, forcing the lien holder—generally, the lender—to sell the property in a foreclosure sale. Such sales are posted in the classified section of local newspapers, with times and locations of the event included in the listing. Foreclosed Fannie Mae–owned homes are sold through real estate brokers and listed in local MLS systems. Your real estate agent can help you locate various Fannie Mae–foreclosed properties currently available in your geographic area. In addition, you can review a list of Fannie Mae–owned properties on your own by visiting www.fanniemae.com.

Keep in mind that with a foreclosed home, you're always taking a gamble. While you may pay less than market value for the property, the home itself may be in need of substantial repair and maintenance, particularly if the last owner let things go over the period when she was failing to make her mortgage payments. This is complicated by the fact that you may not be able to have the home inspected until after the sale. Because you generally can only view these properties from the outside before you buy, you don't know whether major plumbing, electrical, or structural repairs will be necessary to make the house livable. And, you'll likely be purchasing the property as-is, which means you'll be responsible for all repairs that need to be done.

Finally, title issues may present a problem. You may need to evict the prior owners. Also check your state's right of redemption laws, as some allow former owners to "buy back" the home for the winning bid amount, effectively leaving the home buyer back at square one in the house-hunting process.

Real estate auctions, which may include foreclosed homes as well as high-end homes for sale by their owners, are another way to purchase a home. Real estate auctions come in three varieties: absolute, minimum-bid, and reserve. At an absolute auction, the home goes to the highest bidder, and there are no set minimums or reserves. At a minimum-bid auction, the sellers accept the highest bid above an established sales price. Reserve auctions allow sellers to set a hidden "reserve price" that is above the minimum starting bid and not revealed to bidders until it has been met. Should the bidding not exceed that reserve, the seller does not have sell the property.

The seller generally determines the type of auction set for the home, particularly if that seller is a government entity. However, many sellers choose to rely on professional auctioneers for advice and support throughout the process. While auctions certainly present opportunities not available in the general marketplace, they

If you're interested in purchasing a foreclosed property, check out the Department of Housing and Urban Development's foreclosure database (www.hud.gov/homes/index.cfm?). Such homes may present valuable opportunities for buyers, particularly those looking for starter homes that may need some TLC.

When a homeowner with a HUD-insured mortgage can't meet the payments, the lender forecloses on the home. HUD then pays the lender the balance of the loan and takes possession of the home. At that point, the home is sold at market value, based on a recent appraisal, to any potential buyer who has the cash—or who can qualify—to purchase the home. These homes vary in price, but most are affordable for low- and moderate-income Americans. The homes are sold as-is, without warranty, so it's up to the buyer to have the home inspected prior to buying to ferret out any defects or problems that might require repair.

Buyers looking to purchase HUD homes should start by finding a participating real estate agent, who in turn submits bids on your behalf during a designated offer period. When that period ends, the highest reasonable bid is accepted. If your bid is accepted, HUD will notify your real estate agent, usually within forty-eight hours. At that point, your agent will help you through the rest of the process. For more information about how this works, see HUD's booklet "Buying Your Home—Settlement Costs and Helpful Information," available at its Web site, www.hud.gov.

Opportunities Through HUD

don't necessarily guarantee bargain basement prices. In a hot real estate market, for example, a significant number of interested parties might attend the auction and bid for the home, pushing the price up to—or even above—the going market value.

If you're considering an auction purchase, be sure to check out the auction firm's credentials, as well as its track record and level of professionalism. If possible, go in person to another real estate auction conducted by the same auction company to get a feel for how things work before game-day arrives. That way, you'll be better positioned to place your bid when the time comes.

For Sale by Owner (FSBO)

The active real estate market of the last few years has prompted some home sellers to "go it alone," forfeiting the assistance of a real estate agent. In these situations, the seller generally sets his own price—hopefully (but not always) based on what he believes to be comparable recent home sales in the area—and sticks a sign in the yard to attract potential buyers. Most of the time, such sellers are attempting to save the commission that would be paid to the seller's agent, although they may have other motives. The owner may have extensive experience buying and selling homes, or the home may have certain drawbacks that make local real estate professionals believe the home is worth a lower selling price than the seller wants to get. In other cases, the owner may be inexperienced or fail to understand how much value professional real estate agents add to the home-sale transaction.

Sometimes FSBO (pronounced FIZ-bo) sellers will offer a commission to an agent who comes with a buyer, so your buyer's agent will still be compensated by that seller. However, you should be aware that closing the deal could present challenges, especially if the homeowner doesn't have the experience to handle closing his side of the deal professionally. (See pages 112–114 for a discussion of problems that may arise when one party in a real estate transaction is represented and the other is not.)

Criteria for Your Dream Home

In chapter 1, we asked you to think abstractly about the features that are important to you in a neighborhood. Now, as you begin looking at specific homes, it's time to think in more concrete terms. What do you really need to be happy in a neighborhood or a home? What if you find a beautiful three-bedroom home with walk-in closets and a spacious yard for your kids and the dog—but it's in a neighborhood you're unsure of? Is the house worth buying? Let's take a moment to explore in detail some of the important factors you shouldn't overlook as you race from one showing to another.

Location, Location, Location

There is an old saying in real estate that the top three factors in choosing where to live are location, location, and location. But what about location makes it such an important factor? Different people value different characteristics in their surroundings—so how do you decide which location is right for you?

Ideally, you should have two or three locations or neighborhoods in mind as you look for homes. This will give you more flexibility as you consider homes to purchase. Questions to answer when looking at neighborhoods include:

- Are the homes and yards well kept? The condition of these homes will affect the value of the home you purchase.

- Are the homes visually appealing? Are there vacant lots nearby, and, if so, why? Do home exteriors appear to be well-maintained (painted, roofs repaired, walkways in good shape)? Do you like—or can you live with—the architectural styles?

- Are the homes in an area that floods when it rains?

- Does the neighborhood have an established homeowners' association and/or covenants that govern the way in which owners maintain, upgrade, and remodel their homes?

- Are there unsightly structures nearby (such as a gas station or cell phone tower)?

- Are the homes private? Note that trees, shrubs, and fences can provide adequate privacy.

- Will maintaining the grounds be manageable for you?

- What does the area immediately surrounding the neighborhood look like?

- Are the homes close to grocery stores and other shopping venues? Or, if you prefer, is the area rural and remote?

- How close are banks, houses of worship, hospitals, libraries, dog parks, movie theaters, and other cultural venues?

- Are there good public and/or private schools nearby? (See below for more on schools.)

- Are there public facilities, such as parks and community centers, nearby?

- What is the crime rate in the neighborhood and surrounding areas? (Stop by the police station and request records of robberies, burglaries, assaults, and other criminal activity in the neighborhood.)

- Are there any registered sex offenders living in the area and, if so, how close to the home/neighborhood do they live? Megan's Law requires all such offenders to register with their states, which typically have Web sites where the public can search specific areas for registered offenders. In California, for example, residents can visit www.meganslaw.ca.gov to obtain the latest information.

- Is the crime rate in the neighborhood increasing, decreasing, or staying the same?

- Does the neighborhood have a high percentage of owner-occupants? Many non-owner residents could mean a steady flow of new neighbors, not all of whom will be diligent about caring for their properties. (Your real estate agent should be able to get you this information.)

- What is the traffic like, and how will it affect your drive to and from work and other activities? Will you have an easy commute to work, school, or major metropolitan areas?

- How close is it to major airports? If your job requires you to do a lot of traveling, this would be an important factor to consider.

Some of this information may be easy to come by, and some of it may not be as readily available. Crime statistics are available at the local police department, as noted above, while school rankings and locations can be obtained from the local school board. One of the best ways to learn about specific neighborhoods is by getting out and talking to people who live and work there every day. Drive through the area at different times of day and on different days of the week to get a good idea of the neighborhood's characteristics at various times of day and night, talk to the neighbors, and visit nearby schools and local businesses.

School Exams

If you have school-age kids or are planning to have children in the future, you're probably interested in the quality of local schools. Even home buyers without school-age children should know a little about their prospective school district, since home property taxes usually support public schools in the municipality or region (if a regional school district serves the town). In addition, home prices are usually affected by a school district's reputation.

Pop Quiz

At the beginning of your home search, it's advisable to have at your fingertips some basic school statistics. Here are a few key questions to ask your real estate professional:

- How do the local schools perform in state evaluations?

- Has the school district or any of its teachers received state or federal teaching honors? (Examples include Blue Ribbon School status or the Presidential Awards for Excellence in Math and Science Teaching. More information is available at www.ed.gov.)

- What percentage of children in local schools are performing at or above grade level?

- How much time is your child likely to spend traveling to and from school each day?

- On average, how many children are there per class? Per grade? In each school overall?

- What is the student-teacher ratio? (The fewer students per teacher, the more likely your child is to receive individualized attention. However, this may vary greatly from one school to another and from one teacher to another.)

- What percentage of high school seniors pursue higher education?

This information should be available at the county offices where the school is located (this office is usually referred to as the "county superintendent of schools"). Check the state's official Web site and the U.S. Department of Education Web site to find out what honors the school has earned. The local public library is often a good source of school statistics as well, and while you're there you may discover programs that the library offers in cooperation with the schools.

Real estate Web sites typically provide useful school data. For example, visitors to www.remax.com can find school facts by selecting "School Information" from any listing page. For an example of such a school snapshot, see Figure 1.3 on page 25.

Because school information is so important to many home buyers, real estate agents tend to know a great deal about local schools, including test scores, unusual or unique characteristics, and curriculum offerings. Many agents are happy to provide this information to potential home buyers, upon request. In addition, once an agent gets to know what's important to a buyer, she can offer insights tailored to that buyer's particular concerns.

Finally, there are several private companies that offer online comparisons for a small fee. Try searching the Internet for the term *compare schools* and the geographic area you are considering. Check the date of the results to make sure you are getting the most up-to-date information.

Real estate agents can also provide information and advice on private and/or parochial schools, as well as on special-needs programs designed for children who may need more attention than the typical school can provide. If you're basing your buying decision on the proximity to such schools and programs, be sure to do your research in this area before making your final decision.

Finals

Once you've narrowed down your neighborhood choices, look for more in-depth details about the local schools. Before deciding to make an offer on a home, you might want to know:

- How will your child get to school? If by school bus, where are the stops located? And will you have to pay extra for this bus service?

- Are the school district's test scores improving over time?

- What technology (such as computers, Internet access, and use of laptops) does the school district provide to students and how is it used by them?

- How extensively are parents involved in the schools? Is there widespread parental support of educational initiatives?

- How does the school grade students or otherwise measure student performance?

- For high schools, how many Advanced Placement classes are offered and in what subjects?

- What sports programs does the district offer? And are sports programs for girls comparable to those for boys?

- What other extracurricular programs are offered? Is there a music or drama program? How about a literary magazine or a school newspaper that publishes student work? What about clubs?

Look at school grounds as well. Does the school your child(ren) will be attending when you first move in have safe playgrounds? What about the other schools in the district? Are any new construction projects planned for the district? Check to see if the school system has a Web site with more information.

Property Value Stability

When you purchase a home, you're buying an investment in your future. So pay close attention to issues like **property value stability**, which indicate whether homes in a specific area are increasing in, maintaining, or losing value. If home values are on the decline in your target area, then you should look more closely at why this is happening—and whether you're willing to invest in a property that could drop in value—before proceeding with a purchase.

In many markets, home values have risen steadily over the past few years. However, property values in any real estate market go up or down. This is another important issue that home buyers should keep in mind when evaluating a particular neighborhood. Property values fluctuate based on two primary factors:

1. The demand for homes in the neighborhood (that is, the level of competition for homes in a specific location).

2. The availability of homes in a particular neighborhood.

Buying a home in an area with stable or rising property values is likely to be a better investment than purchasing a home in an area with uncertain or falling property values. If you ask your real estate agent or another knowledgeable person about the number of home listings in a neighborhood, the average length of time those listings remain unsold, and the average sale prices, you can begin to get a handle on the neighborhood's property value trends.

One of the ways your real estate agent determines property value stability is by preparing and analyzing a **comparative market analysis** (CMA), which pulls together home-sale data available through the local MLS. To complete the CMA, your agent researches comparable sales data for three to four homes in the vicinity of the one you're considering buying, focusing on properties with similar features. Known as market comps, these houses are roughly equivalent in size, number of rooms, age, and so on, to the home you have your eye on. The agent will also walk through and around the home, adding the benefit of his experience to the MLS data, to arrive at an estimated value for the property. He then issues a report (often including photographs), providing information about these past sales and comparing the market comps to the home you're looking at.

The recent resale prices (obtained through the CMA) should be higher than they were both one and five years ago. One measurement that a CMA will often reveal is the selling price per square foot of different homes in the area. As a result, even if the recently sold homes being compared are bigger or smaller than the one you're considering, you should be able to figure out whether sale prices for comparable homes in the area are on an upswing, relatively stable, or going down.

Another factor affecting property value stability is whether new, competing developments are on the drawing board or under construction in or near the neighborhood. Similarly, major road construction projects or other commercial developments planned for the immediate vicinity may have an impact on property values. Also consider whether the home is in a well-established, desirable community or in a developing neighborhood that is attracting a large number of new residents. Finally, see if homes for sale in the area are receiving multiple offers. This is an indication that such homes are in demand, which, as noted above, usually means that property values will remain high in the foreseeable future.

The physical appearance of a neighborhood can offer clues as to whether property values will remain stable. On a street where homes are well-kept, lawns are maintained, remodeling is evident, and the neighborhood has an attractive, neat quality about it, homeowners are usually investing time and money in maintaining their property's value. Trust your gut instincts on this one. If a quick look around the neighborhood reveals junk cars in the neighbors' yards and a half-completed paint job on the house across the street, it may be wise to look elsewhere for a home that displays property value stability and/or growth.

Other Requirements for Your "Dream Home"

Sometimes a bit of luck helps in your home search. However, the better prepared you are for the search process, the more likely you are to get "lucky" and find a terrific home. Here are five final questions to ask yourself before you get the house hunt rolling. If you answer these questions ahead of time, finding the right home to meet your needs will be much easier:

1. How much square footage do I need to live comfortably?

2. How many bedrooms and bathrooms does my family require?

3. How much storage space do I need?

4. How big a lot or yard do I need for my family and for any pets?

5. What other specific wants or needs do I have that will help to filter out any potential homes that might not suit my tastes?

When viewing homes, be sure to address any issues that affect your lifestyle. If you have one or more dogs, for example, you may prefer a home with plenty of outdoor space. If you have cats, then a home that includes a screened-in enclosure might be desirable, so that the felines can enjoy the outdoor air while still remaining safely confined. If you need handicap accessibility, you'll require a property that is either already modified for those needs, or one that can be easily adapted. Say, you are or will be living with someone who is elderly or disabled. You should be on the lookout for a home with at least one bedroom on the first floor, or one where you could add a ramp outside the front door for easy access. And if you have small children who love to play outside, then it's important for you to choose a home with a yard big enough for a swing set and/or other outside toys. These and other lifestyle issues should be front and center as you make your way through the home, and around the outside of the property.

As you're shopping around, be sure to factor in future needs. A new addition to your family, for example, could find you growing out of a two-bedroom house more quickly than you anticipated.

Your real estate agent will schedule home showings (see below) and/or attend open houses with you in an effort to whittle down your list of choices. To ensure that you're not spending an inordinate amount of time driving from home to

Survival Toolkit

On the Fence

You've thought about what you want, you've taken steps to improve your financial picture, but you still aren't sure that you're ready to buy a home just yet. What should you do? Dan Jimenez, broker-owner of RE/MAX City Horizons in Denver, suggests that you consider setting up a way to receive regular information about available homes and market conditions while you decide whether to take that final step toward homeownership.

"There are two easy ways to do this," Jimenez says. "You can track the market by registering with www.remax.com or other reliable Web sites or by contacting an agent." When you register with an online source, you can enter certain parameters, such as price and location, and learn about new listings via an e-mail alert system. If you contact an agent, Jimenez says, you should be honest about your time line and make it clear that you are not actively looking for a home at this time. You may find that one or two agents can't provide you with the regular information you're looking for, but keep searching—eventually you're likely to find one who will.

Jimenez says that many of his clients, who are first-time buyers and former renters, are surprised to discover the wide breadth of housing options and just how affordable some homes can be. "They're amazed that they can get a home and pay the same, or even less, than they're paying in rent," says Jimenez. "Very often, they'll make an offer on a home, even though they never intended to purchase."

home, agents use your criteria list and financial qualifications to cull through the available choices to arrive at a manageable number. Many agents will also give you a booklet containing printed information (with photos, if available) for homes that you've looked at. Often, the booklet will include a "Notes" section where you can jot down information about each home. Be sure to note if you liked the fireplace, or were enthralled by the home's cathedral ceilings—or if that second-floor, loft bedroom would be just perfect for little Ethan and Joey to share. Having this information at your fingertips will help you compare the homes at a later time, particularly if you're looking at multiple homes in one day, or over a weekend.

Show and Tell

If a home seems to be right up your alley, your agent can arrange for a more thorough look inside at a showing, your opportunity to walk through a home and give it a thorough once-over to see if it's right for you. At a first showing, an agent takes you on an initial tour of the home, while a second showing illustrates that your interest in the home goes beyond just having a peek inside. This second time around allows you to scrutinize the home more methodically, ask further questions of the real estate agent and/or homeowner, and decide if the home is worth pursuing.

When you first pull up to the home for the showing, think about what is known as curb appeal in real estate circles. This term refers to your first impression of a home, as seen from the street. Is the home an attractive color, and is the paint in good condition? Is the landscaping appealing? Is the grass in good shape? Is the home's roof visibly in need of repair? These and other factors will contribute to your first impression of the home.

When it comes to the showing process itself, always use proper etiquette. For example, remove your shoes at the door, if asked, and converse with the home's owners, should they be home at the time. Even if the home's exterior doesn't meet your standards, you should still be courteous and walk through it. Homeowners thrive on feedback, and a "no show" may be misconstrued by some as an insult. Put yourself in their shoes, and be considerate throughout this process.

Address: _____ Name of Town: _____

Home Details

Style (ranch, colonial, bi-level, etc.): _____ Number of floors: _____

Number of bedrooms: _____ Number of bathrooms: _____

Room-by-Room Notes

Bedrooms: _____ Living room: _____

Dining room: _____ Kitchen (eat-in?): _____

Den/Office: _____ Basement: _____

Attic (ample storage space?): _____

Detached storage space _____

Amenities

Type of heating: _____ Central air-conditioning: ☐ Yes   ☐ No

Kitchen range (☐ Gas, ☐ Electric, ☐ Other): _____

Fireplace(s): ☐ Yes   ☐ No   In which room(s): _____

Built-in appliances (dishwasher, microwaves, central vacuums): _____

_____

Garage (1-car, 2-car?): _____ Parking arrangements: _____

Yard: _____

Porch/Terrace/Balcony: _____

Other (pool, sunroom, greenhouse, etc.): _____

_____

Once you're inside the home, your agent will take the lead role in showing the property. When viewing the home, watch for telltale signs of its level of upkeep, the home's layout and flow, the privacy of sleeping and working spaces, and other issues of importance to you as a buyer. Look out for any subtle tricks that the seller has used to make the home more appealing, such as a carpet that covers a flaw in the floor, or a fresh paint job that hides a patch of mold on the wall. Be alert to smells as well. A moldy smell in the basement may signal a flooding or leakage problem. These types of flaws may be expensive to fix, no matter how good the repair or patchwork appears to the naked eye.

As you go through the home, take notes using a worksheet like the one on page 176. Mark down not only the facts (the address, observations about the neighborhood, the number of bedrooms and bathrooms, etc.), but also the pros and cons from your perspective. If one bathroom needs remodeling, for example, make note of this. If the split living room/dining room floor plan is particularly enticing, be sure to record this feature. These notes will come in handy, especially if you're viewing multiple homes over a short period.

As you look around the home, remember to keep in mind the big picture. It's very easy to get caught up in a home that looks terrific inside, but that's located far from a school or is lacking various amenities you had your heart set on. As you attend showings, keep your core criteria and the following facts in mind:

- New home listings come onto the market every day. So if you don't find a home that suits your needs today, there's a good chance you'll find one tomorrow, or the next day.

- As a buyer, it's your right to go through the home with a fine-tooth comb. Turn on faucets, flip on light switches, flush the toilet(s), open the closets, and look in the attic. Even though you'll probably hire a home inspector to go through the home checking for any structural flaws, you should still investigate those aspects of the home that are important to you before buying.

- Take extensive notes and save any home flyers provided by real estate agentsand/or home sellers for future reference. Make a special file for these flyers so you don't have to scout around for them when you want to compare one home to another.

- Interior decor that doesn't suit your taste is no reason to walk away from a home in the right neighborhood at the right price. Redecoration can be fun.

- Or, enjoy what's already there. A beautifully decorated dwelling can save you time and energy. While sellers often take their furnishings and decorations with them, everything is negotiable. If a seller is moving out of state, for example, you may be able to arrange for some or all of the furnishings or other items to remain in the home. Bear in mind that a solid antique bench or a gorgeous Oriental rug doesn't necessarily signify a structurally sound home.

- The more homes you see, the better you'll be able to pinpoint what you want and how closely each house matches your ideal. Be patient and realize that the first few homes you see may not be "perfect fits." Trust that you will eventually find the right home for you—and that it will be well worth the wait!

No matter how quickly you imagine that you can find the right house, it could take much longer than expected. Don't ever let anyone push you into making the biggest financial decision of your life, even if you're in a market where homes are bought and sold at the speed of light. Make the decision for yourself, and only when you feel that you've seen enough options to be able to select the best one.

Home Maintenance

When considering the cost of homeownership, new buyers tend to focus on their first monthly mortgage payment. In doing so, they neglect to think about home maintenance. During the first year or so (particularly for existing homes, as opposed to newly constructed properties), you'll likely be "customizing" your home to meet your needs. Extra costs can range from a $2 paper towel holder to be installed in your kitchen to a $1,000 roof repair or a $2,500 air-conditioning system.

If you had a home inspection (see next chapter), your new home probably won't need immediate, high-cost repairs. One way to avoid surprises during your first year as a homeowner is to figure out exactly how much it will cost to maintain the home before it becomes your responsibility. You can learn some of this information from the current owners, or from any contractors who may have worked on the home in the past (ask the owners for the contractors' names, what work was performed, and when it was performed).

During this investigation, try to find out what routine maintenance work needs to be performed on a regular basis. It's a good idea to ask the following questions:

- Do the gutters need to be cleaned out regularly? Tall, leafy trees near the home are a good tip-off that autumn means gutter cleanup.

- Do any of the windows or skylights leak?

- Does the home have any other "quirks" that require regular maintenance or attention? For example, a surge protector that shuts off the home's electrical system at the first sign of a surge in electric current (sometimes caused by a lightning strike at a nearby substation) may need to be repaired or replaced, especially if the home is located in an area prone to lightning strikes.

Now is also a good time to ask about monthly bills, if you haven't done so already. Ask the owners:

- How much the monthly electricity bill is (both in the summer and the winter)

- How much they typically spend on heating fuel (if applicable), and where they-buy it

- What the cost is of pool maintenance, including cleaning, chemical treatments, and seasonal preparation, if applicable

- Whether they've had to pay any homeowners' association assessments (mainly applicable for condos and townhouses, and less so for single-family dwellings)

- How much the homeowners' association fees typically increase from year to year, if applicable

- How much they pay for lawn care and maintenance each year

- What they spend on pest control each year

- How often they paint the home's exterior (five to ten years is typical), and how much it costs to do so

- Whether there are any other home maintenance–related bills that they pay on a monthly, quarterly, or annual basis

In addition to regular maintenance costs (or to provide a long-term solution to such recurring costs), you may want to consider remodeling, which we'll discuss next.

Survival Toolkit

And the House Came with It

Even though you may have visions of specific features you want in your dream home, your final selection may surprise even you. Every experienced real estate agent has at least one story about a buyer who insisted on viewing only properties with a corner fireplace or a two-car garage or an extra room for sewing. Certainly, everyone visualizes himself in the perfect home with all the amenities possible—even if those features might never be used or needed.

Your real estate agent has listened carefully to your requests, demands, and desires. Perhaps she has even shown you several homes that fit these criteria. Then, she does something that throws you for a loop. She takes you to a home that, from the outside, bears no resemblance to the type of home you told her you want to buy. Maybe it's a Mediterranean style, and you made it clear that you would buy nothing but a Tudor. Or, it's not on a cul-de-sac, but on a corner lot and two blocks from a school. Has she lost her mind? Probably not.

In addition to listening to your list of preferences, your agent has also observed you—during the interviews, the home showings, the discussions in the car between showings, and so forth. She has gotten to know you. And, because of her experience, she innately has begun to understand not only what you say you want, but also what you're not saying. It's as if she has a sixth sense about what might be the perfect home for you.

You may try to rush through the showing. Perhaps you're thinking, "I am not living in this Mediterranean-style home." But when your agent unlocks the front doors (double engraved hardwood), suddenly your anger dissipates, and a warm, calming glow settles upon you.

You see it—the one feature in a home that you absolutely must have. It could be the sunken fireplace conversation pit, the exquisite garden adjacent to the covered, tiled patio, or the breakfast nook with a bay window overlooking a tree-lined brook. It might even be that thirty-by-forty-foot workroom just behind the garage. Whatever it is—it is the feature you didn't know you even wanted or needed (and now, having seen it, it's the one feature you simply can't live without). But your real estate agent suspected it might appeal to you, and hoped you would like it.

What just happened? Well, you had the strangely unsettling but ultimately amazing "I bought the [insert that feature here] and the rest of the house came with it" experience. And, that is wonderful, because you found the place you can truly call "home"!

To Remodel . . . or Not

During your home search, you'll likely encounter a number of dwellings that have real potential, but that fail to suit your needs to a T. You may find a fixer-upper, for example, at a great price and in the right neighborhood. Or, you might wander into a home that's slightly smaller than you wanted, but it's located on a large lot with ample room for expansion.

In these situations, the word *remodel* will likely come to mind before you even sign a purchase contract. Because a home's location often takes precedence over its internal features, remodeling may be a good option for some buyers. Let's explore some of the basics of remodeling, including project financing and some potential pitfalls to avoid.

Buying to Remodel

Buying a home to instantly turn it into a construction zone may not have been what you had in mind when you started your house hunt; but when the right opportunity comes along, doing just that could be the best option. Millions of other homeowners have already discovered the value of remodeling. In fact, according to Remodeling magazine, the home improvement industry is booming all over the nation, and in 2005 reached about $117 billion in volume, 8 percent higher than the previous year.

Every year, *Remodeling* magazine publishes an annual "Cost Versus Value Report," which emphasizes that remodeling a home not only improves its livability for you, but also enhances your home's appeal for potential buyers down the road. According to the magazine's 2005 report, the highest remodeling paybacks come from updating kitchens and baths, and from adding home offices and other modern amenities to older homes. Recoupments or paybacks are defined as the percentage of the total investment that a homeowner earns back (or "recoups") upon selling the home.

The National Association of the Remodeling Industry breaks the paybacks down even further by showing just how much various improvements can net a homeowner. See Table 8.1 for a summary of some of the more profitable home improvements.

As you can see in the table, the payoff associated with remodeling projects can be significant. Remember, too, that as costs of such upgrades escalate over time, the improvements themselves will also increase in value. Keep in mind that you may not always be able to recoup your entire investment, and that some improvements bring a greater return than others.

Sticking to Your Budget

All homeowners dream of adding space, closets, and modern amenities to their existing homes, but what many don't realize is how quickly the costs of such projects can add up. A simple kitchen remodeling job, such as the replacement of cabinet doors and countertops, can easily cost more than $5,000, while a bathroom

TABLE 8.1	REMODELING PAYBACKS	
Projects with the highest return	**Average cost**	**% of cost recouped**
Upgrade kitchen	$ 6,368	101%
Revamp kitchen	$20,078	93%
Upgrade bathroom	$ 6,269	85%
Add bathroom	$11,441	92%
Add family room	$28,736	86%
Add master bedroom suite	$19,210	85%
Add sunroom	$21,998	71%
Re-side exterior	$ 8,592	67%

overhaul can run as high as $10,000, depending on the materials and labor involved.

To make your remodeling project successful, keep to a budget, follow a careful remodeling plan, and pay attention to the details. You should also be fully involved in the project from its first stages through the final installation. Interior design consultants offer these tips to help you keep your project under control and on track:

- Establish a budget and communicate your budget parameters to design consultants and contractors whenever that's appropriate. Don't overstate the amount you want to spend when you're talking to salespeople or interior designers. Spelling out how much you can spend on your remodeling project will help them guide you to products that fit within your budget right from the start. If a professional can't work within your budget, she should tell you so up front.

- Budget for emergency expenditures. Set aside about 10 percent of your budget for unexpected costs. If you sign a contract for the maximum figure you can afford, there's no room left for sudden cost increases or project changes that may arise once the project is under way. Money left over at the end can be used for accessorizing the room without going over budget.

- Choose the best bid, which may not always be the lowest bid. Keep in mind that you're not going to get something for nothing. Be very skeptical if a contractor drops his bid to underprice someone else's lower bid. Some contractors cut costs by cutting quality. To save time and money, do research into brands that the contractor proposes to use, either online or at home improvement stores, before construction begins.

- Get a detailed contract. Include specific product names, model numbers, finishes, and sizes in the contract. The more you have written down, the less likely it is that there will be misunderstandings or substitutions of inferior quality materials. Specify in writing items such as the number of electrical outlets in each new room, the materials to be used on the kitchen backsplash, the brand that you have agreed should be used for paint or countertops, and similar details. With this detailed agreement, you can double-check that you are getting what you're paying for and the contractor will find it harder to take any shortcuts.

- Remember that a little goes a long way when it comes to remodeling. For example, anything that increases the kitchen's functionality, durability, and eye appeal will pay off for the homeowner. So even the most outdated kitchen may not need an entire overhaul.

- Leave room for future upgrades. Consider your new kitchen or bathroom a work in progress. Ask for professional help in planning the project in stages. You might consider adding interior storage to cabinets later on, instead of right now. A less expensive new floor or countertop can be upgraded when you're in a better financial position and ready for the change.

- Keep an open mind about alternative products that give you the same or similar results. For example, consider vinyl flooring or even ceramic tiles in place of more expensive marble tiles. If you spend some time researching and comparison-shopping, you are likely to find several products at affordable prices that can yield the same beautiful finished look for your room.

- Work with what you have. Consider construction techniques like cabinet refacing, a process that uses the existing cabinetry foundation and costs 40–50 percent less than installing brand-new cabinets. Or, simply try updating the kitchen hardware (drawer knobs and handles, for example) to give it a fresh look without draining your budget.

- Check the progress of the project regularly. Ask the general contractor for progress reports every few days. This will keep you informed and alert you to slowdowns or changes that could cost you money later on. Make a personal inspection of the project every day, if possible. If you see something you don't like or don't understand, discuss it with the contractor. Catching a problem early on—and addressing it—is usually less expensive than waiting until the project proceeds further. However, avoid making changes once the project is under way because changes cost money.

- Do one project at a time. It's easy to get swept up in the remodeling process, and find yourself renovating more than you originally planned to. Resist the temptation to add a few furniture-like cabinets in the dining room to match the ones in the kitchen or expand the bedroom closet. Remember that the items on your wish list that you cannot afford right now could always be financed at a later date.

- Think like an investor. When it comes to home improvements, try to take emotion out of the equation. If you treat your home as an investment, then you profit by making "smart" and "seamless" additions and improvements.

- Make sure you get all required permits from your town building department before contractors begin work. Many towns also require local building inspectors to approve certain types of work for safety reasons. Find out what permits or inspections are needed beforehand.

Handy home buyers can save a lot of money by doing some or all of the remodeling work themselves. The fact that national hardware chains target these do-it-yourselfers with products and services makes it particularly easy to plan out such projects, purchase the required materials, and get the job done on your own. Be sure to figure in the time that you'll need to spend making repairs and the cost of materials before coming up with a figure to cover the total remodeling cost.

Whether you want to roll up your sleeves and start on a remodeling project right after you buy your home is entirely up to you. Keep in mind that there are some legitimate arguments both in favor of and against buying a home that requires obvious renovation before it's in move-in condition. Weigh the real costs of renovation—in both your time spent researching and supervising, and your money spent on materials and labor—against the hidden value of the property that you hope to realize through your remodeling efforts. Be sure to consider your renovation investment based on neighborhood trends, your personal wishes, and what the next home buyer is likely to find appealing. Remember that a successful remodeling job should do more than just help you live more comfortably—it should add value and flexibility to your home.

Talk to your lender about financing options for your proposed renovation, discuss the project(s) with a designer or contractor, get solid cost estimates, and confer with your real estate agent about area property values, home buyer trends, and related market information to help you decide whether a home that requires remodeling is right for you.

CHAPTER NINE

For What It's Worth

O nce you decide on the home you want to buy, you are ready to begin the purchase process. This usually involves three steps: negotiating the terms of the sale (including the price and the closing date), inspecting the property, and finalizing the financing and purchase.

In this chapter, we're going to focus on how to make an offer, how to deal with counteroffers, and what to do if you find yourself in a bidding war. We'll also discuss the ins and outs of inspections—the last part of the purchase process before closing.

Let's Make a Deal

Let's assume that you've found the home you've been looking for, and you're ready to make the owners an offer. How much should you offer for the home? First, look at comparable home sales in the area—and in particular, look at the sale price per square foot for homes with similar layouts and, if possible, similar interiors. You real estate agent should be able to help you pinpoint this information. Another good resource is your local property tax collector's office, which may post recent sales data and comparable housing information online. Next, consider how long the house has been on the market, and how long homes in the area generally stay on the market before being sold. The longer the home has been available, the more flexible the seller may be on price. Then, estimate how many repairs, or how much remodeling or redecorating, the house will require before you move in. How many of those repairs do you want the seller to make, and how many are you willing to perform yourself? Also consider whether you're able to bend when it comes to the length of time before you move into the house.

For new homes, determine whether the building cost per square foot matches that of comparable homes in the area and whether the lot location is a highly desirable one (such as in an up-and-coming suburban area into which many well-to-do families and professionals are moving). Also check out the builders themselves—their reputations in the market and their track record for selling quality homes.

Seller's Markets Versus Buyer's Markets

In chapter 4, we touched on seller's markets and buyer's markets. Put simply, these terms refer to the real estate climate in a given area at a given time, and indicate which party—buyer or seller—has the upper hand when it comes to negotiations. A seller's market is characterized by low inventory (or fewer-than-average homes for sale), high property appreciation, and a greater number of buyers than sellers. In this environment, homes sell quickly and at higher prices, making it more difficult for buyers to gain bargaining power.

In a buyer's market, on the other hand, available homes are usually plentiful and prices flexible. The opposite of a seller's market, this environment typically finds buyers snapping up desirable homes for less money and on more favorable terms. While a buyer's market is certainly the preferable climate for you as a buyer, your real estate agent can help you navigate any type of market through effective negotiating strategies, research, and knowledge.

Buying in Difficult Markets

No one wants to overpay for a home. However, if homes in your desired area are selling quickly, you will need to adjust your offer strategy accordingly. An offer that is too low, or carries too many conditions, is unlikely to be accepted in such markets. For example, suppose a home's asking price is $200,000. If, according to past sales research, that home is priced properly, then you probably shouldn't lowball the seller with a paltry $175,000 offer—particularly if that's the home you really want. Doing so may offend seller, who probably is already entertaining other offers.

If, however, that $200,000 home seems overpriced and has been on the market for several months, then a lower offer is likely warranted. Discuss these and other negotiating issues with your real estate agent before having him proceed with any offer. He can clue you in to current market conditions and offer guidance on appropriate offers for your region.

The Offer and Acceptance Process

So you've found a home you'd like to buy and you have some sense of what you'd like to offer. Now what? At this point, you present the seller with a purchase offer. A purchase offer is a potential contract to buy the property, which is written up and delivered to the seller of a house (usually by your real estate agent to the seller's agent). It includes the amount you're willing to pay for the home plus any other conditions that would have to be met for the sale to go forward. Each such additional condition is usually referred to as a contingency to the sale. For example, you may want to make the sale dependent on your obtaining a loan to buy the house. This would be written into the offer as a mortgage contingency. Other popular contingencies require that the home successfully pass an inspection before the sale can proceed, or that the buyers first sell their current home before committing to purchase the new home. (See pages 191–192 for more about contingencies.)

When you make your offer, you generally include an **earnest money** deposit to bind this agreement. This deposit may be in the form of a personal check, a cashier's check, or cash, and the amount is highly dependent on the market. The amount deposited is kept in the trust account of an escrow or title company, the trust account of the real estate company that is handling the listing, or in the trust account of an attorney representing the seller, and is not turned over to the seller until the closing, when it is usually applied toward the purchase price. Retained in escrow, that money may be subject to forfeiture should you back out of the contract for particular reasons. Typically, if you terminate the contract due to circumstances beyond your control (such as an inability to obtain a mortgage or failure of the property to pass inspection), then the money is returned to you. However, the money may be forfeited to the seller if you default on the contract for an unacceptable reason, such as deciding that you want another home. By getting preapproved for a mortgage and choosing your home with care, you can generally avoid such difficult situations.

There is no "standard" offer form; rather, you and the seller can modify, delete, and/or add whatever you wish to the agreement, which your real estate agent can provide. Those modifications must be agreed upon and signed by both parties, and will be used to create the purchase and sale agreement, a written contract signed by the buyer and seller, stating the terms and conditions under which a property will be sold. (See Appendix B for a sample purchase agreement.)

Each state or local Board of Realtors has its own version of the purchase agreement, although the wording may be modified substantially by the time the deal is actually agreed to by the buyer and seller. Be sure to include the following in the written agreement:

- A list of all items you'd like left in the home. These are considered conveyed items, meaning that they "go with the house." Be specific. You don't want to walk into the home expecting to see area rugs, only to find out that the seller grabbed them on his way out the door.

- The actual costs that will have to be paid at closing, and who (buyer or seller) will be responsible for those payments.

- The proposed closing date.

- Concerns you may have with the property in question (such as items that you want the seller to repair prior to closing).

- Any contingency clauses you or your agent feel will protect your interests, such as an inspection clause or a mortgage contingency clause (see below for more information on these clauses).

Once all parties have agreed on the sale terms and signed the purchase agreement, they are generally obligated to complete the sale of the home in accordance with these written terms.

Contingencies: Leaving the Back Door Open

There can be many twists and turns in the home-buying process. When you make your offer, it's wise to include certain protections to help you prepare for the unexpected. Perhaps the home of your dreams has some extensive water damage that you didn't notice (or that was concealed) when you walked through it with your agent. Or perhaps your ability to go through with the purchase is compromised in some way—such as your failure to obtain a mortgage commitment. Should you find yourself in a situation like one of these, you need to make sure you have an exit strategy. Here are the most common contingencies buyers include when making an offer on a home:

Mortgage Contingencies

Also known as a financing contingency, a mortgage contingency protects buyers who must seek financing to pay for their homes. Typical mortgage contingencies allow you to cancel the real estate deal should you be unable to obtain a mortgage commitment from a lender.

The mortgage contingency should include some specific parameters, such as the amount of the mortgage needed, the maximum interest rate you're willing to pay, and the term of the mortgage. It should also specify the amount of time you have to seek this commitment, such as thirty to sixty days. Pay close attention to the length of time your mortgage commitment is good for. If it expires before you close on the home, you could find yourself with a purchase agreement for a home you can no longer afford to buy, should the lender change the terms of the mortgage or opt not to grant you the loan.

Inspection Contingencies

As mentioned above, these contingencies protect you if an inspection reveals serious damage or structural problems with the home. A central air-conditioning unit may be malfunctioning, for example, or there could be roof leaks that have gone undetected for years. If such problems surface, you can cancel the deal without sacrificing your earnest money deposit. Such contingencies typically include inspections of both the home and the property it sits on, as well as tests for termites and other pests, radon, lead paint, and an inspection of the septic system. The contingency will likely specify a time period in which these inspections must occur. We'll discuss inspections in depth later in this chapter.

Home-Sale Contingencies

This contingency applies to buyers who currently own a home, staking the purchase of another home on their ability to sell their current property. These are tricky waters to navigate. With such a contingency in your offer, you might lose your competitive edge in the seller's eyes; however, you may need to sell your current property to fund your new one. In these situations, one option you may hear about is the seventy-two-hour clause, which is also known as a first right of refusal. With this provision, if another buyer comes along and wants to buy the same home you do, you have seventy-two hours to either waive the home sale contingency and proceed with the sale or cancel the sale (and get back any earnest money from the seller).

In deciding whether or not to include a home-sale contingency in your offer, weigh just how much you want this home against just how quickly you can (and how quickly you need to, financially speaking) sell your existing home. If, for example, you can afford to pay the mortgage, utilities, and upkeep on two homes at once, then you may want to take that risk. Also, if you can obtain a bridge loan (discussed in chapter 3), to be paid off when your previous home is sold, then you may also want to go ahead with the purchase. On the other hand, if your local real estate market is "slow" by industry standards—which means your existing home may not sell as quickly as you need it to—then you should rethink your choice of purchasing a new home before unloading the existing property. If you find yourself in this situation, seek advice from your real estate agent and/or an experienced real estate attorney.

Offers and Counteroffers

Once you've made your offer, the seller has three options: She can accept it, reject it, or come back with a **counteroffer.** The first two are self-explanatory, but the commonly used third option requires some explanation, particularly if this is your first home purchase. Since everything is negotiable, it's unlikely that the sellers will accept your first offer exactly as it's written. They may feel the offered price is too low, or they may object to other contingencies or requirements you've included in your offer. A counteroffer is treated as a new offer whose goal is to strike a compromise between what the buyers want and what the sellers need. The counteroffer helps buyers and sellers arrive at a price and terms and conditions that work for both parties.

Survival Toolkit

Making Your Offer Complete

Does your offer fully protect your interests? When writing offers, Brooks Benham, broker-associate with RE/MAX Accord in Castle Pines, Colorado, advises buyers to include an inspection contingency. "That will allow them to seek remedies for any defects on the house, or back out, if need be," says Benham.

Next up is the financing contingency, which he suggests for all buyers, even those who have prequalification letters. That's because such promises are usually contingent upon verification of certain items, such as whether the buyer still has a job when the property closes.

Also include an appraisal contingency in the offer, says Benham, to ensure that the property is indeed worth the purchase price (or more). Finally, he says, most contracts also include a title commitment, to make sure that the property is free and clear of any liens or other encumbrances. (See chapter 10 for a discussion of title searches.)

Here's an example of how a counteroffer works. Let's say you offered $190,000 for a home that was listed for $195,900. Let's also say that you included in the purchase offer a closing date of forty-five days from the time the seller accepts your offer. When the seller receives that offer, he feels that the price is a bit low, and that he'd rather close within thirty days, so that he can move into his new home as quickly as possible. Rather than rewriting the offer, the seller would counteroffer, stating that he's willing to accept all terms and conditions of your offer with the exception of the closing date and the price. Instead, he'd like $193,000 and thirty days to closing. Now the ball is back in your court. At this point, you have three options: You can reject the counteroffer, get your deposit back, and walk away; you can accept his counteroffer; or you can respond with a counteroffer of your own. For example, if the thirty-day closing period is okay with you but the price is still too high, you could counteroffer with, say, a $191,500 sale price.

As you've probably already guessed, this counteroffer process continues until either everyone is satisfied with the terms and price of the home sale or one or both of the parties walks away from the deal. It usually takes one or two rounds of negotiation to reach agreement. A seller isn't obligated to accept offers in order, and can pick and choose among multiple offers. If, for example, buyer #1 offers $150,000 at a noontime showing, and buyer #2 offers $155,000 at a 2 p.m. showing the same day, the seller is free to take the higher offer. Offers can be made at any time, and real estate agents generally carry with them the necessary forms to write them up on the spot. If you're engaging in a series of offers and counteroffers, consult with your real estate agent or attorney about whether continued negotiations are wise, or if it would be more prudent to seal the deal now, rather than risking the home of your dreams by engaging in three more rounds of negotiations.

Bidding Wars

Even if you present the seller with what you consider to be a fair offer, you may still find yourself dragged into a bidding a war. If you have your heart set on a particular home, and if that home also appeals to other buyers, be prepared for some tough negotiations.

If you're buying in a seller's market, it's crucial to keep on your toes at all times. Deals are often made very quickly, and to win them you have to hustle. Obtaining a mortgage preapproval is a good first step, since it shows the seller that you're serious about buying, and that you can afford his home. Talk to your agent about earnest money amounts, since the amount of cash that you put down can also give you leverage in a bidding war. A buyer who forks over 2–3 percent (that is, $4,000 to $6,000 on a $200,000 home), for example, will likely have an edge over one who writes a check for $1,000.

As the seller reviews the bids, she'll likely counter the best offers to find out which of the potential buyers is willing to pay more for her home. This is the time to make your best offer, since you may not get another chance, particularly in a hot market. If buyer #2 improves his bid by $3,000 more than you do, then the seller is entitled to take it and seal the deal. In a seller's market, it's advisable to look past the monetary considerations and write up a deal that includes as few contingencies as possible. For example, the seller who needs to move quickly probably won't be inclined to accept an offer that includes a ninety-day period before closing or a contingency that states that you can't close on the home until your existing dwelling sells.

To win a bidding war, you need to keep your emotions out of the process, and go into it with a level head, the highest price that you're willing and able to pay, and an educated view of the current market conditions. And remember that there are new opportunities coming on the market every day. The next home you see might be even better than the last one.

Negotiating Through Your Agent

If you're working with a real estate agent, she will generally handle the direct negotiating on your behalf, and with your support. She'll work either with the listing agent, who is representing the seller, or directly with the owner. Expect your agent to come to you with all offers and price adjustments—and with solid advice on

Survival Toolkit

Negotiating Tips for Buyers

Brooks Benham, broker-associate with RE/MAX Accord in Castle Pines, Colorado, offers the following tips to help make any negotiation go smoothly:

1. Work with your real estate agent to learn about the market, including how much homes are selling for and how long homes are staying on the market.

2. Successful negotiating involves limited contingencies. Start with the standard contingencies (financing, home inspection, and so forth) and go from there.

3. Be a ready, willing, and able buyer (the concept sounds simple enough, but it's not always easy to put into practice).

4. Try to be responsive to the seller's time frame. A seller who is moving out of state in a month, for example, will be more apt to work with a buyer who is willing to meet that demanding schedule as opposed to one who needs three months to close.

5. Find out what the seller's motivating factors are (perhaps by having your agent talk to the selling agent about the seller's current situation), and use that knowledge to bolster your bargaining power. Say you find out that the sellers are getting divorced and need to sell their home quickly to finalize their divorce settlement. In such situations, you may have more leverage than another prospective buyer may if you offer a shorter time frame from contract to closing.

6. Realize that money isn't everything, and that asking instead for certain concessions (such having the seller leave a specific appliance or pressure wash a tile roof) can be a valuable negotiating tool.

7. Some home sellers might just be testing the water to see if they can ge their ideal price. Try to negotiate with people who are highly motivated to sell; otherwise you are wasting your time.

8. Remember that everything is give-and-take when it comes to negotiating to buy a home. You may stand to lose a property to a higher offer if you play the nickel-and-dime game too long.

Ultimately, you want the seller to feel like a winner—even though you are getting exactly what you want out of the home purchase.

how to counter or respond to those offers. Just how much leeway you give your agent in negotiating is up to you. If you've been through home-buying negotiations before, then you may want to take a more active role in the process. Here are some steps that your agent may take to help strengthen your negotiating position:

- Promptly deliver your offer to the seller and/or the seller's real estate agent.
- Present a strong case for you, the serious and financially stable buyer who has researched the market and presented the best offer around.
- Provide third-party, professional testimony to substantiate the strength of your offer (in the form of a complete Comparative Market Analysis on the home).
- Gauge the reaction of the seller to the offer and determine the best strategy, based on that response.
- Determine what changes to the offer might result in the optimal combination of price, timing, and terms.

An agent with strong negotiating skills, a clear head, and experience working on a buyer's behalf can often mean the difference between getting a good deal or a raw deal. In certain cases, she can also help you avoid losing the home altogether, particularly if you get into a head-to-head bidding war with another potential buyer. If you're buying a home on your own, without the help of an agent, you may wish to pick up one of the many books that deal with negotiating, and brush up on any tactics that will prove valuable in a competitive housing market. Similarly, consider talking to a friend or family member who has been through the process about his experiences.

Home Inspections

Several inspections will take place between signing the purchase contract and closing on your new home. One of them is a home inspection, which banks don't generally require, but which real estate agents and other professionals nearly always press for. Typically, homes are professionally inspected within seven days of acceptance of the purchase agreement. A good home inspector will advise you about the condition of your chosen home, inform you about any maintenance issues, and search for hazards such as radon, termites and other pests, lead paint, and urea formaldehyde foam insulation.

Inspectors are hired and paid by home buyers. Rates for a home inspection range from $150 to $500 and higher, depending on the location and size of the home. Attorneys, real estate agents, and past customers generally refer home buyers to inspectors; however, most home inspectors also advertise in the local Yellow Pages. The American Society of Home Inspectors lists its members on its Web site at www.ashi.org, as does the National Association of Certified Home Inspectors (http://www.nachi.org/).

Your real estate agent will likely be on site during the inspection, but you should consider being there as well, if you can. Not all buyers are able to attend their home inspections, but those who do come away from the experience with greater insight into their investment. Being on site as the inspector wends his way through the home provides an excellent opportunity for buyers to learn from an expert about construction, maintenance, and repairs that may be needed in the future. Below are some issues you should look out for as you accompany your inspector through the home (and which your inspector will be carefully studying):

- **Foundation:** Are there any obvious cracks or shifts?
- **Exterior:** Is the home going to need repairs, a new paint job, or landscaping in the immediate future?
- **Lot:** Is the drainage system effectively funneling water away from the house? This is best tested during a good rainstorm, although your home inspector should be able to help you determine how well the drainage works under any conditions.
- **Roof:** Does it appear to be new, old, or of an unknown age? What is its overall condition?
- **Walls:** When you stand parallel to the wall and eyeball it, does it look straight?
- **Evidence of leaks:** Check inside and outside the house. Look at all ceilings and at areas around windows for stains and other signs of past or present leaks.
- **Basement or crawl space:** Is there dampness? Is there adequate insulation?

- **Attic:** How does the interior of the roof look?

- **Quality and workmanship:** Examine the home as a whole, and pay attention to any physical additions that have been made to the home.

- **Energy efficiency:** Does the home appear to be sealed tightly? Are there noticeable gaps under doors or around windows?

- **Electrical:** Does anything appear to be malfunctioning?

- **Plumbing:** Turn on faucets and tubs. Flush the toilets. Are there any unusual noises?

- **Appliances:** How old are the stove, dishwasher, refrigerator, and microwave (if included)? Are they clean, and in working condition?

- **Heating/cooling systems:** Do the systems appear to be doing a good job of properly controlling the home's temperature? Are there any obvious signs of potential failure (worn belts, bent fan cages, or blades, etc.)?

- **Mold:** Are there signs of moisture or mold on the home's walls, in the attic, or outside the home near, for example, air-conditioning units? Pay attention to smells in the home as well. A moldy smell may be a telltale sign of mold that's not visible.

Be sure to ask the inspector to quantify any vague descriptions (such as a bathroom tub that's been described as "fair" on a "good, fair, or poor" scale). Spend some time familiarizing yourself with the report. The more information that's provided, the easier it will be to understand the overall condition of the home and the surrounding land. For example, a walk around the outside of the home with the inspector can clue you into any defects or issues that might exist within the home's structure—particularly issues that aren't noticeable from the curb or from the inside of the home, such as roof problems or issues with major systems.

Tom Beritelli, broker-owner at Wyckoff, New Jersey–based RE/MAX Real Estate Enterprises, encourages all his home buyers to have thorough home inspections completed before purchasing a home. "They're buying an item that's entirely too expensive not to have it inspected," reasons Beritelli, who typically recommends to buyers a selection of professionals who are members of the American Society of Home Inspectors. He adds, "We like those inspectors because we can be sure that, at the very least, they follow the minimum standards in the industry."

When reviewing the home inspection report with the buyer, Beritelli usually points to the summary page first (this may be at the end of the report) to give buyers an overview. "The report itself runs twenty to forty pages, and can be fairly overwhelming," says Beritelli. "If you start with the summary, and then go back and thoroughly review any problem areas, it's much more manageable."

Resolving Problems

The American Society of Home Inspectors likens a home inspection to a physical examination from a doctor: When problems or symptoms of problems are discovered, the inspector may recommend further evaluation or remedies. Here are five steps to take to ensure that you have a clear picture of exactly what took place—and what was discovered—during the inspection:

1. Review the inspection report, and obtain any and all details about the inspector's findings.

2. Look for items in the report that may indicate possible health hazards, such as the presence of lead paint, radon, or asbestos.

3. Keep an eye out for other issues that could be costly to repair in the near future, such as cracked foundations, leaky roofs, and old central air-conditioning systems that don't run properly.

4. Give the home seller a copy of the report. Notify (or have your agent notify) the seller in writing of the findings and any needed repairs.

5. Obtain estimates for those repairs, and request in writing that the seller either adjust the selling price accordingly or fix the problems prior to closing.

What happens from this point on isn't always cut-and-dried, so talk to your real estate agent about how to handle the remediation process. Sometimes an agent may suggest that you make the repair yourself after closing (if that's financially feasible). For example, if it's an issue that can be resolved by hiring a contractor to come in and, say, replace an air handler for a cooling system for $1,500, it may be worth the cost.

This is especially true in hot housing markets, where another buyer may be waiting in the wings to snap up that $350,000 home you keep picturing yourself in. In those cases, handling the repair yourself may be the smartest choice. Some sellers will split the cost with you, and others may raise the price of the home so that you may, in turn, get a larger mortgage to help cover the cost. Note that this practice is feasible only if the appraisal supports a price increase. Otherwise, the lender may frown upon this practice and decide not to make a loan on the property. (See pages 203–205 for more on appraisals.) If, however, a $150,000 home is in sore need of a $20,000 roof repair or an $8,000 rewiring of the electrical system to bring it up to code, then you may want to seriously consider whether or not to purchase the home—particularly if the seller refuses to cough up the money for the repair.

Ultimately, if your inspection turns up unexpected problems, find out exactly how much it will cost to repair the defects, and then weigh the positives against the negatives. Obtain repair estimates from licensed contractors, and look at your options. Keep in mind that everything is negotiable and turn to your real estate agent for help in creating a win-win solution.

Survival Toolkit

Buying a Home "As Is"

If you're purchasing a home "as is," then you can ask the seller to repair any defects, but you can't expect him to follow through. That's because he's selling you the home in the condition that it was in when you wrote the contract, and while he is required to disclose any defects that he knows about the property, he isn't obligated to fix these flaws.

Consider carefully whether you want to go the route of buying a home "as is." Repairs to roofs and complex electrical systems can be quite costly. By writing a home inspection contingency into your purchase contract, you'll be able to protect yourself from major expenses, while retaining your right to buy the home if the discovered issues are manageable for you, as the buyer.

Home Inspections Required Here

At RE/MAX Real Estate Specialists in Long Beach, California, sales associate Valerie Condon remembers a time twenty-five years ago when she used a single-page contract to sell homes. Disclosures, or statements revealing information that might not otherwise be evident (such as flaws in the property) were unheard of back then, and the words home inspection were rarely uttered in the typical real estate office. Over the last two decades that single-page contract has morphed into a fifteen-page tome (including about eight pages of addendums). Disclosures tacked onto the contract add about fifty more pages, give or take a few.

This evolution has pushed Condon to require home inspections on all home sales. "I don't even give my clients an option. I tell them that we're going to have an inspection, lay out how much it will cost them, and explain that, at the very worst, they'll be out the cost of the inspection should they need to pull out of the deal for any reason," says Condon. "The best-case scenario is that they'll know they're not buying a money pit."

Ultimately, Condon says, thoroughness counts, even if it means finding a defect that kills the sale she worked so hard to put together. "I've seen agents use inspectors who are less detail-oriented, but I think agents do everyone an injustice when they try to skimp on this important step," Condon explains. "I prefer knowledgeable, local inspectors who know our market well and who can provide the best possible, unbiased assessment of the home."

Working in an area of the state where two-bedroom, one-bath homes built in the 1940s are selling for $1 million, Condon says she has seen buyers waiving their right to inspect, particularly in multiple-offer situations. When working with anxious buyers who are concerned that their offers will be turned down if they include an inspection contingency, Condon says she finds creative ways to make the offer more enticing without eliminating that important protection.

"Early on I talk to buyers about positioning themselves to win in multiple-offer situations, which have always been common in our market," Condon says. "We'll use a large deposit, figure out what the seller's motivation and time frame are, and seek out other ways to position them to win, instead of giving up contingencies that are designed to protect them."

Property Disclosures

Property disclosures are designed to protect buyers from purchasing homes with hidden defects of which the sellers had prior knowledge. As a result, most states now require sellers to complete one or more forms disclosing the existence (or the absence) of defects in the sale property even before such information is requested by a potential buyer. (See Appendix B for a sample of such a disclosure.)

"Mandatory disclosure can reveal and bring to the forefront issues that may not be as apparent today, but that will pop up in adverse weather conditions or other instances," says Dick Helminiak, a sales associate with RE/MAX Preferred Associates in Toledo, Ohio. "This helps reduce the 'buyer beware,' aspect of home buying and shifts the focus to treating the buyer fairly."

The property disclosures required by the states vary from state to state. According to Dennis Steed, broker-owner at RE/MAX Crossroads in Strongsville, Ohio, the Buckeye State requires three disclosures for all transactions: a residential property disclosure (discussed above); the agency disclosure, which outlines the relationship between the agent and her client; and a lead-based paint disclosure. (Federal law requires that, for homes built prior to 1978, sellers notify buyers of known lead-paint hazards.) Steed recommends that buyers check their state's Real Estate Commission or ask a local real estate agent or attorney for details on exactly what sellers are required to disclose, and how.

Appraisals: Your Lender's Due Diligence

When you buy a home, your property serves as collateral for the mortgage. For this reason, the lender obtains (and the buyer pays for) an independent assessment of the property's value, and typically turns to a local appraiser to handle this task. To ascertain the value, the appraiser charges a fee (which varies from about $150 to $300, depending on the home's value and how much work the appraiser has to do) to estimate the home's value in a specific housing market. Appraisers use two different methods to determine a home's value:

1. **Sales comparison approach:** This is the most commonly used method for existing homes. An appraiser estimates a subject property's market value by comparing it to similar properties (known as comps or comparables) that have sold in the area.

2. **Cost approach:** More useful for newly constructed homes, this method takes into account how much it would cost to replace the structure if it were destroyed. Understand that the appraiser does not determine sale price, nor is he charged with trying to meet the purchase price agreed upon between buyer and seller.

The appraiser produces an appraisal report for the property, which includes some or all of the following components:

- An accurate description of the property

- A purpose statement for the appraisal (for example, to determine the market value of a home that is for sale)

- An evaluation of the overall real estate market in the area

- The neighborhood in which the home is located (a subdivision, or an established neighborhood of relatively new homes, etc.)

- The data and criteria used to determine the property's value, including three or more comparable sales and cost-approach figures

- Photos of the home in question, as well as photos of the comparable homes used in the appraisal

- A final estimated value

- Any special conditions relating to the property, including issues that might adversely affect the property's value (such as its location in a floodplain).

- The appraiser's certification and signature

- Estimate of the average sale time for the property

The appraisal serves as the final piece of the puzzle your lender uses in determining the size of the mortgage it is willing make on the property. The loan may be declined, for example, if the property is appraised for an amount lower than the negotiated sale price. Other factors that show up in the appraisal, such as an "estimated time to sell the property" that's longer than the area average, may also affect a lender's final decision. Expect the lender to review the appraisal carefully before determining whether or not the property qualifies to serve as collateral for your mortgage loan.

Homeowner's Insurance

Once you've signed a contract for your home, it's time to start thinking about getting homeowner's insurance for the property. This policy must be in effect from the date of closing. What you include in your policy will depend on where your home is located and the value of your home. If the home is located in a floodplain, for example, you'll need to add coverage in case of a flood. And if your home is in a hurricane-prone state like Florida, then you should make sure that your hurricane deductible (the amount you'll pay out of pocket to rebuild and/or repair the home following hurricane damage) reflects the actual costs of rebuilding in the event of hurricane damage.

Homeowner's insurance can be obtained from a number of sources, but most people rely on local insurance brokers who represent one or more companies. These agents are licensed in their respective states, typically by a state department of insurance or some other governing body. A good place to start your search is with the insurance company that is already insuring your automobile. When selecting a plan, Homeowner's-1 (HO-1) is the most basic and popular, covering fire, flood, theft and major breakage, among other contingencies. Your insurance representative can point you in the direction of more complex options that may be better suited to your individual needs.

One good way to compare insurance providers and estimate what your insurance premium might be is to go online and enter the words *homeowner insurance quotes* into a search engine. From any of the sites that pop up, you'll be able to search various options offered by insurance firms and get a good idea of what kind of premium you'll be paying, and what type of coverage will be offered in return.

The Final Stage Is Near:
What to Do

As you prepare for closing, gather together all the paperwork and other items needed for the closing. These materials include:

- A certification that, at the time of closing, the house is free of termites. This is awarded by a professional pest control firm that inspects (separately of any home inspection) and confirms that the home is free of wood-destroying insects.

- A certification stating that the home is radon-free.

- A bank check or certified check made payable to the appropriate party. Note that personal checks will not be accepted.

- The insurance policy on the property, effective from the date of closing.

- Each borrower's driver's license or other form of photo ID.

Your real estate agent should supply a written or verbal checklist of events that will take place over the next few days or weeks. And while every real estate deal is unique, most do follow a certain chain of events that starts with the signing of the purchase contract and ends at closing. Here are some final issues to consider as you prepare to close:

- Determine the date of closing, and be sure all parties agree to the date that's been selected.

- Make sure the contract states the correct purchase price. You don't want to pay more than the agreed-upon amount.

- For new homes: Obtain a warranty from the builder that covers defects in workmanship or materials in ceilings, doors and door frames, the roof or windows, the septic system, the foundation, the furnace and heating systems, the well and plumbing systems, and electrical wiring, plus any ancillary features, such as a pool, a deck, a tennis court, and the like. You might also consider asking the builder to establish an escrow account for any work not completed. If so, be sure the amount in the escrow account is sufficient to cover the additional work. Discuss this issue with the builder, and with your real estate agent, to determine how much will be necessary.

Prior to closing, you or your agent should:

- Find out if you'll be asked to pay any extras at closing, such as a prorated share of fuel, maintenance fees, or taxes.

- If the home is to be a **joint tenancy** (co-owned by two or more persons), determine if all parties need to be present at the closing.

- Provide the lender with a copy of the purchase offer (a step that's usually handled by a real estate agent) and a copy of the listing data from the MLS system (if the lender requests it).

- Let your lender know how many days the contract allows for you to obtain financing.

- Specify to the lender that you need written confirmation when your financing is approved.

- Make sure the seller's agent receives a copy of your written confirmation of financing.

If you've followed the steps outlined in this chapter, you can take a deep breath. Your home's been appraised, you've obtained homeowner's insurance, and you've crossed a lot of other tasks off your "to do" list. Congratulations! All this hard work will pay off soon, as you make your way to the closing table to seal the deal. In the next chapter, we'll discuss the final stage of the home-buying process: closing day.

CHAPTER TEN

The Grand Finale: Closing

C losing day can be both exhausting and exhilarating. On one hand, you know that weeks or months of preparation are finally coming to an end, and that within just a few hours you'll be driving away from the closing table with the keys to your new home jangling from your keychain. On the other hand, you'll be asked to sort through and sign mounds of paperwork, not all of it drafted in plain English. The reality of becoming a homeowner may hit you at this point, as visions of mortgage bills, property tax invoices, and repair bills begin to dance in your head.

One way to help guarantee a smooth closing is by coming to the table prepared. Your real estate agent and other real estate professionals (such as an attorney) can assist you with this process, but building up your own education and knowledge about what to expect will also go a long way toward ensuring a good experience on closing day.

In this chapter, we'll fill you in on the kind of paperwork and documents you're likely to see during your closing. Remember that every transaction is different, and that some lenders or title companies may use different versions of these forms.

How It Works

The hours leading up to closing day will be filled with many last-minute issues to resolve, as well as the all-important **walk-through,** which typically occurs the day before or the day of closing. During this walk-through, you and your real estate agent will once again go through the home and make sure that everything is as it should be, and that you're indeed purchasing the same home—with all the contents you expected—that you fell in love with a few weeks or months before during your first and second showings. If you discover that something is amiss, your agent will usually step in and negotiate the issue with the seller's agent to try to clear up any issues before the closing begins.

Then, it's off to the closing table, where you'll finalize the purchase that you've been working on since the day you signed the contract. You'll likely find yourself signing more papers than you ever have before in a single sitting. Don't be alarmed—this mound of paperwork is to be expected. The closing or settlement agent will work with the lender to prepare and record all the necessary documents. This agent is generally selected by the lender and is typically an attorney, a representative of the title company, or an officer of the escrow company. The settlement agent oversees the closing and makes sure that everything that needs to be done during the closing is actually completed.

At this time, the title, or legal ownership of the house, is transferred from seller to buyer by means of a **property deed** (see page 212). Before closing your loan, your lender will commission a complete title search by a reputable title insurance company that guarantees that the home you're buying is free from any claims against the property. This close examination of all public records that involve title to a specific property is meant to verify that there are no liens or other claims, say, for nonpayment of bills by the seller, against the property, other than those scheduled to be satisfied at closing, such as the seller's mortgage. A title search verifies that all former owners have formally given up their rights to the property, and generally encompasses documents filed within the last thirty years. In some states, a title agency handles this task, while in others an attorney is charged with reviewing title searches and clearances (the removal of any liens).

While at the closing table, you also present your homeowner's insurance policy (if you haven't done so already); pay applicable closing costs (see below); and sign important documents, such as the mortgage note guaranteeing that you will repay your home loan. The closing agent disburses the closing funds—including commissions paid to the agents and other fees—to the appropriate parties and files the necessary paperwork with the county recorder and other government entities.

Other professionals present at the closing may include real estate agents involved in the transaction and the buyer's and/or seller's attorney. Closings generally take an hour or more to complete, and are held at a location specified in the purchase agreement (typically chosen by the seller), unless other arrangements are agreed upon. This is not the time to rush or be rushed, so take as much time as you need to review the documents carefully. It's natural to be excited about the prospect of finally getting the keys to your new home. But by taking the time to read through every document before you sign it, whether a day before or at the closing table—and by asking questions of the closing agent, the real estate agent, the seller, and your attorney—you'll know exactly what's expected of you as a new homeowner.

The Process Step by Step

There's no such thing as a "typical" closing. Different financial situations, mortgage options, and the requirements associated with such loans can create various scenarios. However, closings generally follow a standard choreography, including the following:

- Producing proof of homeowner's insurance.
- Reviewing your HUD-1 settlement statement for any typographical errors, added fees, or other issues. (If you recall from chapter 7, the HUD-1 statement is a complete rundown of all closing costs, and who is responsible for them.)
- Handing over a cashier's or certified check to cover your closing costs, any prepaid expenses (such as property taxes), and your down payment balance.

Survival Toolkit

Deeds

There are two main types of deeds that you may encounter during the home-buying process. One is a property deed, or the piece of paper that transfers title to your new house at the closing. The other is a **deed of trust,** the document that you execute in connection with your home loan.

In the past, property deeds were signed, sealed (by wax), and delivered. Now, the seller need only sign and deliver it (that is, hand it over to you). Once you have accepted it, the title of the property is yours, and you are responsible for it. There are different kinds of property deeds, which reflect different ways to transfer ownership. Examples include warranty deeds (where the seller fully warrants a **clear title** to the property), grant deeds (the most common type of deed used to transfer property from a seller to buyer), and quitclaim deeds (which convey only the grantor's rights or interest in real estate, without stating the nature of the rights and with no warranties of ownership). Property deeds have to meet a certain set of rules in order to be valid. The legal requirements vary from state to state, but, in general, deeds must be in writing and be signed in accordance with state law. They must also describe the property in detail (that is, its legal description). The deed is recorded with the county or state to give public notice of the property's change in ownership status.

The second type of deed you may see at closing is a deed of trust. A deed of trust is similar to a mortgage but involves three parties instead of two. The buyer still pledges the house as collateral for the home loan, but this pledge is held by a third party (the trustee). The trustee has the power to sell the home and give the proceeds to the lender if the buyer fails to make his loan payments.

- Going over documents, of which there could be many or few, depending on your individual situation. Expect the closing agent to go over all of these with you as you sign or initial them.

- Setting up an escrow account to pay for homeowner's insurance, property taxes, interest, and private mortgage insurance (PMI), if applicable. See below for more on escrows.

- Signing and dating all mortgage documents, including the promissory note and either a mortgage or a deed of trust (see box above).

- The lender presenting the mortgage check to the closing agent, to cover the mortgage amount.

- Receiving the property's title via a property deed that the seller signs and hands over to your mortgage holder.

- The closing agent or attorney recording all legal documents—including the warranty deed.

- Walking away from the closing table with the keys to your new property!

These steps may sound complicated—and they can feel overwhelming—but with the help of your agent (and possibly your attorney), you'll accomplish each one smoothly and with as little stress as possible. As your closing approaches, here are a number of other important factors to consider.

What to Know about Escrow

During the home-buying process, a neutral third party (usually a lender, a title company, or a real estate attorney), known as an escrow agent, holds money and/or documents that pertain to the sale of the home. These items are kept "in escrow" until all conditions of the sale are satisfied. If those conditions aren't met, and if the sale is canceled, then the escrow agent disburses the funds and/or documents to the appropriate parties.

Money for future payment of property taxes and insurance may also be held in an escrow account until it's time to pay for those items. As we discussed earlier (see chapter 2), if your loan amount is more than 80 percent of the home's appraised value, your lender may require that your monthly mortgage payment include an amount to cover these expenses, which would be placed in escrow.

Paper, Paper Everywhere

At closing, you may feel overwhelmed by the flurry of papers you'll be confronted with. Just how big your stack of paperwork grows is directly related to the mortgage company you choose and the closing coordinator with whom you work. Barbara Weinberg, broker/owner at RE/MAX East of the River in Manchester, Connecticut, says she's seen the pile come in at two inches (5 cm) thick. As such, she advises buyers to come to the meeting prepared to review and sign a great many important documents.

Weinberg urges buyers to thoroughly review any financial documents before signing them: These may not always reflect the same interest rates or terms that were, say, advertised in the newspaper. For the best information, Weinberg points buyers to their good-faith estimates (see chapter 7), which lenders are required by law to share with borrowers. A good real estate agent and real estate attorney can also provide guidance, as they have likely helped many buyers review such documents in the past.

"The real key to dealing with the paperwork and the forms you'll be asked to sign and review is to educate yourself," says Weinberg. "Pay attention to the advice and information that your agent gives, and use that knowledge to make the best decisions."

Before closing day arrives, there are several steps you can take to ensure a good experience. One or two days before closing, for example, you should obtain a copy of your HUD-1 statement from the closing agent and review it thoroughly, questioning any inaccuracies or errant fees. (By law, your lender must provide you with a written estimate (the good-faith estimate discussed earlier) of closing costs within three days of accepting your mortgage application, and will usually follow up with an exact figure one business day prior to closing.) Your real estate agent will work with the closing agent to iron out any issues that could have resulted from simple miscommunications. In some cases, the issues may run deeper—such as a predatory lending situation (see chapter 7), in which the mortgage lender adds unexpected fees to the final HUD-1 statement—so be sure to nip them in the bud long before you sit down with pen in hand on closing day.

During your review of the HUD-1 statement, go over all the calculations. Make sure that you're being given credit for all your deposits, and that the statement accurately reflects any other items agreed upon between you and the seller. Also pore over the lender, title, and escrow fees to make sure they match the good faith estimate—or that any additional costs are indeed warranted. Finally, check any mathematical calculations that appear on the form. It's always a good idea to come to the closing table with calculator in hand.

Here are the other basic forms that you may be asked to review and/or sign at the closing table:

Abstract of title Provides a listing of every document that has been recorded within the past thirty years about this particular piece of property.

Acknowledgment of reports A document that assures that the buyer has seen all reports (such as surveys and termite inspections) related to the property.

Affidavits Sworn statements in writing by the borrower. A name affidavit, for example, is a document certifying that you are who you say you are.

Deed The legal document transferring, or conveying, title to a property. See page 212 for more on deeds.

Escrow analysis A detailed itemization of the escrow account used in servicing your loan.

Home appraisal The lender is required by law to provide a copy of the appraisal, if you request a copy in writing within a reasonable time in advance of the closing.

Itemization of amount financed Like the Truth-in-Lending statement, this document summarizes the finance costs, such as points, associated with your loan.

Loan application Your signature on the loan application at the closing table confirms that the information you gave when you first applied for the loan—such as your employment and marital status—has not changed.

Monthly payment letter This letter breaks down your monthly payment into principal, interest, taxes, insurance, and any other monthly escrows.

Mortgage The legal document specifying the lender's interest in the property you're buying and your guarantee to repay the debt. It puts a lien on the home as security for the loan, thus allowing the bank to foreclose if you default on the promissory note.

Mortgage-location survey The boundary survey indicating whether there are any encroachments on the property.

Promissory note Your written promise to repay a specified amount over a specified period.

Real Estate Settlement Procedures Act (RESPA) statement A statement that acknowledges that you have been informed about how the closing process works, and that you fully understand all the closing documents and financial obligations related to your mortgage.

Tax authorization This document grants permission to your local real estate taxing authority to send tax bills directly to your loan servicer, so that payments may be made from the loan's escrow account (this is only applicable if you're using a PITI loan, with property taxes and insurance folded into your monthly loan payment).

Tax and utility receipts Municipal and state receipts acknowledging that various fees have been paid by the seller, or that they will be paid by the buyer.

Title policy Issued by the title company, this policy protects you from any claims made against the property before you bought it, and is often mailed to buyers a few weeks after closing.

Truth-in-Lending Statement Also known as "Regulation Z," this is a federal law that requires lenders to disclose fully, and in writing, the terms and conditions of a particular mortgage. Terms and conditions disclosed on this form include the annual percentage rate (APR), the way in which the funding will change hands, the total finance charges, the amount financed, and the terms of the loan.

If your "pile" of paper includes a large number of these documents, don't despair. They're simply included to minimize the issues that you and/or the lender have to deal with postclosing. Read through the documents carefully, consult with your real estate agent and/or attorney, and be sure that you fully understand what you're signing before you write your name on the dotted line.

Common Closing Costs

Closing costs are defined as the bundle of fees associated with the buying or selling of a home. Certain fees are automatically assigned to either the buyer or the seller; other costs are either negotiable or dictated by precedents set by the local market. As a buyer, you can expect to pay various fees at the closing table, including the down payment, loan fees (such as the application fee, discount points, and so forth), prepaid interest, inspection fees, appraisal costs, mortgage insurance, and more. We'll look at each of these—and the many other fees you can expect—in detail shortly. Also keep in mind that the seller has her own list of closing costs, including expenses such as:

- Paying off the existing mortgage loan on the property

- The broker's commission for selling her home

- Transfer taxes (taxes that are paid when title changes hands from one owner to another)

- Documentary stamps on the deed (this is paid to your local government for registration of a deed or mortgage, and is calculated as a percentage of the purchase price or the value of the mortgage)

- Prorated property taxes (taxes on the property that are prorated at closing, or assessed and divided proportionately between buyer and seller)

Closing costs typically fall into one of two categories: nonrecurring (items paid one time, and never again, such as appraisal fees) and recurring (costs paid for throughout the period that you own your home, such as homeowner's insurance and property taxes). Here's a breakdown of various fees you may incur when purchasing your home, grouped into nonrecurring and recurring costs. It's important to note that not all these costs will appear on your good-faith estimate, nor are lenders required to show all of them on the estimates that they provide to home buyers.

Survival Toolkit

Closing Details

In evaluating closing costs, Charlotte Van Steyn, broker and co-owner of RE/MAX Premier Choice in Columbus, Ohio, says buyers should start with the lender's good-faith estimate (GFE). Review the form carefully, she says, and understand that these numbers will ultimately be transferred to the HUD-1 settlement form. She encourages home buyers to get a copy of the GFE when they apply for the loan and remember to keep it handy for reference throughout the transaction. "As closing day approaches, you want to make sure that those numbers correlate with the numbers on the HUD-1," says Van Steyn. She also sees this as a precautionary measure against predatory lending, since it can prevent a lender from "embellishing" the numbers as the HUD-1 settlement form is prepared, based on the GFE. "The buyer who doesn't pay attention to this detail could potentially pay thousands of dollars more than she should for a mortgage," she explains.

Lastly, Van Steyn advises buyers to double-check the other financial obligations involved with homeownership, such as property taxes, community development fees (paid for by the builder, and passed on the homeowner), condo fees, homeowners' association fees, and any others that may be "attached" to the property and transferred to you upon purchase. "You should know about these fees well in advance of arriving at the closing table," says Van Steyn. "But it's important to take another look at them during the closing process to understand exactly what additional financial obligations you are assuming by buying the home."

Nonrecurring Closing Costs

The following are typical nonrecurring fees you may be confronted with at the closing table. Whether or not a particular fee applies to your home purchase depends on any number of factors, from the type of home you're buying (single family, condo, townhouse, etc.) to the kind of mortgage you're getting, the covenants on your property, if any, and the like.

Appraisal fee   An appraisal is a determination of the value of your property, reached by a professional appraiser and based on recent sales information for similar properties, the condition of the property, and the neighborhood's anticipated impact on future property values. Typical fees for appraisals range from $250 to $500.

Appraisal review fee   Charged by some lenders, and ranging from $65 to $150, this fee covers the routine review of your property's appraisal as a quality-control measure, particularly on high-priced properties.

Courier fee   A $25–50 fee charged to cover the costs associated with transporting loan documents between the lender, the title firm, attorneys, and others involved in the settlement process.

Credit report fee   As you read earlier in this book, lenders review your credit history before approving your loan. This fee is usually about $20 to $60, depending on the type of credit report that your lender requires.

Document preparation   This fee, which averages about $200, dates back to a time when lenders hired document preparation firms to draw up their loan documents. Technology has made the task easier for the lenders, who charge the fees for handling the services in-house.

Escrow account   At closing, you may be required to establish initial reserve funds in an escrow account if the lender will be paying homeowner's insurance premiums, property taxes, and/or other expenses on your behalf.

Flood certification fee   This fee is charged by an independent service that makes the determination as to whether or not the property is located in a federally designated flood zone.

Flood-monitoring fee   Lenders may charge this fee to maintain monitoring of flood zone maps, to remain current regarding the effects on your property from the government's frequent remapping of such zones.

Home inspection Buyers typically pay for the home inspection, which costs about $200 to $500, depending on geographic location and the size of the home. The inspection is usually paid for by the buyer, and generally includes a thorough examination of the home's major systems and structures, as well as the overall structural soundness of the home.

Home warranty This optional item is not always included on the good-faith estimate, but may show up on the final document that you sign at closing. Often paid for by the seller (ask your real estate agent about this feature), a home warranty usually covers such items as the major appliances included in the sale, should they break down within a specified time.

Typically, the warranty covers the electrical and plumbing systems, the furnace and range, the roof, and other items, for one year from the date of closing. If something under warranty breaks, the homeowner calls the warranty company, which dispatches a plumber, an electrician, a roofer, or other professional to repair or replace the item in question. The homeowner pays a small deductible, and the warranty company covers the rest. When the home warranty period expires, many insurers approach the new homeowner about extending it for an annual fee.

Homeowners' association transfer fee For buyers purchasing condominiums or homes in neighborhoods that are governed by a homeowners' association, this fee is charged to transfer all the property's ownership documents and records to the new owner. (Fees vary on this one, depending on the annual or quarterly dues payable to the specific community.)

Lender's inspection fee This fee applies mainly to newly constructed homes. Because a newly built home is generally not completed during the time of appraisal, lenders charge this fee at closing to cover the cost of verifying that the home is indeed complete and ready for occupancy.

Loan discount Often referred to as loan discount point(s), this is a one-time charge by lenders or brokers to lower the interest rate they would otherwise offer on the loan. Again, points are measured as a percentage of the loan, with each point equal to 1 percent of the total loan amount.

Loan origination fee Also referred to as "points," with one point being equal to 1 percent of the mortgage loan. Lenders charge loan origination fees in exchange for evaluating and processing a loan.

Loan tie-in fee Paid to a settlement agent (such as a title company, a lawyer, or an escrow firm) to compensate for services provided in dealing with the lender. Fees vary by agent.

Mortgage broker fee These are fees paid to a mortgage broker, should you use one in obtaining your loan. Assessed as points—where one point equals 1 percent of the total sale price—these fees vary by broker and transaction size. Broker processing fees may also be included in this line, and can help you understand exactly how much your broker is charging you for his services.

Notary fees By notarizing a form, a notary confirms that the person who signed the document presented identification at the time the document was signed. Notarized documents give more assurance that such documents are proper and authentic. Most official loan documents include two to three forms that require notarization, which runs about $10 to $15 per form.

Pest inspection (or termite inspection) Usually required by the lender and paid for by the buyer (for $50 to $150, on average), this inspection certifies that the property is free of termites and/or other wood-destroying insects. If repairs are required, the amount to cover those repairs may vary. As discussed in chapter 9, the seller will usually pay for the most serious repairs, but buyers should understand that this is a negotiable item.

Prepaid interest Because mortgage loans can close on any day of the month, and because mortgage payments are generally due on the first of every month, expect to pay a certain amount of "prepaid interest" at closing. This amount covers the interest due from the time the loan closes until your first payment is due. If, for example, you close on the fifteenth of the month, then you pay fifteen days of prepaid interest.

Recording fees A number of loan documents need to be filed with the county recorder, and buyers pay a fee of about $35 to $75 (depending on geographic region) to have this work done.

Sub-escrow fee Typically charged by the title insurance company, this $200 to $250 fee compensates the title company for work related to the title search, completed prior to and at closing.

Survey fee Your lender may require a property survey for the home you're purchasing. Unlike a title and deed, which describe the property boundaries, a survey actually locates the boundaries of the property and charts the location of improvements that have been made. After closing, the survey will come in handy when you want to make your own improvements—or if your neighbor argues with you about the location of his lot lines. Surveys cost about $150 to $300, and are paid for by the buyer at closing.

Tax service fee Some lenders pay an independent service to monitor your prompt payment of property tax bills, since those payments take precedence over any other liens against the home (including your mortgage), should your home be foreclosed upon. Borrowers pay anywhere from $65 to $85 as a one-time, flat fee for this service.

Title insurance This kind of insurance assures buyers that the homeowner they're buying the property from has what is known as clear title to the property, meaning that it is free from any liens or other claims against it. The lender requires this coverage to ensure that the new mortgage loan will be paid off first—after Uncle Sam, that is— should the home be foreclosed upon. The cost of the policy is usually a function of the value of the property, and can be paid for by the purchaser and/or the seller.

Underwriting fee This fee covers the evaluation of a loan application to determine the risk involved for the lender, and it ranges from about $325 to $500, depending on the lender and the geographic location. The fee covers the lender's use of Automated Underwriting Systems (AUS) to assess the credit risk of loans that they make.

VA funding fee If you're taking out a loan through the Department of Veterans Affairs (VA), your closing statement will include a fee that the VA charges for guaranteeing your loan. The cost ranges from 2 to 3 percent of the total loan, depending on whether or not you've tapped your VA loan eligibility in the past.

Wire transfer fee A $25 to $50 fee charged by some lenders to cover the cost of moving mortgage funds (by electronic wire transfer) to the appropriate parties (such as the attorney or title company) to ensure that those funds are available for closing.

Recurring Closing Costs

Here are the main recurring costs that you're likely to see on your closing statement:

FHA mortgage insurance premiums The Federal Housing Administration requires a mortgage insurance premium (MIP), payable by everyone who participates in its home-buying programs. An up-front premium of 1.5 percent of the total loan amount is paid at closing (this premium may be financed as part of the total mortgage amount). There is also a monthly MIP amount included in the PITI of .50 percent.

Flood insurance If the home you're purchasing is located in a floodplain, your lender will ask you to purchase flood insurance before finalizing the loan. This type of insurance protects homeowners against losses from a flood, and is purchased and administered separately from your basic homeowner's insurance policy. Coverage for flood damage is available from the federal government under the National Flood Insurance Program, but is sold by licensed insurance agents. Flood insurance is also available for properties located in areas that are at a low risk of flooding. This type of insurance is available directly from insurance providers. Check out FEMA's Web site tool for determining a property's flood risk at: www.floodsmart.gov/floodsmart/pages/riskassesment/findpropertyform.jsp.

Homeowner's insurance To ensure that your property is protected—and, that your mortgage lender recoups the loan price if your home is damaged or destroyed—you're required by your mortgage lender to take out a homeowner's insurance policy. (Even if you're buying your home outright, without a mortgage, no homeowner should be without homeowner's insurance.) This policy covers possible damage to your home itself (some policies also cover the contents of the home) and the surrounding property as a result of natural disasters like hurricanes and tornados, as well as fire and theft. Most insurers require the prepayment of your first year of coverage at closing. If you're purchasing a condominium, your homeowners' association fees will likely cover this insurance through an **impound account,** a reserve maintained by a lender for paying property taxes and insurance premiums on behalf of the homeowner.

Mortgage insurance Some lenders require borrowers to pay their mortgage insurance premiums a year in advance, to cover the lender and a portion of the losses in case the borrower defaults on the loan. These days, most lenders allow this premium to be paid monthly, although you may be asked to allocate two months' worth of premiums as an initial deposit into your impound account if you're purchasing a condo.

Property tax impounds If your mortgage loan incorporates an impound account, the lender will require you to deposit between two and ten months' worth of property taxes into that account, depending on what time of year the loan closes. If, for example, you close in June, then you will have to pay the real property taxes remaining on the property for the balance of the year. If, however, the seller has prepaid the taxes for the year, you'll have to refund the seller for your share.

This money is used to pay the annual property tax bill on your property, and will preclude you from having to shell out a lump sum to cover this expense every year. Instead, a portion of your monthly mortgage payment will be allocated for this expense.

Because every lender operates differently, discuss any "red flags" on your good-faith estimate and HUD-1 settlement statement early in the process. A specific fee, for example, that looks higher than what was originally quoted, should be questioned. Or, a list of new fees added to the good-faith estimate should also be cause for concern. While the fees noted in this chapter are among those most commonly imposed, lenders can add other fees—some of which are warranted and some of which are not. If something in the settlement papers troubles you, talk over the issue with your lender, your real estate agent, and your attorney before proceeding.

Enlisting the Seller's Help

You know what to expect on your closing statement, but did you know that—like the rest of the real estate transaction—some of the fees you see on the settlement statement are negotiable? No, that doesn't mean you can talk a title insurance firm into a lower fee, but it does mean that you and/or your real estate agent can negotiate with the home seller (and her agent) to share some of the closing costs.

In fact, buyers and sellers often include closing costs in their negotiations, both for major and minor fees. If, for example, that rattling air-conditioning system seems like a candidate for replacement sooner rather than later, then the seller may agree to pay for the home inspection. On the other hand, a buyer may agree to pay a seller's full asking price in exchange for the seller paying all the allowable closing costs (generally, this includes the nonrecurring costs). Items that the seller may pay for include appraisal and title fees, taxes, points, and attorney fees, among others.

Whether a seller will pay any of the closing costs hinges on a few key factors, including market trends. In a market where buyers are lined up behind you, ready to write checks, don't expect too much leeway in this area. Other considerations include the condition of the home itself and the sellers' personal circumstances (if they're anxious to move right away and no other offers are coming in, you'll have some leverage when it comes to closing costs).

Your real estate agent can be a good source of information in this regard, since she's probably handled many a transaction in which the seller and buyer negotiated over the payment of closing costs. Be sure that all terms and conditions are written into the purchase agreement (you don't want a seller developing selective amnesia on the day the settlement statements are distributed), and that they're agreed upon by all parties.

Avoiding Closing Table Traumas

It's a day carefully selected, prepared for, and anticipated by all parties involved. For these reasons, closing day should, ideally, proceed as follows: Buyer and seller meet with the appropriate third parties, sign oodles of papers, get their copies, and go off into the sunset, pleased with the transaction.

Unfortunately, it doesn't always work that way. With the countless regulations and requirements surrounding property transactions, the many different personalities to contend with, and the sheer emotion tied to the home-buying and home-selling process, closing day can quickly turn into a nightmare. Caught early enough, many problems can be addressed before the big day, but even more are usually ready to rear their ugly heads at the closing table. By working with a knowledgeable real estate agent who can guide you through the process, and by staying on top of issues as they arise, you can ensure a much smoother closing table experience.

Stranger than Fiction

What better way to help you avoid closing table trauma than to give you a few real-life examples from real estate professionals who have made countless trips to the closing table? In the sections that follow, six different agents share their closing table horror stories, how they solved them, and what you can learn from their experiences. Here are their tales, as told by the individual agents.

"Closing Funds? What Closing Funds?"

There we were at the closing table, said one agent, with all documents signed by both parties. The seller relinquished the keys, and the closing agent asked the buyer for the cashier's check to cover the balance of the down payment and the closing costs. His reply? "I loaned the money and don't have it with me." Everyone thought he was kidding, but he wasn't. Because the agent was representing both parties, everyone turned to her with a "What now?" look.

The agent whisked the buyer off to another room and found out that he'd lent the money to a family member. She then consulted with the closing agent, who negotiated for a forty-eight-hour stay from the lender as well as from the seller of the property, who was furious. She then informed the buyer that he would lose the $25,000 in escrow if he didn't come up with the remaining $15,000 within the forty-eight-hour deadline. Everyone did some nail biting for those two days, but the buyer turned up with the money at the last minute.

From this experience, buyers can learn that not coming to the closing table with the right closing funds, and in the right format (usually a cashier's check), can hold up the deal and cause needless aggravation and ill will. And avoid any "big loans" to family members in the days leading up to your closing!

"Oops, I Forgot I Was Married!"

Agent and seller were sitting at the closing table when the attorney acting as the closing agent reviewed the paperwork for the first time and discovered that the seller was married. Unaware of this, the buyer's and seller's attorneys had drawn up the papers to reflect that she was transferring title to the property as a single woman. However, it turned out that she was just about to finalize a divorce—but wasn't yet officially "single." Therefore, she needed her husband's signature to close the transaction.

Luckily, this marital breakup was amicable, so the problem was rectified quickly. Closing was delayed for about an hour and a half as the seller tracked down her husband, who came over to the office during his lunch hour to sign the papers. Obviously, the situation could have been far worse, and could have resulted in the transaction not going through at all.

As a buyer, you need to be prepared for the unexpected. Real estate deals can and sometimes do fall through. Talk to your agent about eventualities to prepare for, and how to protect yourself in the contract—and be sure to share with both your agent and your attorney any relevant financial and personal details that may have an impact on the sale.

"Heck No, We Won't Fix It"

Before this agent's buyer signed the contract, she inserted clauses stating that it was up to the seller to repair the home's sprinkler system, ripped screens, a toilet that wouldn't flush, and a few broken window cranks. Both buyer and seller signed the contract, but inspections a few weeks later revealed that the broken items had not yet been repaired. The buyer's agent asked the seller's agent for a list of items that the seller would fix, but never received it. On closing day, the seller stated flat out that he had no intention of making those repairs. For two hours the buyer's agent served as mediator between the two, trying to get the deal closed. Finally, both parties agreed that the seller would pay the buyer $500 to do the repairs, which totaled about $1,000, essentially splitting the difference.

After this experience, the agent always recommends that all parties initial any contract repair clauses. However, you should also keep in mind that no matter how the contract reads, there's always someone who just doesn't care.

"Did I Say *These* Appliances?"

Upon walk-through, one agent and his buyers immediately noticed that the seller had removed the high-end washer and dryer that were supposed to be included with the home, and had replaced them with an old, rusted pair. The contract, which itemized what appliances were included, didn't state the name or make of the items, so the buyers had no legal recourse and they were extremely upset.

After calming them down, the buyers' agent spoke with the listing agent who was also appalled at what the seller had done. Together, the agents agreed to chip in $500 each to the buyers—out of their own pockets—so the new homeowners could buy comparable appliances.

Since that experience, the agent itemizes the make, model, and other identifying details of all appliances that come with the home, and then includes the words "as seen on this date" next to each item. He encourages buyers to incorporate this kind of detailed itemization into all their contracts because of how effectively it locks in everything that the buyer saw in the home on that particular date.

The Case of the Missing ID

Once this agent found a buyer for an elderly couple's condominium, they discussed the closing process, inspections, and other requirements. The couple sat very attentively through it all, listening to everything she told them, including the requirement that they would both need driver's licenses or photo IDs at the closing table. But when the parties arrived, the woman pulled out a Social Security card and said, "This is how I get on a plane. Isn't it good enough?"

Luckily, there was a county office that issues photo IDs nearby, so the agent took the seller over there and came back in under an hour with a photo ID.

The lesson here is that both buyers and sellers should pay close attention to their agent's instructions, and bring the appropriate paperwork with them to prevent delays at the closing table. Don't be afraid to ask for a checklist of what to bring—it may save you a lot of trouble on the big day.

As you can see, buying a home takes a lot of advance study and other preparation, with the "final exam" coming on closing day. Come into the experience with a positive attitude and the realization that, like many other buyers who came before you, you'll probably have a mild case of writer's cramp to contend with when it's all over. Once the money and keys are transferred, you'll be free to enjoy your new abode. We'll discuss exactly how to go about doing that, beginning with the physical move, in the next chapter.

CHAPTER ELEVEN

You've Got the Keys— Now What?

During the home-buying process, all roads lead to the closing table, where you get the keys to your new home and depart as the owner of the dwelling you've been dreaming about for months. There's nothing quite like walking away from the closing table knowing that all the work you've put into buying a home has finally come to fruition. It's time to celebrate by going out for a nice dinner, popping a bottle of bubbly, and just enjoying the moment.

However, you haven't quite reached the end of the journey. There is the move to consider, services to start and/or transfer, and maybe even repairs or upgrades to be made before the transaction is truly "closed." In this chapter, you'll learn how to navigate these complex waters to become a successful, satisfied homeowner.

Your Agent Can Still Help! With What?

The sale may be closed, but that doesn't mean your real estate agent can't help with the moving and relocation process. Well connected in their communities, agents can often point you in the direction of reputable plumbers, electricians, carpenters, landscapers, and other home-repair and -maintenance people you'll need to call on to address issues relating to your home. Realizing that their business depends on both referrals to new customers and repeat business from past customers, real estate agents pride themselves on their ability to serve as a one-stop shop for clients—even those who have already moved past the closing table.

Some agents, for example, own their own moving vans, which they rent on an hourly or daily basis. Others hand out booklets filled with business cards from contractors, roofers, house cleaners, and the like, whom they know and trust to provide good service to new home buyers. Talk to your agent about these and other referral services she offers. Because you've already established a trusting relationship with your agent, who better to turn to for help and advice once you've purchased a home?

Prep Your Home

Before you move into your new home, you may have to make some repairs, replace some appliances, or do some cleaning. For example, you may need to remove carpeting and install other flooring if you're allergic to the dander found on the former owner's dog—before you can move in.

You'll also need to get the utilities—such as phone, water, electricity, cable, and Internet service—set up, preferably before you move in. A deposit may be required for some of these services, unless you're already doing business with the companies that offer them. A power company, for example, may require a deposit for a new customer. You can talk to the previous owner about what providers he used and then call those companies to set up service—or choose a different one, if more than one is available in your area.

Ask the seller to leave you any area telephone books or community directories so you can look up the names of local contractors to handle necessary repairs and remodeling. Your real estate agent may also know a good, affordable company to handle the work. Personal referrals are usually the best way to find a contractor, since you can ask pointed questions about the company's workmanship and timeliness on other projects.

We recommend that buyers prepare for the first few days in their new home by putting together a few staples that are essential to have on hand even before the moving van arrives with your furniture. Among these necessities are the following:

Get on Track Early

- toilet paper
- paper towels
- paper cups
- light bulbs (one or two are sure to burn out the minute you move in!)
- a broom and dustpan
- tension rods to hang curtains
- snacks and drinks
- sponges or countertop wipes
- trash bags
- dishwashing detergent
- hand soap (and lotion) for kitchen and bathrooms
- cleaning products

Choosing Your Mover

If you're going to hire a moving company to relocate your belongings, make sure that you're not only getting the best price for the services, but that you're also hiring a reputable, trustworthy firm that will take care of your home's contents and guard against damage en route to your new home. Start by evaluating your needs. Ask yourself the following questions:

> Do I need someone who can work within a tight time frame, or are my moving dates relatively flexible?

Am I moving locally or long distance?

Do I need someone to pack my belongings for me?

Do I need someone to transport valuable and/or fragile items? (Some companies specialize in handling fragile goods.)

Do I need someone who can unpack the goods upon delivery?

Do I need storage facilities?

How much insurance coverage do I need, in case something goes wrong during the move?

Do I need someone who can organize and set up my belongings in the new home?

Do I need help decorating? (Like many industries, the moving sector has branched out into nontraditional services like home décor to serve its customers.)

Most moving companies will tailor their services around your needs and your budget. Because selecting a mover is more involved than just selecting the first company you see in the phone book, be sure to start the process four to six weeks before the actual move. Search online (try http://www.remax.com/residential/moving_assistance/index.htm), ask your friends and family for referrals, check with your real estate agent, and/or contact a trade association like the American Moving and Storage Association (AMSA). AMSA-certified movers and van lines are companies that have voluntarily agreed to abide by a Code of Conduct that requires complete disclosure of moving information to consumers, written estimates of charges, timely service, and prompt response to claims and complaints. AMSA's Web site (www.moving.org) offers many useful tools, such as a consumer handbook and a Find a Mover link. (While the association doesn't recommend individual movers, it does provide a member list from which to choose.) Other useful links on the AMSA Web site include Find a Certified Moving Consultant, How to Choose a Mover, How to Get an Estimate, and How to Plan Your Move.

Mover's Rates and Fees

Moving companies usually base their prices on the weight of the goods being hauled, how far they're being moved, and the time and energy required for extra services (such as packing and unpacking) that you ask for. Other firms may charge by the hour; still others will estimate the price based on the number of rooms of furniture and goods being moved. To get a handle on the cost of your move, check out the estimating calculators that some companies have on their Web sites. There you can key in the number of rooms, the amount of furniture, and the number of boxes you're moving, and subsequently receive a price quote.

AMSA advises consumers to obtain estimates directly from several moving companies (preferably two to four) before making a decision. The timing of your move may have an impact on the final cost. Summer season and the first and last days of each month are typically the busiest times for movers. Other factors that may affect the cost of your move include where you move (moves between metropolitan areas may be less expensive than moves to remote locations), and how much you move (charges are often based on weight and distance). Along with the rates and charges, be sure to factor in insurance to cover your home's contents, exactly how pickup and delivery will work, and the time it will take to do the job. Finally, if you're pleased with the results of your move, you may want to tip the moving company personnel. Use your judgment on the amount, and be sure to include a snack and a drink for all the moving company personnel, if you're so inclined.

Carrier Liability

In choosing a mover, you also need to consider what claims protection you have, should something go wrong: Carrier liability is based on **valuation,** which is typically determined by weight. Valuation applies only to cases in which carrier negligence can be proven, such as if the movers drop your Steinway piano down a flight of stairs. Liability coverage falls into one of three categories:

- **Standard coverage:** Movers provide their customers with minimum insurance for every item. This coverage is based on weight alone, and is required by law to be at least sixty cents per pound (.5kg).

- **Assessed-value coverage:** This coverage is based on how much it would cost to replace the assessed value of your property, should the damage be caused by carrier negligence. This coverage is more costly than standard coverage.

- **Full-replacement-value coverage:** Based on how much you would have to pay to replace any of your property if it were damaged due to carrier negligence, this coverage—the most expensive—requires the carrier to pay for a replacement of any piece of property damaged.

Final Considerations

Before making your final selection, also consider the additional services offered by the mover. If, for example, you're relocating to accept a new job—and you need to get up to speed at your new workplace quickly—then the extra bucks to have someone pack up and unpack your home's contents may be worth it. If, however, you're retiring to a new area and working within a flexible time frame, it may pay for you to take the time to pack and unpack yourself. Or you may even decide that moving yourself is the most efficient choice.

Once you've selected the mover, you'll probably be asked to sign a confirmation or agreement that states the nature of the relationship, when it will start and end, and exactly what is expected of both parties. If the agreement doesn't reflect what was discussed, ask questions and have it modified to meet your needs before signing it. Check all dates, terms, and prices, and be sure to give your movers a reminder call a few days before moving day to confirm that everything is on track.

Do It Yourself?

If you're moving to a new home that's located close to your current home, or if you're just the DIY (do it yourself) type by nature, then you may want to handle the moving process on your own. With enough friends, trucks, and time (mainly for packing and unpacking), you'll be able to relocate without the expense of using a moving company.

Rental-truck rates are often figured on a per-day basis, with some offering unlimited mileage and/or providing extra services and conveniences (such as pack-

Making the Move

Ilene Winegard, broker-owner at RE/MAX Heritage in East Providence, Rhode Island, says that, when working with moving companies, the most important first step is to get several estimates and then hold the companies to those estimates. "Moving companies typically are required by law to come within about 10 percent of their estimate," says Winegard. She recommends that buyers consider using the expanded services that moving firms offer, such as packing and unpacking your belongings, in order to save both time and hassle involved with packing an entire house, then unpacking it on the other end.

She also notes that movers can vary greatly in how they charge for moving services. For example, one mover in her area recently told her that he charges by the hour and/or the minute for his services, and includes a fuel surcharge for out-of-state moves. As a result, someone moving from East Providence, Rhode Island, to neighboring Massachusetts could pay an extra $600 to $800, just for crossing state lines.

Before getting into the moving process, Winegard advises home buyers to clean out their attics, garages, and basements, and to hold one or more garage sales to unload anything that hasn't been used in a year or more. This step has several advantages: It can net you a few dollars, it can eliminate the need for storage space, it can save on moving costs, and it can keep you from cluttering up your new home.

ing boxes). If you're moving locally, mileage will be less of an issue. In such cases, the fees will be based on the number of hours or days that you keep the truck.

When you rent a truck, the rental company will likely ask you for a valid driver's license (to ensure that you're an authorized and legally qualified driver), a major credit card (for payment or as a form of security), proof of insurance (to verify that you are personally covered in case of an accident), and a deposit. The company may also ask you the details of your trip and anticipated vehicle usage, such as destination, pickup and drop-off times, and the type of cargo being hauled. Most will also offer optional rental insurance, covering accidents involving personal injury and/or damage to cargo, as well as limited loss and damage waiver coverage, which releases you from any liability resulting from loss or accidental damage to the vehicle.

For DIY movers, there are also firms that will deliver a van, a trailer, or even a cargo container to your home, leave it in the driveway for you to fill, and then come back to move it to your destination, where you unload it yourself. One firm that offers this service is PODS, whose Web site (www.pods.com) offers you a very detailed look at dimensions, prices, and availability of its moving products.

If you're moving yourself, there are several expenses you should budget for. For example, you may need special equipment to handle bulky items, such as pianos and washing machines. Often, a dolly (which can usually be rented from the same place where you obtained the moving truck) will do the trick. If you're moving a long distance and plan to tow your car, you'll need a tow bar. Inquire at your local self-moving company for more information about these items, and be sure to figure in these expenses when budgeting for the move. Also, don't forget to factor the cost of gas or diesel into the equation. Estimate high, particularly if you're moving to a new state, as fuel prices tend to vary from one location to another.

To get a better sense of just how much your DIY move is going to cost, AMSA offers a useful cost analysis, found in the worksheet on page 237. The list can be particularly helpful for first-time movers (or those who haven't moved in several years), who are unaware of the many costs associated with a DIY move. Fill in the worksheet with your own numbers, leaving blank any that don't apply to your specific situation. We'll discuss budgeting for your move in more detail in the next section.

WORKSHEET	**CALCULATING ACTUAL DO-IT-YOURSELF COSTS**

1. Truck rental charge (include total charge for packing, loading, driving, and unloading): $ _____

2. Rental deposit: $ _____

3. Trailer package or automobile hitch: $ _____

4. Wear and tear, if you drive your personal vehicle (40.5¢ per mile $ _____

5. Daily insurance rate, if you rent a truck or van: $ _____

6. Furniture pads: $ _____

7. Appliance dollies: $ _____

8. Value of your time (for you and other family members involved in the packing, loading, driving, unloading, and unpacking):* $ _____

9. Cost of boxes, cartons, tape, and other packing materials (plus trash and landfill fees for getting rid of the debris after your move is finished): $ _____

10. Fuel charge (estimate approximately $2.75 per gallon/10 miles per gallon): $ _____

11. Appliance service cost (special preparation for handling and moving appliances): $ _____

12. Warehouse/storage rental cost: $ _____

13. Additional truck rental to deliver goods to and from the storage warehouse: $ _____

14. Additional costs (child care, back brace, food, hotels, tolls, etc.): $ _____

Your Total Estimated Self-Move Cost: $ _____

*One way to arrive at this figure is to multiply total hours spent moving by the number of people involved by the going rate for such labor (such as $15 per hour) in your area.

Courtesy of the American Moving and Storage Association

The most successful DIY movers are the ones who get the right combination of manpower and hauling capability lined up well in advance. That means rounding up as many friends, family members, coworkers, and vehicles as you can, to ensure that the job gets done swiftly and efficiently. Don't forget to provide snacks and drinks (especially bottled water) to your helpers, who will appreciate the extra effort you've made to keep them comfortable while they help you move into your new home.

Moving In

Now that you've decided how you're going to move—whether you're going hire movers or attempt it on your own—it's time to start preparing for the actual move. The moving process can begin as soon as you take possession of the home, or sooner if you make arrangements to do so with the seller. For this discussion, it will be assumed that you'll be moving in on or (preferably) after the actual closing day.

Your Moving Time Line

To make the transition as smooth as possible, you should be thinking about this task during the weeks leading up to the actual closing day. The American Moving and Storage Association (AMSA) and RE/MAX offer the following time line of tasks to prepare for the big move:

Eight Weeks Before Moving Day

☐ Solicit in-home estimates from three moving companies. Check out the free mover referral service at www.moving.org, the Web site of the American Moving and Storage Association.

☐ Begin making an inventory of furniture that you will be moving.

☐ Obtain U.S. Post Office Change of Address forms (turn these in at least one month prior to your move, to ensure proper handling of your mail.)

☐ Contact new schools to determine which of your children's records will need to be transferred.

If your move is work-related, some of your moving expenses may be tax deductible. If you're eligible to do so, you can deduct from your federal income tax return both the cost of physically moving household goods from one place to another and travel and lodging expenses incurred during the trip to your new home. To deduct moving expenses, you must meet both of the following conditions as set forth by the IRS:

Tax-Deductible Moves

- **The distance test:** The new job site must be at least fifty miles farther from your former home than was your previous job site. If you are a new entrant into the job market, your new primary job location must be at least fifty miles from your former residence. For example, if your prior job was three miles from your former home, your new job must be located at least fifty- three miles from that former home.

- **The time test:** You must work full time as an employee in the general location of your new home for at least 39 of the 52 weeks following the move. Alternatively, you may work full time as a self-employed individual for both 39 of the 52 weeks and 78 of the 104 weeks immediately following the move. (This tax requirement can be met either with one job or through a series of full-time positions.)

Automotive expenses, such as gas and oil, are also tax deductible, as long as accurate records are kept. (Or, you can take the standard 15 cents a mile tax deduction instead.) Parking fees and tolls may be tax deductible, but general car repairs, maintenance, insurance, or depreciation of your car are not.

According to the IRS, you generally can consider deducting moving expenses incurred within one year from the date you first reported to work at the new location. It is not necessary to begin working at the new location before moving, as long as you actually do go to work in this location within the specified period.

You do not have to itemize deductions to deduct moving expenses, but you must complete and attach Form 3903, Moving Expenses, to your Form 1040. For more information, refer to Publication 521, Moving Expenses (available on the IRS Web site at www.irs.gov). Form 3903 and Publication 521 are available for download or you may request a copy by calling 1-800-829-3676.

- [ ] Obtain a detailed floor plan of your new house (specifying the size of each room), and begin deciding what furniture to move.

- [ ] Begin to establish relationships with new health care professionals (doctors, hospitals, dentists, pharmacists, etc.).

- [ ] Find new veterinary professionals, if necessary.

- [ ] Locate new financial institutions and open accounts.

- [ ] Set up accounts with new utility companies.

- [ ] Clean out your closets.

- [ ] Begin gathering all valuable personal papers.

- [ ] Begin to notify credit card companies of your change of address.

Six Weeks Before Moving Day

- [ ] Notify friends and family of your new address.

- [ ] Choose a mover (see pages 231–234 for tips on selecting the right mover for your needs).

- [ ] Send out any drapes or area rugs for repair or cleaning.

- [ ] Hold a garage sale or make donations to charity of anything that you won't be taking to your new home.

- [ ] Make the necessary travel plans for long-distance moves (hotels, planes, trains, and so forth).

- [ ] Begin notifying all companies that bill you of your change of address.

- [ ] For self-movers: Reserve your equipment (see pages 234–238 for guidelines on managing a do-it-yourself move).

- [ ] Contact your children's current schools about transferring school records.

- [ ] Unless the mover is doing the packing, *start packing*!

Four Weeks Before Moving Day

- [ ] Transfer medical, dental, and prescription information to new health care providers.

- [ ] Begin using up food supplies.

- [ ] Make arrangements for child care the day of the move.

Three Weeks Before Moving Day

- [ ] Gather copies of all vehicle registration and insurance records and put them in one place, so that you will be prepared to show them to moving/rental companies, if required.

- [ ] Transfer veterinary records.

- [ ] Reserve any elevators, loading docks, or parking areas you will need on moving day

- [ ] Notify your current state's Motor Vehicle Bureau of your new address.

Two Weeks Before Moving Day

- [ ] Arrange to move pets, if you are not taking them with you.

- [ ] Have your vehicle serviced, if you're traveling by car.

- [ ] Enjoy a final favorite family activity in your current residence/neighborhood.

- [ ] As soon as the home is vacant, have utilities turned on at your new home (water, phone, electric, gas, cable, Internet service, etc.).

One Week Before Moving Day

☐ Cancel newspaper delivery.

☐ Dispose of all items that cannot be transported (such as flammable items like kerosene or other fuel substances).

☐ Have a final family dinner at your favorite restaurant.

☐ Defrost and dry all refrigerators and freezers that are being moved. Drain and dry all waterbeds.

☐ Disconnect all major appliances in preparation for the move.

☐ If you are packing yourself, all packing should be finished.

☐ Make sure you have enough medication to last at least two weeks.

One Day Before Moving Day

☐ Set aside enough clothing for two weeks, for access while you're traveling to your new home and for use during the initial days of your residence there.

☐ Turn off and back up all computers.

☐ Get a good night's sleep!

Moving Day

☐ Be available on all loading days. Movers will have questions.

☐ Accompany the driver as he prepares your inventory of household goods. Ask questions if the driver lists the condition of some of your items as worse than what you think they are.

☐ Carefully read and complete the bill of lading. This is the legal contract between you and the mover; treat it accordingly.

☐ Make sure you have copies of the bill of lading and all inventories before the driver leaves.

☐ Before the driver leaves, take a final walk through the house, checking all closets and storage areas to make sure nothing was left behind.

☐ Provide the driver with contact information, such as a cell phone or pager number, in case he needs to reach you during the course of the move.

☐ Take down the driver's truck number, agency name, and all contact information, including his cell phone number. This will make it easier to reach the driver if you have questions or if your plans change.

☐ Make sure the driver has the correct address of your new home or storage facility.

☐ Provide the movers with a clean water supply (either individual bottles of water or cups with jugs of water).

☐ Put the items that will be traveling with you—clothes, car registrations, driver's licenses, and the like—in one place, such as a bathroom that has been previously packed or in the vehicle that you will be taking with you. This will help prevent them from mistakenly being loaded onto the truck.

☐ Valuables (such as cash, jewelry, photographs, important papers, and so on) should be taken with you personally or sent ahead by a trackable service such as UPS or FedEx.

☐ Keep things in perspective. No matter how well prepared you are, things occasionally go wrong. Fido will chase the neighbor's cat and disappear just as you're about to leave. Junior will decide that he has to have the toy in the bottom box of a stack of boxes. Everyone you know will drop by for one last chat. Try to relax—this is all a normal part of moving.

After Moving In:

☐ Begin unpacking.

☐ Have any new furniture delivered. Have old appliances connected and new appliances delivered.

☐ Arrange to have utilities turned off in your old home, or transferred to the name of the new homeowner.

☐ Plan a family activity away from your new home. Explore your new hometown.

☐ Arrange for debris pickup.

☐ Verify that all bills are now coming to your new address.

☐ Thirty days following delivery, pay any final bills with the moving company, if necessary.

Following this list can help ensure a smoother transition from your current home to your new abode. Not everything listed here will apply to your situation, but the time lines and steps will give you a good idea of exactly what goes into a successful move.

Settling into Your New Home

Once the movers have left, don't be overwhelmed. MoveSource.com advises new homeowners to begin one step at a time. Start with the easy jobs. Put toilet paper in the bathrooms, paper cups by the sink, and trash bags in every room. Put light bulbs in the most important fixtures, and hang up your shower curtain. If you've packed curtains and tension rods, hang them in the bedroom windows. If you didn't bring curtains, slide a tension rod through the top hem of any sheet; it will at least give you temporary privacy. If you have a pet, make sure all doors and windows are closed before you let Fifi explore the house. Don't take her out without a leash until you've checked your yard for hidden exits, such as holes dug under the fence or spaces where a post is missing.

Hints for an Easier Delivery Day

The American Moving and Storage Association offers the following five tips for a smoother delivery day, or the day on which your household goods are delivered to your new home:

1. Have estimated moving funds available as either cash, a certified check, or a money order. If you are paying by credit card, you will need to make those arrangements before your possessions are loaded onto the moving van.

2. Check carefully for damaged or missing items at the time of delivery, and be sure to make note of these on the inventory before the movers leave.

3. Supervise the unloading and unpacking.

4. Complete your unpacking as quickly as possible.

5. When possible, make arrangements for the closing on the new house to be a day or two before your movers are scheduled to arrive at the new home. This will help reduce the stress of having to be available for the movers and having to concentrate on the closing at the same time.

Following the tips listed here and throughout the chapter should minimize problems on delivery day. However, should you need to resolve a problem with your mover, visit www.moving.org for information on dispute resolution.

Introduce your pets to the neighborhood through frequent walks. Eventually, they'll get to know the area well enough to find their way home, if necessary.

Although you'll want to get some basic food supplies right off the bat, there's no need to start cooking meals immediately. You can always have pizza; check your telephone directory for other possibilities. Give yourself a chance to relax, and recognize that you can't do everything at once.

Remember: It takes a while to settle into a new home. If you first take care of the kitchen, the bedrooms, and the bathrooms, everything else should fall into place fairly easily. Now is the time to try new furniture arrangements, but don't hang up pictures and mirrors right away. Otherwise, you'll have holes in your walls if you change your mind later.

Take the time to get to know your neighborhood and your neighbors. Slowly but surely, you'll get all the boxes unpacked and everything put away. Within a few weeks, you'll have turned your new house into a home.

Children and Pets: Your Most Precious Cargo

According to John Lane of RE/MAX Advantage 1, in Chesterfield, Michigan, "Moving can be a very emotional time for adults, but for children the adjustment can be even more extreme." He offers these strategies to help make the transition much easier for the little ones:

- Include your children when making plans for the move. If possible, take them with you when you are looking for your new home.

- If you are moving to a distant place, both you and your children can learn about the new area together. The Internet, the local library, the local chamber of commerce, tourist bureaus, and state agencies are good sources of information.

- Children can use dolls, boxes, and a wagon to get a sense of what moving means through playacting. Children can use the toys to act out their own version of "moving," and to become more familiar and comfortable with the process.

- If you are going to need a baby-sitter on moving day, reserve one beforehand.

- Let the children join in the fun of helping to decide how to decorate and arrange their new rooms.

- Take the time to make a "last visit" to places your family is fond of.

- Encourage your children to keep in contact with their friends. Have them exchange addresses and, if possible, suggest having them invite their friends to come visit them at their new home.

- Prepare a package for each one of your children, containing their favorite toys, clothing, and snacks. Make sure to label each package with the child's name, and let each one open that package first when they get to their new home. That way, they'll have their comfort clothing and foods on hand as they're adjusting to their new environment.

- Survey your new home for loose steps, low overhangs, and other accidents-waiting-to-happen. Watch your children carefully until everyone becomes familiar with your new home.

- Take a break with the family as soon as the major unpacking is done. Don't try to do everything as soon as you arrive.

Your move may entail other challenges for your children, such as changing schools and making new friends. The first few weeks in a new school may be difficult for children. Follow their progress closely and, if any problems arise, do not hesitate to arrange meetings with teachers. If you are moving during the school year, you may have to pre-enroll children in their new schools before you actually move. Check with school officials to get their advice and suggestions.

Pets need some special care, too, says Lane, who advises new home buyers to talk to their veterinarian about ways to make the move easier on their animals. Here are some suggestions to consider:

- Animals get used to the local water, so many vets recommend taking along a supply from your old home. It may keep your pet from developing an upset stomach on the road.

- Remember to bring along an ample supply of pet food, treats, and any necessary medicines for your pet—enough to last you through the first two weeks or so in your new home.

- Identify a vet in your new neighborhood as soon as possible.

- Don't leave your pet unsupervised outside for long periods at first. Be sure that your pet stays close to home (and in your yard). Find out whether there areother animals in the neighborhood who tend to pay unexpected visits.

- Get to know which neighbors have pets, and determine whether your pets will get along.

By taking these steps, your children and pets will have a less stressful moving experience, and a happier introduction to their new home.

It's Your Move

Perhaps your plan is to round up a hoard of friends on a Saturday afternoon, load your home's contents into a rental truck or trailer, and transport it a few miles down the road. Or perhaps you're going to hire a mover to pack up your home, move everything across the country, and then unpack it when it arrives. No matter which way you're going about it, the basic tenets of moving are the same: Think ahead, be prepared, and do the necessary homework before proceeding.

As you learned from the information and tips offered in this chapter, it's never too early to start thinking about and preparing for a move. Even if it's going to be six months before you move into your new domicile, you can start culling through your belongings and holding garage sales right now. And the best part of moving is that, when all the furniture is delivered and the boxes are unpacked, you and your family will have a wonderful new home to enjoy and cherish as your own!

Welcome Home!

Buying a home is an exciting experience. And like any adventure, it's filled with surprises around every corner—some good; some not so good. By reading this book, using the resources cited in each chapter, and following the guidelines and advice offered by the many agents whose expertise fills these pages, you should be prepared to get out there and begin the home-buying process (if you haven't already).

As you have no doubt noticed by now, a large number of RE/MAX real estate brokers and agents were interviewed for this book. Not only do these agents share their stories of working with buyers, but they also share their experience and knowledge with you, the reader. Whether this is your first home-buying experience, or one of many that you've already undertaken, we know that their advice—combined with the information provided in this book—will help ensure that your house hunt is both successful and rewarding.

Your New Home and You

Once you've moved into your new home, you'll likely spend several weeks (or even months) making the place "your own." That means bringing in your existing furniture and decorations, buying new items, and sprucing up the home by replacing carpeting and painting to suit your taste, all in the name of personalizing the space to your liking. While this process may be tedious, it's definitely worth the effort because you wind up with a home that you and your family can cherish and enjoy for years to come.

An Ongoing Investment

Unlike renting, purchasing a home is an investment in your future. Because properties typically appreciate in value over time, it's wise to maintain your home and make improvements to it. Should you eventually decide to move—either because you're looking for more space as your family grows, relocating for a new job, downsizing as you prepare to enjoy your retirement years, or you're ready to sell for any other reason—your home should bring you a profit. So the TLC you put into your home now and in years to come can pay off down the road.

One way to safeguard your investment is to make your mortgage payments on time, every time. That way, you'll continually improve your credit score and open up future opportunities to borrow on credit, such as when you're ready to move again.

A Lifelong Relationship

The relationship you've forged with your real estate agent doesn't have to end on closing day. You may want to retain that agent when the time comes to sell your home, or to purchase a second home. If you're pleased with how she handled your home purchase, you may also refer friends, family members, and coworkers to her, because real estate agents generally rely on referrals to generate business. Also remember that real estate agents have connections in a variety of industries: They can usually point you in the direction of good handymen, contractors, roofers, landscaper architects, and other postsale service providers.

The RE/MAX Difference

Not all real estate agents are alike. We're proud of RE/MAX's agents, who are among the most reputable, competent agents working in the field today. Here are some quick facts about RE/MAX International and its agents:

- RE/MAX has more than 6,500 full-service offices in the United States, Canada, the Caribbean, Mexico, Europe, South Africa, the Pacific Rim, and Europe.

- RE/MAX sales associates currently work in sixty-three countries and speak over thirty-nine languages.

- Today, RE/MAX sales associates proudly number over 120,000 full-time, professional agents worldwide.

- The typical RE/MAX sales associate averages more than thirteen years of experience as a real estate professional.

- RE/MAX sales associates earn, on average, more professional real estate credentials based on educational achievement than industry competitors—the result of an ongoing commitment to boosting their professional expertise.

- About 70 percent of RE/MAX sales associates' business comes from repeat business or referrals from past customers and friends—much higher than the industry average.

- Miracle Home®: A home listed by RE/MAX may be designated as a Miracle Home®. When it is, RE/MAX sales associates will make a contribution on behalf of the listing and/or sale to the local hospital affiliated with the Children's Miracle Network. Funds raised in the community remain in the area to benefit local children.

Each RE/MAX office is locally owned and independently operated and is staffed by independent contractor associates who have earned the highest in professional designations and certifications to ensure their clients receive quality, knowledgeable services.

The Home of Your Dreams

RE/MAX sales associates share yet another common goal: helping buyers get into the homes of their dreams. Knowing that buying a home is the most significant financial decision that people make in their lifetimes, they take their job of matching consumers with the right dwellings very seriously. With this book in hand and a reputable, experienced agent in your corner, you'll be equipped to make the best purchase decision possible. We wish you the best of luck, and look forward to helping you find the home of your dreams.

Real Estate Licensing Agencies in North America

Courtesy of ARELLO
(Association of Real Estate License Law Officials)

ALABAMA
Alabama Real Estate Commission
1201 Carmichael Way
Montgomery, Alabama
36106-4350 USA
FAX 334/270-9118
Telephone 334/242-5544

ALASKA
Division of Occupational Licensing
Alaska Real Estate Commission
550 W. 7th Avenue, Suite 1500
Anchorage, AK 99501 USA
FAX 907/269-8156
Telephone 907/269-8160

ALBERTA
Real Estate Council of Alberta
340, 2424 4 Street SW
Calgary, Alberta Canada T2S 2T4
FAX 403/228-3065
Telephone 403/228-2954

ARIZONA
Department of Real Estate
2910 N. 44th Street, Suite 100
Phoenix, Arizona 85018 USA
FAX 602/468-0562
Telephone 602/468-1414

ARKANSAS
Real Estate Commission
612 South Summit Street
Little Rock, Arkansas 72201-4740 USA
FAX 501/683-8020
Telephone 501/683-8010

BRITISH COLUMBIA
Real Estate Council of British Columbia
900–750 West Pender Street
Vancouver, British Columbia
V6C 2T8 Canada
FAX 604/683-4117
Telephone 604/683-9664

CALIFORNIA
State of California
Department of Real Estate
Post Office Box 187000
Sacramento, CA 95818-7000 USA
Consumer Information Line:
916/227-0864
Licensing & Education Inquiries:
916/227-0931

COLORADO
Department of Regulatory Agencies
Division of Real Estate
1900 Grant Street, Suite 600
Denver, Colorado 80203 USA
FAX 303/894-2683
Telephone 303/894-2166

CONNECTICUT
Department of Consumer Protection
Occupational and Professional
Licensing Division
165 Capitol Avenue, Room 110
Hartford, Connecticut 06106 USA
FAX 860/713-7239
Telephone 860/713-6150

DELAWARE
Real Estate Commission
861 Silver Lake Blvd., Suite 203
Dover, Delaware 19904 USA
FAX 302/739-2711
Telephone 302-739-4522 ext. 219

DISTRICT OF COLUMBIA
Board of Real Estate
941 North Capitol Street, NE,
Room 7200
Washington, DC 20002 USA
FAX 202/442-4528
Telephone 202/442-4320

FLORIDA
Division of Real Estate
400 W. Robinson Street, Suite N801
Orlando, Florida 32801-1757 USA
FAX 407/317-7260
Telephone 407/481-5662

GEORGIA
Real Estate Commission
Suite 1000 - International Tower
229 Peachtree Street NE
Atlanta, Georgia 30303-1605 USA
FAX 404/656-6650
Telephone 404/656-3916

GUAM
Dept. of Revenue & Taxation
Post Office Box 23607
GMF Barrigada, Guam 96921
FAX 671/472-2643
Telephone 671/475-1844

HAWAII
Real Estate Commission
335 Merchant Street, Room 333
Honolulu, Hawaii 96813 USA
FAX 808/586-2650
Telephone 808/586-2643

IDAHO
Real Estate Commission
Post Office Box 83720
Boise, Idaho 83720-0077 USA
FAX 208/334-2050
Telephone 208/334-3285

ILLINOIS
Office of Banks and Real Estate
500 East Monroe Street, Suite 200
Springfield, Illinois 62701 USA
FAX 217/782-3390
Telephone 217/785-9300

INDIANA
Professional Licensing Agency
302 W. Washington Street, Room EO34
Indianapolis, Indiana 46204 USA
FAX 317/232-2312
Telephone 317/232-2980

IOWA
Real Estate Commission
19208 SE Hulsizer Avenue
Ankeny, Iowa 50021-3941 USA
FAX 515/281-7411
Telephone 515/281-5910

KANSAS
Real Estate Commission
Three Townsite Plaza, Suite 200
120 SE 6th Avenue
Topeka, Kansas 66603-3511 USA
FAX 785/296-1771
Telephone 785/296-3411

KENTUCKY
Real Estate Commission
10200 Linn Station Road, Suite 201
Louisville, Kentucky 40223 USA
FAX 502/426-2717
Telephone 502/425-4273

LOUISIANA
Real Estate Commission
Post Office Box 14785
Baton Rouge, Louisiana
70898-4785 USA
FAX 225/925-4431
Telephone 225/925-4771

MAINE
Real Estate Commission
35 State House Station
Augusta, Maine 04333-0035 USA
FAX 207/624-8637
Telephone 207/624-8603

MANITOBA
Securities Commission
1110 - 405 Broadway
Winnipeg, Manitoba R3C 3L6 Canada
FAX 204/948-4627
Telephone 204/948-4627

MARYLAND
Real Estate Commission
500 N. Calvert Street
Baltimore, Maryland 21202-3651 USA
FAX 410/333-0023
Telephone 410/230-6200

MASSACHUSETTS
Real Estate Board
239 Causeway Street, Suite 500
Boston, Massachusetts 02114 USA
FAX 617/727-2669
Telephone 617/727-2373

MICHIGAN
Department of Consumer and
Industry Services
Bureau of Commercial Services
Post Office Box 30243
Lansing, Michigan 48909 USA
FAX 517/241-9280
Telephone 517/241-9288

MISSISSIPPI
Real Estate Commission
Post Office Box 12685
Jackson, Mississippi 39236-2685 USA
FAX 601/932-2990
Telephone 601/932-9191

MISSOURI
Real Estate Commission
Post Office Box 1339
3605 Missouri Blvd.
Jefferson City, MO 65102 USA
FAX 573/751-2777
Telephone 573/751-2628

MONTANA
Board of Realty Regulation
Post Office Box 200513
301 South Park
Helena, Montana 59620-0513 USA
FAX 406/841-2323
Telephone 406/444-2961

NEBRASKA
Real Estate Commission
Post Office Box 94667
Lincoln, Nebraska 68509-4667 USA
FAX 402/471-4492
Telephone 402/471-2004

NEVADA
Department of Business & Industry
Real Estate Division
2501 E. Sahara Ave., Suite 102
Las Vegas, Nevada 89104-4137 USA
FAX 702/486-4275
Telephone 702/486-4033

NEW HAMPSHIRE
Real Estate Commission
State House Annex
25 Capitol Street, Room 435
Concord, New Hampshire
03301-6312 USA
FAX 603/271-1039
Telephone 603/271-2701

NEW JERSEY
Real Estate Commission
20 West State Street
Post Office Box 328
Trenton, New Jersey 08625-0328 USA
FAX 609/292-0944
Telephone 609/292-8280

NEW MEXICO
Real Estate Commission
1650 University Blvd., NE, Suite 490
Albuquerque, New Mexico 87102 USA
FAX 505/246-0725
Telephone 505/841-9120 or
800/801-7505

NEW YORK
Division of Licensing Services
84 Holland Avenue
Albany, New York 12208-3490 USA
FAX 518/473-2730
Telephone 518/473-2728

NORTH CAROLINA
Real Estate Commission
Post Office Box 17100
Raleigh, North Carolina
27619-7100 USA
FAX 919/872-0038
Telephone 919/875-3700

NORTH DAKOTA
Real Estate Commission
314 East Thayer Avenue
Post Office Box 727
Bismarck, North Dakota
58502-0727 USA
FAX 701/328-9750
Telephone 701/328-9749

NORTHWEST TERRITORIES
Consumer Services
#600 5201-50th Avenue
Yellowknife, Northwest Territories
X1A 3S9 Canada
FAX 867/873-0152
Telephone 867/873-7125

NOVA SCOTIA
Real Estate Commission
7 Scarfe Court
Dartmouth, Nova Scotia
B3B 1W4 Canada
FAX 902/468-2533
Telephone 902/468-3511

OHIO
Division of Real Estate
and Professional Licensing
77 South High Street, 20th Floor
Columbus, Ohio 43215-6133 USA
FAX 614/644-0584
Telephone 614/466-4100

OKLAHOMA
Real Estate Commission
Shephard Mall
2401 NW 23rd, Suite 18
Oklahoma City, Oklahoma 73107 USA
FAX 405/521-2189
Telephone 405/521-3387

ONTARIO
Real Estate Council of Ontario
3250 Bloor Street West
East Tower, Suite 600
Toronto, Ontario M8X 2X9 Canada
FAX 416/207-4820
Telephone 416/207-4800

OREGON
Real Estate Agency
1177 Center Street NE
Salem, Oregon 97301-2505 USA
FAX 503/378-2491
Telephone 503/378-4170

PENNSYLVANIA
Real Estate Commission
Post Office Box 2649
Harrisburg, Pennsylvania
17105-2649 USA
FAX 717/787-0250
Telephone 717/783-3658

PUERTO RICO
Real Estate Board
Post Office Box 9023271
San Juan, Puerto Rico 00902-3271
FAX 787/722-4818
Telephone 787/722-0136 or
787/722-2122

QUÉBEC
Association des Courtiers et Agents
Immobiliers du Québec
6300 Auteuil, Suite 300
Brossard, Québec J4Z 3P2, Canada
FAX 450/676-7801
Telephone 450/676-4800

RHODE ISLAND
Department of Business Regulation
233 Richmond Street, Suite 230
Providence, RI 02903 USA
FAX 401/222-6654
Telephone401/222-2255

SASKATCHEWAN
Real Estate Commission
231 Robin Crescent
Saskatoon, Saskatchewan S7L 6M8
Canada
FAX 306/373-5377
Telephone 306/374-5233

SOUTH CAROLINA
Department of Labor Licensing
& Regulation
Real Estate Commission
Post Office Box 11847
Columbia, South Carolina
29211-1847 USA
FAX 803/896-4404
Telephone 803/896-4400

SOUTH DAKOTA
Real Estate Commission
425 E. Capitol
Pierre, South Dakota 57501 USA
FAX 605/773-4356
Telephone 605/773-3600

TENNESSEE
Real Estate Commission
500 James Robertson Parkway
Davy Crockett Tower, Suite 180
Nashville, Tennessee 37243-1151 USA
FAX 615/741-0313
Telephone 615/741-2273

TEXAS
Real Estate Commission
Post Office Box 12188
Austin, Texas 78711-2188 USA
FAX 512/465-3910
Telephone 512/465-3900

UTAH
Division of Real Estate
Post Office Box 146711
Salt Lake City, Utah 84114-6711 USA
FAX 801/530-6749
Telephone 801/530-6747

VERMONT
Office of Professional Regulation
Real Estate Commission
81 River Street, Drawer 9
Montpelier, Vermont 05609-1106 USA
FAX 802/828-2368
Telephone 802/828-3228

VIRGIN ISLANDS
Department of Licensing
and Consumer Affairs
Golden Rock Shopping Center
Christiansted, St. Croix 00820
FAX 340/778-8250
Telephone 340/773-2226

VIRGINIA
Department of Professional
and Occupational Regulation
3600 West Broad Street
Richmond, Virginia 23230 USA
FAX 804/367-2475
Telephone 804/367-8526

WASHINGTON
Department of Licensing
Business and Professions Division,
Real Estate
Post Office Box 9015
Olympia, Washington 98507-9015 USA
FAX 360/586-0998
Telephone 360/664-6500

WEST VIRGINIA
Real Estate Commission
300 Capitol Street, Suite 400
Charleston, West Virginia 25301 USA
FAX 304/558-6442
Telephone 304/558-3555

WYOMING
Real Estate Commission
2020 Carey Avenue, Suite 100
Cheyenne, Wyoming 82002 USA
FAX 307/777-3796
Telephone 307/777-7141

Sample Real Estate Forms

Real estate forms come in all shapes and sizes. Where some may take just one page to get their point across, others go on for what seems to be forever, covering many bases to ensure a smooth transaction. In this section, you'll find several key forms that you're likely to come across during the home-buying process, including:

- A Residential Sale and Purchase Contract
- A Seller's Real Property Disclosure Statement
- A Summary Home Inspection Report
- A Non-Exclusive Buyer Representation Contract
- A Disclosure and Consent to Dual Agency Form
- An Exclusive Buyer Representation Contract

It's important to note that not all states require these forms, and that each may have its own variation of the document. For example, the Non-Exclusive Buyer Representation Contract, Disclosure and Consent to Dual Agency Form, and Exclusive Buyer Representation Contract we've included here—courtesy of the Illinois Association of Realtors—all comply with the laws of the State of Illinois and should not be used in other states. So check with your real estate agent or attorney for those forms that are specific to your location.

Residential Sale and Purchase Contract
FLORIDA ASSOCIATION OF REALTORS®

1* **1. SALE AND PURCHASE:** _____ ("Seller")
2* and _____ ("Buyer")
3 agree to sell and buy on the terms and conditions specified below the property described as:
4* Address: _____
5* _____ County: _____
6* Legal Description: _____
7* _____ Tax ID No: _____
8 together with all improvements and attached items, including fixtures, built-in furnishings, built-in appliances, ceiling fans, light
9 fixtures, attached wall-to-wall carpeting, rods, draperies and other window coverings. The only other items included in the
10* purchase are: _____
11* _____
12* _____
13* The following attached items are excluded from the purchase: _____
14* _____
15 The real and personal property described above as included in the purchase is referred to as the "Property." Personal property listed
16 in this Contract is included in the purchase price, has no contributory value and is being left for **Seller's** convenience.

17 PRICE AND FINANCING
18* **2. PURCHASE PRICE:** $_____ payable by **Buyer** in U.S. currency as follows:
19* **(a)** $_____ Deposit received (checks are subject to clearance) _____, _____ by
20* _____ for _____ ("Escrow Agent")
21 *Signature* *Name of Company*
22* **(b)** $_____ Additional deposit to be delivered to Escrow Agent by _____,
23* _____ or _____days from Effective Date (10 days if left blank)
24* **(c)** _____ Total financing (see Paragraph 3 below) (express as a dollar amount or percentage)
25* **(d)** $_____ Other: _____
26* **(e)** $_____ Balance to close (not including **Buyer's** closing costs, prepaid items and prorations). All funds paid
27 at closing must be paid by locally drawn cashier's check, official bank check, or wired funds.
28* **3. FINANCING:** (Check as applicable) ❏ **(a) Buyer** will pay cash for the Property with no financing contingency.
29* ❏ **(b) Buyer** will apply for the financing specified in Paragraph 2(c) at the prevailing interest rate and loan costs based on
30* **Buyer's** creditworthiness (the "Financing") within _____ days from Effective Date (5 days if left blank) and provide **Seller** with a
31* written Financing commitment or approval letter ("Commitment") within _____ days from Effective Date (30 days if left blank)
32 ("Commitment Period"). **Buyer** will keep **Seller** and Broker fully informed about loan application status, progress and
33 Commitment issues and authorizes the mortgage broker and lender to disclose all such information to **Seller** and **Broker**. Once
34 **Buyer** provides the Commitment to **Seller**, the financing contingency is waived and **Seller** will be entitled to retain the deposits
35 if the transaction does not close by the Closing Date unless (1) the Property appraises below the purchase price and either the
36 parties cannot agree on a new purchase price or **Buyer** elects not to proceed, or (2) another provision of this Contract requires
37 the deposits to be returned. If **Buyer**, using diligence and good faith, cannot provide the Commitment within the Commitment
38 Period, this Contract will be terminated and **Buyer's** deposits refunded.

39 CLOSING
40 **4. CLOSING DATE; OCCUPANCY:** Unless extended by other provisions of this Contract, this Contract will be closed on
41* _____, _____ ("Closing Date") at the time established by the closing agent, by which time **Seller** will (a) have removed all
42 personal items and trash from the Property and swept the Property clean and (b) deliver the deed, occupancy and possession, along with
43 all keys, garage door openers and access codes, to **Buyer**. If on Closing Date insurance underwriting is suspended, **Buyer** may
44 postpone closing up to 5 days after the insurance suspension is lifted. If this transaction does not close for any reason, **Buyer** will
45 immediately return all **Seller**-provided title evidence, surveys, association documents and other items.

46 **5. CLOSING PROCEDURE; COSTS:** Closing will take place in the county where the Property is located and may be conducted by
47 mail or electronic means. If title insurance insures **Buyer** for title defects arising between the title binder effective date and recording
48 of **Buyer's** deed, closing agent will disburse at closing the net sale proceeds to **Seller** and brokerage fees to Broker as per
49 Paragraph 19. In addition to other expenses provided in this Contract, **Seller** and **Buyer** will pay the costs indicated below.
50 **(a) Seller Costs: Seller** will pay taxes and surtaxes on the deed and recording fees for documents needed to cure title; up to
51* $_____ or _____% (1.5% if left blank) of the purchase price for repairs to warranted items (**"Repair Limit"**);

52* **Buyer** (____) (____) and **Seller** (____) (____) acknowledge receipt of a copy of this page, which is Page 1 of 7 Pages.
53 FAR-8 Rev. 10/04 © 2004 Florida Association of REALTORS® All Rights Reserved

54· and up to $_____ or _____% (1.5% if left blank) of the purchase price for wood-destroying organism
55· treatment and repairs (**"WDO Repair Limit"**); Other: _____
56 **(b) Buyer Costs: Buyer** will pay taxes and recording fees on notes and mortgages; recording fees on the deed and financing
57· statements; loan expenses; lender's title policy; inspections; survey; flood insurance; Other: _____
58 **(c) Title Evidence and Insurance: Check (1) or (2):**
59· ❑ **(1)** The title evidence will be a Paragraph 10(a)(1) owner's title insurance commitment. ❑ **Seller** ❑ **Buyer** will select the title
80· agent. ❑ **Seller** ❑ **Buyer** will pay for the owner's title policy, search, examination and related charges. Each party will
61 pay its own closing fees.
62· ❑ **(2) Seller** will provide an abstract as specified in Paragraph 10(a)(2) as title evidence. ❑ **Seller** ❑ **Buyer** will pay for
63 the owner's title policy and select the title agent. **Seller** will pay fees for title searches prior to closing, including tax
64 search and lien search fees, and **Buyer** will pay fees for title searches after closing (if any), title examination fees and
65 closing fees.
66 **(d) Prorations:** The following items will be made current (if applicable) and prorated as of the day before Closing Date: real
67 estate taxes, interest, bonds, assessments, association fees, insurance, rents and other current expenses and revenues of
68 the Property. If taxes and assessments for the current year cannot be determined, the previous year's rates will be used with
69 adjustment for exemptions and improvements. **Buyer** is responsible for property tax increases due to change in ownership.
70 **(e) Special Assessment by Public Body:** Regarding special assessments imposed by a public body, **Seller** will pay (i) the full
71 amount of liens that are certified, confirmed and ratified before closing and (ii) the amount of the last estimate of the assessment if
72 an improvement is substantially completed as of Effective Date but has not resulted in a lien before closing, and **Buyer** will pay all
73 other amounts.
74 **(f) Tax Withholding: Buyer** and **Seller** will comply with the Foreign Investment in Real Property Tax Act, which may require
75 **Seller** to provide additional cash at closing if **Seller** is a "foreign person" as defined by federal law.
76· **(g) Home Warranty:** ❑ **Buyer** ❑ **Seller** ❑ **N/A** will pay for a home warranty plan issued by _____ at a
77· cost not to exceed $_____. A home warranty plan provides for repair or replacement of many of a home's mechanical
78 systems and major built-in appliances in the event of breakdown due to normal wear and tear during the agreement period.

79 **PROPERTY CONDITION**
80· **6. INSPECTION PERIODS: Buyer** will complete the inspections referenced in Paragraphs 7 and 8(a)(2) by _____,
81· _____ (within 10 days from Effective Date if left blank) ("Inspection Period"); the wood-destroying organism inspection
82· by _____, _____ (at least 5 days prior to closing, if left blank); and the walk-through inspection on the
83 day before Closing Date or any other time agreeable to the parties; and the survey referenced in Paragraph 10(c) by
84· _____, _____ (at least 5 days prior to closing if left blank).

85 **7. REAL PROPERTY DISCLOSURES: Seller** represents that **Seller** does not know of any facts that materially affect the value
86 of the Property, including but not limited to violations of governmental laws, rules and regulations, other than those that **Buyer**
87 can readily observe or that are known by or have been disclosed to **Buyer. Seller** will have all open permits (if any) closed out,
88 with final inspections completed, no later than 5 days prior to closing.
89 **(a) Energy Efficiency: Buyer** acknowledges receipt of the energy-efficiency information brochure required by Section 553.996,
90 *Florida Statutes.*
91 **(b) Radon Gas:** Radon is a naturally occurring radioactive gas that, when it has accumulated in a building in sufficient
92 quantities, may present health risks to persons who are exposed to it over time. Levels of radon that exceed federal and
93 state guidelines have been found in buildings in Florida. Additional information regarding radon and radon testing may be
94 obtained from your county public health unit. **Buyer** may, within the Inspection Period, have an appropriately licensed person
95 test the Property for radon. If the radon level exceeds acceptable EPA standards, **Seller** may choose to reduce the radon
96 level to an acceptable EPA level, failing which either party may cancel this Contract.
97 **(c) Flood Zone: Buyer** is advised to verify by survey, with the lender and with appropriate government agencies which flood
98 zone the Property is in, whether flood insurance is required and what restrictions apply to improving the Property and rebuilding
99 in the event of casualty. If the Property is in a Special Flood Hazard Area or Coastal High Hazard Area **and** the buildings are built
100 below the minimum flood elevation, **Buyer** may cancel this Contract by delivering written notice to **Seller** within 20 days from
101 Effective Date, failing which **Buyer** accepts the existing elevation of the buildings and zone designation of the Property.
102 **(d) Homeowners' Association:** If membership in a homeowners' association is mandatory, an association disclosure
103 summary is attached and incorporated into this Contract. **BUYER SHOULD NOT SIGN THIS CONTRACT UNTIL**
104 **BUYER HAS RECEIVED AND READ THE DISCLOSURE SUMMARY.**
105 **(e) PROPERTY TAX DISCLOSURE SUMMARY: BUYER** SHOULD NOT RELY ON THE **SELLER'S** CURRENT PROPERTY
106 TAXES AS THE AMOUNT OF PROPERTY TAXES THAT **BUYER** MAY BE OBLIGATED TO PAY IN THE YEAR SUBSEQUENT
107 TO PURCHASE. A CHANGE OF OWNERSHIP OR PROPERTY IMPROVEMENTS TRIGGERS REASSESSMENTS OF THE
108 PROPERTY THAT COULD RESULT IN HIGHER PROPERTY TAXES. IF YOU HAVE ANY QUESTIONS CONCERNING
109 VALUATION, CONTACT THE COUNTY PROPERTY APPRAISER'S OFFICE FOR FURTHER INFORMATION.
110 **(f) Mold:** Mold is part of the natural environment that, when accumulated in sufficient quantities, may present health risks to
111 susceptible persons. For more information, contact the county indoor air quality specialist or other appropriate professional.

112· **Buyer** (_____) (_____) and **Seller** (_____) (_____) acknowledge receipt of a copy of this page, which is Page 2 of 7 Pages.
FAR-8   Rev. 10/04   © 2004   Florida Association of REALTORS®   All Rights Reserved

113 **8. MAINTENANCE, INSPECTIONS AND REPAIR: Seller** will keep the Property in the same condition from Effective Date until
114 closing, except for normal wear and tear ("maintenance requirement") and repairs required by this Contract. **Seller** will provide
115 access and utilities for **Buyer's** inspections. **Buyer** will repair all damages to the Property resulting from the inspections,
116 return the Property to its pre-inspection condition and provide **Seller** with paid receipts for all work done on Property upon its
117 completion. If **Seller**, using best efforts, is unable to complete required repairs or treatments prior to closing, **Seller** will give
118 **Buyer** a credit at closing for the cost of the repairs **Seller** was obligated to make. At closing, **Seller** will assign all assignable repair
119 and treatment contracts to **Buyer** and provide **Buyer** with paid receipts for all work done on the Property pursuant to the
120 terms of this Contract.
121   **(a) Warranty, Inspections and Repair:**
122   **(1) Warranty: Seller** warrants that non-leased major appliances and heating, cooling, mechanical, electrical, security,
123   sprinkler, septic and plumbing systems, seawall, dock and pool equipment, if any, are and will be maintained in working
124   condition until closing; that the structures (including roofs) and pool, if any, are structurally sound and watertight; and
125   that torn or missing pool cage and screen room screens and missing roof tiles will be replaced. **Seller** does not warrant
126   and is not required to repair cosmetic conditions, unless the cosmetic condition resulted from a defect in a warranted
127   item. **Seller** is not obligated to bring any item into compliance with existing building code regulations unless necessary
128   to repair a warranted item. "Working condition" means operating in the manner in which the item was designed to
129   operate and "cosmetic conditions" means aesthetic imperfections that do not affect the working condition of the item,
130   including pitted marcite; missing or torn window screens; fogged windows; tears, worn spots and discoloration of floor
131   coverings/wallpapers/window treatments; nail holes, scratches, dents, scrapes, chips and caulking in bathroom
132   ceiling/walls/flooring/tile/fixtures/mirrors; cracked roof tiles; curling or worn shingles; and minor cracks in floor
133   tiles/windows/driveways/sidewalks/pool decks/garage and patio floors.
134   **(2) Professional Inspection: Buyer** may, at **Buyer's** expense, have warranted items inspected by a person who
135   specializes in and holds an occupational license (if required by law) to conduct home inspections or who holds a Florida
136   license to repair and maintain the items inspected ("professional inspector"). **Buyer** must, within 5 days from the end of the
137   Inspection Period, deliver written notice of any items that are not in the condition warranted and a copy of the inspector's
138   written report, if any, to **Seller**. If **Buyer** fails to deliver timely written notice, **Buyer** waives **Seller's** warranty and accepts
139   the items listed in subparagraph (a) in their "as is" condition, except that **Seller** must meet the maintenance requirement.
140   **(3) Repair: Seller** will obtain repair estimates and is obligated only to make repairs necessary to bring warranted items
141   into the condition warranted, up to the Repair Limit. **Seller** may, within 5 days from receipt of **Buyer's** notice of items
142   that are not in the condition warranted, have a second inspection made by a professional inspector and will report
143   repair estimates to **Buyer.** If the first and second inspection reports differ and the parties cannot resolve the differences,
144   **Buyer** and **Seller** together will choose, and equally split the cost of, a third inspector, whose written report will be
145   binding on the parties. If the cost to repair warranted items equals or is less than the Repair Limit, **Seller** will have the
146   repairs made in a workmanlike manner by an appropriately licensed person. If the cost to repair warranted items
147   exceeds the Repair Limit, either party may cancel this Contract unless either party pays the excess or **Buyer**
148   designates which repairs to make at a total cost to **Seller** not exceeding the Repair Limit and accepts the balance of
149   the Property in its "as is" condition.
150   **(b) Wood-Destroying Organisms:** "Wood-destroying organism" means arthropod or plant life, including termites, powder-post
151 beetles, oldhouse borers and wood-decaying fungi, that damages or infests seasoned wood in a structure, excluding fences.
152 **Buyer** may, at **Buyer's** expense and prior to closing, have the Property inspected by a Florida-licensed pest control business to
153 determine the existence of past or present wood-destroying organism infestation and damage caused by infestation. If the
154 inspector finds evidence of infestation or damage, **Buyer** will deliver a copy of the inspector's written report to **Seller** within 5
155 days from the date of the inspection. If **Seller** previously treated the Property for wood-destroying organisms, **Seller** does not
156 have to treat the Property again if (i) there is no visible live infestation, and (ii) **Seller** transfers a current full treatment warranty to
157 **Buyer** at closing. Otherwise, **Seller** will have 5 days from receipt of the inspector's report to have reported damage estimated by
158 a licensed building or general contractor and corrective treatment estimated by a licensed pest control business. **Seller** will have
159 treatments and repairs made by an appropriately licensed person at **Seller's** expense up to the WDO Repair Limit. If the cost to
160 treat and repair the Property exceeds the WDO Repair Limit, either party may pay the excess, failing which either party may
161 cancel this Contract by written notice to the other. If **Buyer** fails to timely deliver the inspector's written report, **Buyer** accepts the
162 Property "as is" with regard to wood-destroying organism infestation and damage, subject to the maintenance requirement.
163 **(c) Walk-through Inspection: Buyer** may walk through the Property solely to verify that **Seller** has made repairs required
164 by this Contract and has met contractual obligations. No other issues may be raised as a result of the walk-through
165 inspection. If **Buyer** fails to conduct this inspection, **Seller's** repair and maintenance obligations will be deemed fulfilled.

166 **9. RISK OF LOSS:** If any portion of the Property is damaged by fire or other casualty before closing and can be restored within
167 45 days from the Closing Date to substantially the same condition as it was on Effective Date, **Seller** will, at **Seller's** expense,
168 restore the Property and the Closing Date will be extended accordingly. **Seller** will not be obligated to replace trees. If the
169 restoration cannot be completed in time, **Buyer** may accept the Property "as is", in which case with **Seller** will credit the
170 deductible and assign the insurance proceeds, if any, to **Buyer** at closing in such amounts as are (i) attributable to the Property
171 and (ii) not yet expended in making repairs, failing which either party may cancel this Contract. If the Property is a
172 condominium, this paragraph applies only to the unit and limited common elements appurtenant to the unit; if the Property is in
173 a homeowners' association, this paragraph will not apply to common elements or recreation or other facilities.

174* **Buyer** (_____) (_____) and **Seller** (_____) (_____) acknowledge receipt of a copy of this page, which is Page 3 of 7 Pages.
   FAR-8   Rev. 10/04   © 2004   Florida Association of REALTORS®   All Rights Reserved

Residential Sale and Purchase Contract

TITLE

10. TITLE: Seller will convey marketable title to the Property by statutory warranty deed or trustee, personal representative or guardian deed as appropriate to **Seller's** status.

(a) **Title Evidence:** Title evidence will show legal access to the Property and marketable title of record in **Seller** in accordance with current title standards adopted by the Florida Bar, subject only to the following title exceptions, none of which prevent residential use of the Property: covenants, easements and restrictions of record; matters of plat; existing zoning and government regulations; oil, gas and mineral rights of record if there is no right of entry; current taxes; mortgages that **Buyer** will assume; and encumbrances that **Seller** will discharge at or before closing. **Seller** will, at least 2 days prior to closing, deliver to **Buyer Seller's** choice of one of the following types of title evidence, which must be generally accepted in the county where the Property is located (specify in Paragraph 5(c) the selected type). **Seller** will use option (1) in Palm Beach County and option (2) in Miami-Dade County.

(1) **A title insurance commitment** issued by a Florida-licensed title insurer in the amount of the purchase price and subject only to title exceptions set forth in this Contract.

(2) **An existing abstract of title** from a reputable and existing abstract firm (if firm is not existing, then abstract must be certified as correct by an existing firm) purporting to be an accurate synopsis of the instruments affecting title to the Property recorded in the public records of the county where the Property is located and certified to Effective Date. However, if such an abstract is not available to **Seller**, then a **prior owner's** title policy acceptable to the proposed insurer as a base for reissuance of coverage. **Seller** will pay for copies of all policy exceptions and an update in a format acceptable to **Buyer's** closing agent from the policy effective date and certified to **Buyer** or **Buyer's** closing agent, together with copies of all documents recited in the prior policy and in the update. If a prior policy is not available to **Seller** then (1) above will be the title evidence. Title evidence will be delivered no later than 10 days before Closing Date.

(b) **Title Examination: Buyer** will examine the title evidence and deliver written notice to **Seller**, within 5 days from receipt of title evidence but no later than closing, of any defects that make the title unmarketable. **Seller** will have 30 days from receipt of **Buyer's** notice of defects ("Curative Period") to cure the defects at **Seller's** expense. If **Seller** cures the defects within the Curative Period, **Seller** will deliver written notice to **Buyer** and the parties will close the transaction on Closing Date or within 10 days from **Buyer's** receipt of **Seller's** notice if Closing Date has passed. If **Seller** is unable to cure the defects within the Curative Period, **Seller** will deliver written notice to **Buyer** and **Buyer** will, within 10 days from receipt of **Seller's** notice, either cancel this Contract or accept title with existing defects and close the transaction.

(c) **Survey: Buyer** may, at **Buyer's** expense, have the Property surveyed and deliver written notice to **Seller**, within 5 days from receipt of survey but no later than closing, of any encroachments on the Property, encroachments by the Property's improvements on other lands or deed restriction or zoning violations. Any such encroachment or violation will be treated in the same manner as a title defect and **Buyer's** and **Seller's** obligations will be determined in accordance with subparagraph **(b)** above. If any part of the Property lies seaward of the coastal construction control line, **Seller** will provide **Buyer** with an affidavit or survey as required by law delineating the line's location on the property, unless **Buyer** waives this requirement in writing.

MISCELLANEOUS

11. EFFECTIVE DATE; TIME: The "Effective Date" of this Contract is the date on which the last of the parties initials or signs the latest offer. **Time is of the essence for all provisions of this Contract.** All time periods will be computed in business days (a "business day" is every calendar day except Saturday, Sunday and national legal holidays). If any deadline falls on a Saturday, Sunday or national legal holiday, performance will be due the next business day. All time periods will end at 5:00 p.m. local time (meaning in the county where the Property is located) of the appropriate day.

12. NOTICES: All notices will be made to the parties and Broker by mail, personal delivery or electronic media. **Buyer's failure to deliver timely written notice to Seller, when such notice is required by this Contract, regarding any contingencies will render that contingency null and void and the Contract will be construed as if the contingency did not exist. Any notice, document or item given to or received by an attorney or Broker (including a transaction broker) representing a party will be as effective as if given to or by that party.**

13. COMPLETE AGREEMENT: This Contract is the entire agreement between **Buyer** and **Seller**. Except for brokerage agreements, no prior or present agreements will bind Buyer, Seller or Broker unless incorporated into this Contract. Modifications of this Contract will not be binding unless in writing, signed or initialed and delivered by the party to be bound. Signatures, initials, documents referenced in this Contract, counterparts and written modifications communicated electronically or on paper will be acceptable for all purposes, including delivery, and will be binding. Handwritten or typewritten terms inserted in or attached to this Contract prevail over preprinted terms. If any provision of this Contract is or becomes invalid or unenforceable, all remaining provisions will continue to be fully effective. **Buyer** and **Seller** will use diligence and good faith in performing all obligations under this Agreement. This Contract will not be recorded in any public records.

14. ASSIGNABILITY; PERSONS BOUND: Buyer may **not** assign this Contract without **Seller's** written consent. The terms "**Buyer**," "**Seller**," and "**Broker**" may be singular or plural. This Contract is binding on the heirs, administrators, executors, personal representatives and assigns (if permitted) of **Buyer**, **Seller** and Broker.

DEFAULT AND DISPUTE RESOLUTION

15. DEFAULT: (a) Seller Default: If for any reason other than failure of **Seller** to make **Seller's** title marketable after diligent effort, **Seller** fails, refuses or neglects to perform this Contract, **Buyer** may choose to receive a return of **Buyer's** deposit without waiving the right to seek damages or to seek specific performance as per Paragraph **16**. **Seller** will also be liable to Broker for the full amount of the

Buyer (_____) (_____) and **Seller** (_____) (_____) acknowledge receipt of a copy of this page, which is Page 4 of 7 Pages.

235 brokerage fee. **(b) Buyer Default:** If **Buyer** fails to perform this Contract within the time specified, including timely payment of all deposits,
236 **Seller** may choose to retain and collect all deposits paid and agreed to be paid as liquidated damages or to seek specific performance as
237 per Paragraph **16**; and Broker will, upon demand, receive 50% of all deposits paid and agreed to be paid (to be split equally among
238 cooperating brokers except when closing does not occur due to **Buyer** not being able to secure Financing after providing a Commitment,
239 in which case Broker's portion of the deposits will go solely to the listing broker) up to the full amount of the brokerage fee.

240 **16. DISPUTE RESOLUTION:** This Contract will be construed under Florida law. All controversies, claims and other matters in
241 question arising out of or relating to this transaction or this Contract or its breach will be settled as follows:

242   **(a) Disputes concerning entitlement to deposits made and agreed to be made: Buyer** and **Seller** will have 30 days from the
243   date conflicting demands are made to attempt to resolve the dispute through **mediation**. If that fails, Escrow Agent will
244   submit the dispute, if so required by Florida law, to Escrow Agent's choice of arbitration, a Florida court or the Florida Real
245   Estate Commission. **Buyer** and **Seller** will be bound by any resulting award, judgment or order.

246   **(b) All other disputes: Buyer** and **Seller** will have 30 days from the date a dispute arises between them to attempt to
247   resolve the matter through mediation, failing which the parties will resolve the dispute through neutral binding **arbitration**
248   in the county where the Property is located. The arbitrator may not alter the Contract terms or award any remedy not
249   provided for in this Contract. The award will be based on the greater weight of the evidence and will state findings of fact
250   and the contractual authority on which it is based. If the parties agree to use discovery, it will be in accordance with the
251   Florida Rules of Civil Procedure and the arbitrator will resolve all discovery-related disputes. Any disputes with a real
252   estate licensee or firm named in Paragraph **19** will be submitted to arbitration only if the licensee's broker consents in
253   writing to become a party to the proceeding. This clause will survive closing.

254   **(c) Mediation and Arbitration; Expenses:** "Mediation" is a process in which parties attempt to resolve a dispute by
255   submitting it to an impartial mediator who facilitates the resolution of the dispute but who is not empowered to impose a
256   settlement on the parties. Mediation will be in accordance with the rules of the American Arbitration Association ("AAA") or
257   other mediator agreed on by the parties. The parties will equally divide the mediation fee, if any. "Arbitration" is a process in
258   which the parties resolve a dispute by a hearing before a neutral person who decides the matter and whose decision is
259   binding on the parties. Arbitration will be in accordance with the rules of the AAA or other arbitrator agreed on by the
260   parties. Each party to any arbitration will pay its own fees, costs and expenses, including attorneys' fees, and will equally
261   split the arbitrators' fees and administrative fees of arbitration.

262   **ESCROW AGENT AND BROKER**

263 **17. ESCROW AGENT: Buyer** and **Seller** authorize Escrow Agent to receive, deposit and hold funds and other items in escrow and,
264 subject to clearance, disburse them upon proper authorization and in accordance with Florida law and the terms of this Contract,
265 including disbursing brokerage fees. The parties agree that Escrow Agent will not be liable to any person for misdelivery of escrowed
266 items to **Buyer** or **Seller**, unless the misdelivery is due to Escrow Agent's willful breach of this Contract or gross negligence. If Escrow
267 Agent interpleads the subject matter of the escrow, Escrow Agent will pay the filing fees and costs from the deposit and will recover
268 reasonable attorneys' fees and costs to be paid from the escrowed funds or equivalent and charged and awarded as court costs in
269 favor of the prevailing party. All claims against Escrow Agent will be arbitrated, so long as Escrow Agent consents to arbitrate.

270 **18. PROFESSIONAL ADVICE; BROKER LIABILITY:** Broker advises **Buyer** and **Seller** to verify all facts and representations that are
271 important to them and to consult an appropriate professional for legal advice (for example, interpreting contracts, determining the
272 effect of laws on the Property and transaction, status of title, foreign investor reporting requirements, etc.) and for tax, property
273 condition, environmental and other specialized advice. **Buyer** acknowledges that Broker does not reside in the Property and that all
274 representations (oral, written or otherwise) by Broker are based on **Seller** representations or public records. **Buyer agrees to rely**
275 **solely on Seller, professional inspectors and governmental agencies for verification of the Property condition, square footage**
276 **and facts that materially affect Property value. Buyer** and **Seller** respectively will pay all costs and expenses, including reasonable
277 attorneys' fees at all levels, incurred by Broker and Broker's officers, directors, agents and employees in connection with or arising
278 from **Buyer's** or **Seller's** misstatement or failure to perform contractual obligations. **Buyer** and **Seller** hold harmless and release
279 Broker and Broker's officers, directors, agents and employees from all liability for loss or damage based on **(1) Buyer's** or **Seller's**
280 misstatement or failure to perform contractual obligations; **(2)** Broker's performance, at **Buyer's** and/or **Seller's** request, of any task
281 beyond the scope of services regulated by Chapter 475, F.S., as amended, including Broker's referral, recommendation or retention
282 of any vendor; **(3)** products or services provided by any vendor; and **(4)** expenses incurred by any vendor. **Buyer** and **Seller** each
283 assume full responsibility for selecting and compensating their respective vendors. This paragraph will not relieve Broker of statutory
284 obligations. For purposes of this paragraph, Broker will be treated as a party to this Contract. This paragraph will survive closing.

285 **19. BROKERS:** The licensee(s) and brokerage(s) named below are collectively referred to as "Broker." **Instruction to Closing**
286 **Agent: Seller** and **Buyer** direct closing agent to disburse at closing the full amount of the brokerage fees as specified in separate
287 brokerage agreements with the parties and cooperative agreements between the brokers, except to the extent Broker has
288 retained such fees from the escrowed funds. In the absence of such brokerage agreements, closing agent will disburse
289 brokerage fees as indicated below. This paragraph will not be used to modify any MLS or other offer of compensation made by
290 **Seller** or listing broker to cooperating brokers.

291 **Buyer** (____) (____) and **Seller** (____) (____) acknowledge receipt of a copy of this page, which is Page 5 of 7 Pages.
    FAR-8   Rev. 10/04   © 2004 Florida Association of REALTORS® All Rights Reserved

292* _____
293* *Selling Sales Associate/License No.* _____   Selling Firm/Brokerage Fee: ($ or % of Purchase Price) _____

294* _____
295* *Listing Sales Associate/License No.* _____   Listing Firm/Brokerage fee: ($ or % of Purchase Price) _____

296   **ADDENDA AND ADDITIONAL TERMS**

297 **20. ADDENDA:** The following additional terms are included in addenda and incorporated into this Contract (check if applicable):

298* ❏ A. Condo. Assn.   ❏ H. As Is w/Right to Inspect   ❏ O. Interest-Bearing Account   ❏ V. Prop. Disclosure Stmt.
299* ❏ B. Homeowners' Assn.   ❏ I. Inspections   ❏ P. Back-up Contract   ❏ W. FIRPTA
300* ❏ C. Seller Financing   ❏ J. Insulation Disclosure   ❏ Q. Broker - Pers. Int. in Prop. ❏ X. 1031 Exchange
301* ❏ D. Mort. Assumption   ❏ K. Pre-1978 Housing Stmt. (LBP) ❏ R. Rentals   ❏ Y. Additional Clauses
302* ❏ E. FHA Financing   ❏ L. Insurance   ❏ S. Sale/Lease of Buyer's Property ❏ Other_____
303* ❏ F. VA Financing   ❏ M. Housing Older Persons   ❏ T. Rezoning   ❏ Other_____
304* ❏ G. New Mort. Rates   ❏ N. Unimproved/Ag. Prop.   ❏ U. Assignment   ❏ Other_____

305* **21. ADDITIONAL TERMS:** _____
306* _____
307* _____
308* _____
309* _____
310* _____
311* _____
312* _____
313* _____
314* _____
315* _____
316* _____
317* _____
318* _____
319* _____
320* _____
321* _____
322* _____
323* _____
324* _____
325* _____
326* _____
327* _____
328* _____
329* _____
330* _____
331* _____
332* _____
333* _____
334* _____
335* _____
336* _____
337* _____
338* _____
339* _____
340* _____
341* _____
342* _____
343* _____
344* _____
345* _____
346* _____
347* _____

348* **Buyer** (_____) (_____) and **Seller** (_____) (_____) acknowledge receipt of a copy of this page, which is Page 6 of 7 Pages.

FAR-8   Rev. 10/04   © 2004   Florida Association of REALTORS®   All Rights Reserved

235 brokerage fee. **(b) Buyer Default:** If **Buyer** fails to perform this Contract within the time specified, including timely payment of all deposits,
236 **Seller** may choose to retain and collect all deposits paid and agreed to be paid as liquidated damages or to seek specific performance as
237 per Paragraph **16**; and Broker will, upon demand, receive 50% of all deposits paid and agreed to be paid (to be split equally among
238 cooperating brokers except when closing does not occur due to **Buyer** not being able to secure Financing after providing a Commitment,
239 in which case Broker's portion of the deposits will go solely to the listing broker) up to the full amount of the brokerage fee.

240 **16. DISPUTE RESOLUTION:** This Contract will be construed under Florida law. All controversies, claims and other matters in
241 question arising out of or relating to this transaction or this Contract or its breach will be settled as follows:
242   **(a) Disputes concerning entitlement to deposits made and agreed to be made:** **Buyer** and **Seller** will have 30 days from the
243 date conflicting demands are made to attempt to resolve the dispute through **mediation**. If that fails, Escrow Agent will
244 submit the dispute, if so required by Florida law, to Escrow Agent's choice of arbitration, a Florida court or the Florida Real
245 Estate Commission. **Buyer** and **Seller** will be bound by any resulting award, judgment or order.
246   **(b) All other disputes:** **Buyer** and **Seller** will have 30 days from the date a dispute arises between them to attempt to
247 resolve the matter through mediation, failing which the parties will resolve the dispute through neutral binding **arbitration**
248 in the county where the Property is located. The arbitrator may not alter the Contract terms or award any remedy not
249 provided for in this Contract. The award will be based on the greater weight of the evidence and will state findings of fact
250 and the contractual authority on which it is based. If the parties agree to use discovery, it will be in accordance with the
251 Florida Rules of Civil Procedure and the arbitrator will resolve all discovery-related disputes. Any disputes with a real
252 estate licensee or firm named in Paragraph **19** will be submitted to arbitration only if the licensee's broker consents in
253 writing to become a party to the proceeding. This clause will survive closing.
254   **(c) Mediation and Arbitration; Expenses:** "Mediation" is a process in which parties attempt to resolve a dispute by
255 submitting it to an impartial mediator who facilitates the resolution of the dispute but who is not empowered to impose a
256 settlement on the parties. Mediation will be in accordance with the rules of the American Arbitration Association ("AAA") or
257 other mediator agreed on by the parties. The parties will equally divide the mediation fee, if any. "Arbitration" is a process in
258 which the parties resolve a dispute by a hearing before a neutral person who decides the matter and whose decision is
259 binding on the parties. Arbitration will be in accordance with the rules of the AAA or other arbitrator agreed on by the
260 parties. Each party to any arbitration will pay its own fees, costs and expenses, including attorneys' fees, and will equally
261 split the arbitrators' fees and administrative fees of arbitration.

262   **ESCROW AGENT AND BROKER**
263 **17. ESCROW AGENT:** **Buyer** and **Seller** authorize Escrow Agent to receive, deposit and hold funds and other items in escrow and,
264 subject to clearance, disburse them upon proper authorization and in accordance with Florida law and the terms of this Contract,
265 including disbursing brokerage fees. The parties agree that Escrow Agent will not be liable to any person for misdelivery of escrowed
266 items to **Buyer** or **Seller**, unless the misdelivery is due to Escrow Agent's willful breach of this Contract or gross negligence. If Escrow
267 Agent interpleads the subject matter of the escrow, Escrow Agent will pay the filing fees and costs from the deposit and will recover
268 reasonable attorneys' fees and costs to be paid from the escrowed funds or equivalent and charged and awarded as court costs in
269 favor of the prevailing party. All claims against Escrow Agent will be arbitrated, so long as Escrow Agent consents to arbitrate.

270 **18. PROFESSIONAL ADVICE; BROKER LIABILITY:** Broker advises **Buyer** and **Seller** to verify all facts and representations that are
271 important to them and to consult an appropriate professional for legal advice (for example, interpreting contracts, determining the
272 effect of laws on the Property and transaction, status of title, foreign investor reporting requirements, etc.) and for tax, property
273 condition, environmental and other specialized advice. **Buyer** acknowledges that Broker does not reside in the Property and that all
274 representations (oral, written or otherwise) by Broker are based on **Seller** representations or public records. **Buyer agrees to rely**
275 **solely on Seller, professional inspectors and governmental agencies for verification of the Property condition, square footage**
276 **and facts that materially affect Property value.** **Buyer** and **Seller** respectively will pay all costs and expenses, including reasonable
277 attorneys' fees at all levels, incurred by Broker and Broker's officers, directors, agents and employees in connection with or arising
278 from **Buyer's** or **Seller's** misstatement or failure to perform contractual obligations. **Buyer** and **Seller** hold harmless and release
279 Broker and Broker's officers, directors, agents and employees from all liability for loss or damage based on **(1) Buyer's** or **Seller's**
280 misstatement or failure to perform contractual obligations; **(2)** Broker's performance, at **Buyer's** and/or **Seller's** request, of any task
281 beyond the scope of services regulated by Chapter 475, F.S., as amended, including Broker's referral, recommendation or retention
282 of any vendor; **(3)** products or services provided by any vendor; and **(4)** expenses incurred by any vendor. **Buyer** and **Seller** each
283 assume full responsibility for selecting and compensating their respective vendors. This paragraph will not relieve Broker of statutory
284 obligations. For purposes of this paragraph, Broker will be treated as a party to this Contract. This paragraph will survive closing.

285 **19. BROKERS:** The licensee(s) and brokerage(s) named below are collectively referred to as "Broker." **Instruction to Closing**
286 **Agent:** **Seller** and **Buyer** direct closing agent to disburse at closing the full amount of the brokerage fees as specified in separate
287 brokerage agreements with the parties and cooperative agreements between the brokers, except to the extent Broker has
288 retained such fees from the escrowed funds. In the absence of such brokerage agreements, closing agent will disburse
289 brokerage fees as indicated below. This paragraph will not be used to modify any MLS or other offer of compensation made by
290 **Seller** or listing broker to cooperating brokers.

291* **Buyer** (____) (____) and **Seller** (____) (____) acknowledge receipt of a copy of this page, which is Page 5 of 7 Pages.
    FAR-8   Rev. 10/04   © 2004   Florida Association of REALTORS®   All Rights Reserved

Residential Sale and Purchase Contract

292* _____
293* *Selling Sales Associate/License No.*   *Selling Firm/Brokerage Fee: ($ or % of Purchase Price)*_____

294* _____
295* *Listing Sales Associate/License No.*   *Listing Firm/Brokerage fee: ($ or % of Purchase Price)*_____

296   **ADDENDA AND ADDITIONAL TERMS**
297 **20. ADDENDA:** The following additional terms are included in addenda and incorporated into this Contract (check if applicable):

298* ❏ A. Condo. Assn.   ❏ H. As Is w/Right to Inspect   ❏ O. Interest-Bearing Account   ❏ V. Prop. Disclosure Stmt.
299* ❏ B. Homeowners' Assn.   ❏ I. Inspections   ❏ P. Back-up Contract   ❏ W. FIRPTA
300* ❏ C. Seller Financing   ❏ J. Insulation Disclosure   ❏ Q. Broker - Pers. Int. in Prop. ❏ X. 1031 Exchange
301* ❏ D. Mort. Assumption   ❏ K. Pre-1978 Housing Stmt. (LBP) ❏ R. Rentals   ❏ Y. Additional Clauses
302* ❏ E. FHA Financing   ❏ L. Insurance   ❏ S. Sale/Lease of Buyer's Property ❏ Other_____
303* ❏ F. VA Financing   ❏ M. Housing Older Persons   ❏ T. Rezoning   ❏ Other_____
304* ❏ G. New Mort. Rates   ❏ N. Unimproved/Ag. Prop.   ❏ U. Assignment   ❏ Other_____

305* **21. ADDITIONAL TERMS:** _____
306* _____
307* _____
308* _____
309* _____
310* _____
311* _____
312* _____
313* _____
314* _____
315* _____
316* _____
317* _____
318* _____
319* _____
320* _____
321* _____
322* _____
323* _____
324* _____
325* _____
326* _____
327* _____
328* _____
329* _____
330* _____
331* _____
332* _____
333* _____
334* _____
335* _____
336* _____
337* _____
338* _____
339* _____
340* _____
341* _____
342* _____
343* _____
344* _____
345* _____
346* _____
347* _____

348* **Buyer** (_____) (_____) and **Seller** (_____) (_____) acknowledge receipt of a copy of this page, which is Page 6 of 7 Pages.
FAR-8   Rev. 10/04   © 2004   Florida Association of REALTORS®   All Rights Reserved

349 **This is intended to be a legally binding contract. If not fully understood, seek the advice of an attorney prior to signing.**

350 **OFFER AND ACCEPTANCE**
351* **(Check if applicable:** ❑ **Buyer** received a written real property disclosure statement from **Seller** before making this Offer.)
352 **Buyer** offers to purchase the Property on the above terms and conditions. Unless this Contract is signed by **Seller** and a copy
353* delivered to **Buyer** no later than _____❑ a.m.❑ p.m. on _____, _____, this offer will be revoked
354 and **Buyer's** deposit refunded subject to clearance of funds.

355* Date: _____   **Buyer:** _____
356*   Print name: _____

357* Date: _____   **Buyer:** _____
358* Phone: _____   Print name: _____
359* Fax: _____   Address: _____
360* E-mail: _____   _____

361* Date: _____   **Seller:** _____
362*   Print name: _____

363* Date: _____   **Seller:** _____
364* Phone: _____   Print name: _____
365* Fax: _____   Address: _____
366* E-mail: _____   _____

367 **COUNTER OFFER/REJECTION**
368* ❑ **Seller** counters **Buyer's** offer (to accept the counter offer, **Buyer** must sign or initial the counter offered terms and deliver a copy
369* of the acceptance to **Seller** by 5:00 p.m. on _____, _____). ❑ **Seller** rejects **Buyer's** offer.

370* **Effective Date:** _____ (The date on which the last party signed or initialed acceptance of the final offer.)

371* **Buyer** (____) (____) and **Seller** (____) (____) acknowledge receipt of a copy of this page, which is Page 7 of 7 Pages.

Seller's Real Property Disclosure Statement
FLORIDA ASSOCIATION OF REALTORS®

NAME: _____

SELLER HAS ❏ HAS NOT ❏ OCCUPIED THE PROPERTY.

DATE SELLER PURCHASED PROPERTY?_____

IS THE PROPERTY CURRENTLY LEASED? NO ❏ YES ❏ TERMINATION DATE OF LEASE: _____

DOES THE PROPERTY CURRENTLY HAVE HOMESTEAD EXEMPTION? NO ❏ YES ❏; YEAR _____

GENERAL INFORMATION ABOUT PROPERTY:

PROPERTY ADDRESS: _____

LEGAL DESCRIPTION:_____

NOTICE TO BUYER AND SELLER:

In Florida, a Seller is obligated to disclose to a Buyer all known facts that materially affect the value of the property being sold and that are not readily observable. This disclosure statement is designed to assist Seller in complying with the disclosure requirements under Florida law and to assist the Buyer in evaluating the property being considered. This disclosure statement concerns the condition of the real property located at above address. It is not a warranty of any kind by the Seller or any Licensee in this transaction. It is not a substitute for any inspections or warranties the parties may wish to obtain. It is based only upon Seller's knowledge of the property condition. This disclosure is not intended to be a part of any contract for sale and purchase. All parties may refer to this information when they evaluate, market, or present Seller's property to prospective Buyers.

The following representations are made by the Seller(s) and are not the representations of any real estate licensees.

1. CLAIMS & ASSESSMENTS

a. Are you aware of existing, pending, or proposed legal actions, claims, special assessments, municipal service taxing or benefit unit charges or unpaid assessments (including homeowners' association maintenance fees or proposed increases in assessments and/or maintenance fees) affecting the property? NO ❏ YES ❏ If yes, explain: ____

b. Have any local, state, or federal authorities notified you that repairs, alterations or corrections of the property are required? NO ❏ YES ❏ If yes, explain: _____

2. DEED/HOMEOWNERS' ASSOCIATION RESTRICTIONS

Are You Aware:

a. of any deed or homeowner restrictions? NO ❏ YES ❏

b. of any proposed changes to any of the restrictions? NO ❏ YES ❏

c. of any resale restrictions? NO ❏ YES ❏

d. of any restrictions on leasing the property? NO ❏ YES ❏

e. If any answer to questions 2a-2e is yes, please explain:

_____

_____

f. Are access roads private ❏ public ❏? If private, describe the terms and conditions of the maintenance agreement: _____

g. If there is a homeowner association, is membership mandatory? NO ❏ YES ❏, and are fees charged by the homeowner association? NO ❏ YES ❏ If yes, explain: _____

3. PROPERTY-RELATED ITEMS

Are You Aware:

a. if you have ever had the property surveyed? NO ❏ YES ❏ Date: _____

b. if the property was surveyed, did you receive an elevation certificate? NO ❏ YES ❏ Date: _____

c. of any walls, driveways, fences or other features shared in common with adjoining landowners or any encroachments, boundary line disputes, setback violations, or easements affecting the property? NO ❏ YES ❏

d. of any portion of the property that is fenced? NO ❏ YES ❏

If any answer to questions 3a-3d is yes, please explain:_____

_____

_____

Page 1 of 5 Pages.

SRPD-3   Rev. 10/05   © 2005   Florida Association of REALTORS®   All Rights Reserved

4. THE LAND:

Are You Aware:

    a. of any past or present settling, soil movement, or sinkhole problems on the property or on adjacent properties? NO ❏ YES ❏

        i. of any sinkhole insurance claim that has been made on subject property? NO ❏ YES ❏

        ii. if claim made, was claim paid? NO ❏ YES ❏

        iii. was the full amount of the insurance proceeds used to repair the sinkhole damage? NO ❏ YES ❏

    b. of any past or present drainage or flood problems affecting the property or adjacent properties? NO ❏ YES ❏

    c. of any past or present problems with driveways, walkways, patios, seawalls, or retaining walls on the property or adjacent properties due to drainage, flooding, or soil movements? NO ❏ YES ❏

If any answer to questions 4a-4c is yes, please explain: _____

_____

_____

_____

5. ENVIRONMENT:

Was the property built before 1978? NO ❏ YES ❏

Are You Aware:

    a. of any substances, materials, or products which may be an environmental hazard, such as, but not limited to, asbestos, urea formaldehyde, radon gas, mold, lead-based paint, fuel, propane or chemical storage tanks (active or abandoned), or contaminated soil or water on the property? NO ❏ YES ❏ If yes, explain: _____

_____

        i. of any damage to the structures located on the property due to any of the substances, materials or products listed in subsection (a) above? NO ❏ YES ❏ If yes, explain: _____

_____

_____

        ii. of any clean up, repairs, or remediation of the property due to any of the substances, materials or products listed in subsection (a) above? NO ❏ YES ❏ If yes, explain: _____

_____

_____

    b. of any condition or proposed change in the vicinity of the property that does or will materially affect the value of the property, such as, but not limited to, proposed development or proposed roadways? NO ❏ YES ❏

    c. of wetlands, mangroves, archeological sites, or other environmentally sensitive areas located on the property? NO ❏ YES ❏

If any answer to questions 5a-5c is yes, please explain: _____

_____

_____

6. ZONING:

Are You Aware:

    a. of the zoning classification of the property? NO ❏ YES ❏ If yes, identify the zoning classification _____

    b. of any zoning violations or nonconforming uses? NO ❏ YES ❏

    c. if the property is zoned for its current use? NO ❏ YES ❏

    d. of any zoning restrictions affecting additions, improvements or replacement of the property? NO ❏ YES ❏

    e. if there are any zoning, land use or administrative regulations which are in conflict with the existing or intended use of the property? NO ❏ YES ❏

    f. of any restrictions other than association and flood area requirements affecting improvements or replacement of the property? NO ❏ YES ❏

If any answer to questions 6a-6f is yes, please explain: _____

_____

_____

_____

7. FLOOD:

Are You Aware:

    a. if any portion of the property is in a special flood hazard area? NO ❏ YES ❏

    b. does the property require flood insurance? NO ❏ YES ❏

    c. whether any improvements including additions, are located below the base flood elevation? NO ❏ YES ❏

    d. whether such improvements have been constructed in violation of applicable local flood guidelines? NO ❏ YES ❏

e. if any portion of the property is seaward of the coastal construction control line? NO ❑ YES ❑
If any answer to questions 7a-7e is yes, please explain: _____
_____
_____
_____

8. TERMITES, DRY ROT, PESTS, WOOD DESTROYING ORGANISMS:
   a. Do you have any knowledge of termites, dry rot, pests or wood destroying organisms on or affecting any improvements located on the property or any structural damage to the property by them? NO ❑ YES ❑ If yes, explain: _____
   _____

   b. Have you ever had the property inspected for termites, dry rot, pest or wood destroying organism?
   NO ❑ YES ❑ Date of inspection_____If so, what was the outcome of the inspection? _____

   c. Has the property been treated for termites, dry rot, pest or wood destroying organisms? NO ❑ YES ❑ Date and
   type of treatment_____
   _____,Company name:_____
   _____

9. STRUCTURE-RELATED ITEMS:
   Are You Aware:
   a. of any structural damage which may have resulted from events including, but not limited to, fire, wind, flood, hail,
   landslide, or blasting, and which materially affect the value of the property? NO ❑ YES ❑
   b. of any structural condition or, in the case of a homeowner association, any condition in the common elements
   that materially affects the value of the property? NO ❑ YES ❑
   c. of any improvements or additions to the property, whether by you or by others, that have been constructed in
   violation of building codes or without necessary permits? NO ❑ YES ❑
   d. of any active permits on the property which have not been closed by a final inspection? NO ❑ YES ❑
   If any answer to questions 9a-9d is yes, please explain: _____
   _____
   _____
   _____

10. ROOF-RELATED ITEMS:
   Are You Aware:
   a. of any roof or overhang defects? NO ❑ YES ❑
   b. if the roof has leaked since you owned the property? NO ❑ YES ❑
   c. if anything was done to correct the leaks? NO ❑ YES ❑
   d. if the roof has been replaced? NO ❑ YES ❑ If yes, when:_____
   e. If there is a warranty on the roof? NO ❑ YES ❑ If yes, is it transferable? NO ❑ YES ❑
   f. If the roof been inspected within the last twelve months? NO ❑ YES ❑
   If any answer to questions 10a-10f is yes, please explain: _____
   _____
   _____
   _____

11. PLUMBING-RELATED ITEMS:
   a. What is your drinking water source? Public ❑ Private Well ❑ Other Source ❑. If your drinking water is from a well
   or other source, when was your water last checked for safety and what was the result of the test?_____
   _____

   b. Do you have a water conditioning system? NO ❑ YES ❑ If yes, type:_____Owned ❑ Leased ❑ **c.**
   What is the balance owed on the system? $_____
   d. Do you have a sewer ❑ or septic system ❑? If septic system describe the location of each system:_____
   _____

   e. Are you aware of any septic tanks or wells on the property which are not currently being used?
   NO ❑ YES ❑ If yes, explain: _____
   f. Are you aware of any plumbing leaks since you have owned the property? NO ❑ YES ❑ If yes, explain: _____
   _____

   g. Are you aware of any conditions that materially affect the value of the property relating to the septic tank/drain
   field, sewer lines, or any other plumbing related items? NO ❑ YES ❑ If yes, explain:_____
   _____
   _____

12. POOLS/HOT TUBS/SPAS:

    a. Does the property have a swimming pool? NO ❑ YES ❑ Hot tub? NO ❑ YES ❑ Spa? NO ❑ YES ❑

    b. If you answered yes to any part of 12a, was the certificate of completion received after Oct. 1, 2000 for the pool? NO ❑ YES ❑ For the spa? NO ❑ YES ❑ For the hot tub? NO ❑ YES ❑

    c. Check the pool safety features (as defined by Section 515.27, Florida Statutes) your swimming pool, hot tub or spa has: Enclosure that meets the pool barrier requirements ❑ Approved safety pool cover ❑ Required door and window exit alarms ❑ Required door locks ❑ none ❑

    d. Are you aware of any conditions regarding these items that materially affect the value of the property? NO ❑ YES ❑ If yes, explain: _____

_____

_____

13. MAJOR APPLIANCES:

    Indicate existing equipment:

    Range ❑ Oven ❑ Microwave ❑ Dishwasher ❑ Garbage Disposal ❑ Trash Compactor ❑ Refrigerator ❑ Freezer ❑ Washer ❑ Dryer ❑

    Are any of these appliances leased? NO ❑ YES ❑ Are any of these gas appliances? NO ❑ YES ❑

    Is the water heater: owned ❑ leased ❑; Is the water heater: electric ❑ gas ❑

    Are you aware of any problems with these appliances, including whether any of the appliances have leaked or overflowed, since you have owned the property? NO ❑ YES ❑ If yes, explain: _____

_____

14. ELECTRICAL SYSTEM:

    Are You Aware:

    a. of any damaged or malfunctioning switches, receptacles, or wiring? NO ❑ YES ❑

    b. of any conditions that materially affect the value or operating capacity of the electrical system? NO ❑ YES ❑

    If answers to questions 14a or 14b is yes, please explain: _____

_____

_____

15. HEATING AND AIR CONDITIONING:

    Indicate existing equipment:

    Air conditioning: **Heating:**

    Central ❑ Window/Wall ❑ Number of units _____   Electric ❑ Fuel Oil ❑ Gas ❑ Other ❑

    Solar Heating:

    Owned ❑ Leased ❑

    Wood-burning stove: NO ❑ YES ❑

    Fireplace: NO ❑ YES ❑ Describe fireplace equipment: _____

    Are you aware of any defects, malfunctioning or condensation problems regarding these items, since you have owned the property? NO ❑ YES ❑ If yes, explain: _____

16. OTHER EQUIPMENT:

    Indicate existing equipment:

    Security System: NO ❑ YES ❑ Leased ❑ Owned ❑ Connected to Central Monitor ❑ Monthly Fee $_____

    Smoke Detectors: NO ❑ YES ❑, Number of smoke detectors?_____

    Lawn Sprinkler System: NO ❑ YES ❑ Sprinkler water source:_____If well is source, is there an iron filter? NO ❑ YES ❑ Is there a timer? NO ❑ YES ❑ Is the timer automatic? NO ❑ YES ❑

    Garage door openers? NO ❑ YES ❑, Number of transmitters?_____, Humidistat? NO ❑ YES ❑ Humidifier? NO ❑ YES ❑ Electric air filters? NO ❑ YES ❑ Vent fans? NO ❑ YES ❑

    Paddle fans? NO ❑ YES ❑, Number of paddle fans?_____

17. OTHER MATTERS:

    Is there anything else that materially affects the value of the property? NO ❑ YES ❑

    If yes, explain: _____

_____

_____

_____

Page 4 of 5 Pages.

SRPD-3   Rev. 10/05   © 2005   Florida Association of REALTORS®   All Rights Reserved

Seller's Real Property Disclosure Statement

ACKNOWLEDGEMENT OF SELLER

The undersigned Seller represents that the information set forth in the above disclosure statement is accurate and complete to the best of the Seller's knowledge on the date signed below. Seller does not intend for this disclosure statement to be a warranty or guaranty of any kind. Seller hereby authorizes disclosure of the information contained in this disclosure statement to prospective Buyers of the property. Seller understands and agrees that Seller will notify the Buyer in writing within five business days after Seller becomes aware that any information set forth in this disclosure statement has become inaccurate or incorrect in any way during the term of the pending purchase by the Buyer.

Seller:_____ / _____ Date:_____
　　　　　　(signature)　　　　　　　　　　　(print)

Seller:_____ / _____ Date:_____
　　　　　　(signature)　　　　　　　　　　　(print)

RECEIPT AND ACKNOWLEDGMENT OF BUYER

Seller is using this form to disclose Seller's knowledge of the condition of the real property and improvements located on the property as of the date signed by Seller. This disclosure form is not a warranty of any kind. The information contained in the disclosure is limited to information to which the seller has knowledge. It is not intended to be a substitute for any inspections or professional advice the Buyer may wish to obtain. An independent professional inspection is encouraged and may be helpful to verify the condition of the property and to determine the cost of repairs, if any. Buyer understands these representations are not made by any real estate licensee.

Buyer hereby acknowledges having received a copy of this disclosure statement.

Buyer:_____ / _____ Date:_____
　　　　　　(signature)　　　　　　　　　　　(print)

Buyer:_____ / _____ Date:_____
　　　　　　(signature)　　　　　　　　　　　(print)

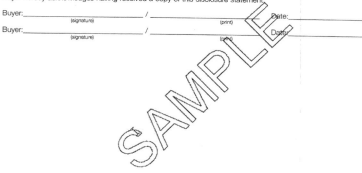

Page 5 of 5 Pages.
SRPD-3　Rev. 10/05　© 2005　Florida Association of REALTORS®　All Rights Reserved

Affirming the American Dream

11260 Wilbur Ave, Sutie 102, Northridge, CA 91326
Tel: (818) 363-7728 Fax: (818) 443-3333 Mobile: (818) 445-4545 Licence #: 12345

SUMMARY REPORT

Client: Mr. & Mrs. Donald Nelson
Realtor: Tina Smith, Stoneybrook Realty

Inspection Address: 12345 Demonstration Street, Great Lakes, New York 123456
Inspection Date: 07/14/2004 Start: 9:00 am

Inspected by: Lorne Steiner

This summary report is intended to provide a convenient and cursory preview of the more significant conditions and components that we have identified within our report as needing service, but could be incomplete. It is obviously not comprehensive, and should not be used as a substitute for reading the entire report, nor is it a tacit endorsement of the condition of components or features that may not appear in this summary. Also, in accordance with the terms of the contract, the service recommendations that we make in this summary and throughout the report should be completed well before the close of escrow by licensed specialists, who may well identify additional defects or recommend some upgrades that could affect your evaluation of the property.

This report is the exclusive property of the Inspection Company and the client whose name appears herewith, and its use by any unauthorized persons is prohibited.

Components and Conditions Needing Service

Exterior

House Wall Finish
House Wall Finish Observations
• Portions of the wood siding are damaged and should be evaluated by a specialist
• Water stains on the walls of the residence indicate uncontrolled run-off
• Areas of the house walls need typical maintenance-type service

Exterior Components
Patio Covers or Gazebos
• The screened-in patio cover appears to be an addition that does have some defects
Windows
• Putty is missing from some of the windows and should be serviced

Structural

Inspection Summary - Page 1

Inspection Address: 12345 Demonstration Street, Great Lakes, New York 123456
Inspection Date/Time: 07/14/2004 9:00 am

Grading and Drainage
Interior-Exterior Elevations
• Grading and drainage is negative or neutral adjacent to the residence and should be monitored

Roof/Attic

Composition Shingle Roof
With Flat Roofed Sections
• The flat-roofed section is significantly deteriorated and needs to be evaluated or serviced
Gutters and Drainage
• The gutters need to be cleaned and serviced to drain properly

Chimney

Living Room Chimney
Chimney Stack or Walls
• There are cracks and washed-out mortar joints in the chimney wall which should be evaluated by a specialist

Plumbing

Gas Water Heaters
Vent Pipe and Cap
• Carbon deposits around the vent pipe confirm inadequate or impaired drafting

Irrigation or Sprinklers
Hose Bibs
• The hose bib in the rear is not insulated against freezing

Electrical

Main Panel
Main Panel Observations
• The panel is a Federal Pacific some components of which have been alleged to be defective
• The panel does not have thirty-six inches of clear space which is mandated
Circuit Breakers
• The panel employs obsolete screw-in fuses that should be evaluated by an electrician

Common Areas

Kitchen
Outlets
• The ungrounded obsolete wall outlets should be upgraded

Bathrooms

Powder Room

This report has been produced in accordance with our signed contract and is subject to the terms and conditions agreed upon therein.
All printed comments and the opinions expressed herein are those of the Inspection Company.
Inspection Summary - Page 2

Inspection Address: 12345 Demonstration Street, Great Lakes, New York 123456
Inspection Date/Time: 07/14/2004 9:00 am

Sink Faucet Valves & Connectors Trap & Drain
• There is little or no water volume on the hot side of the sink faucet

Master Bathroom
  Outlets
  • The outlets should be upgraded to have ground-fault protection

Main Hallway Bathroom
  Tub-Shower
  • The tub-shower valves need new stem washers

Laundry

Single-Car
  Entry Door Into the House
  • The door leading into the house is not fire-rated and should be replaced

Garage

Primary Attic
  Ventilation
  • Ventilation is limited and could be improved

This report has been produced in accordance with our signed contract and is subject to the terms and conditions agreed upon therein.
All printed comments and the opinions expressed herein are those of the Inspection Company.
Inspection Summary - Page 3

ILLINOIS ASSOCIATION OF REALTORS
NON-EXCLUSIVE BUYER REPRESENTATION CONTRACT
(DUAL AGENCY DISCLOSURE AND CONSENT INCLUDED)

In consideration of_____'s ("Brokerage Company hereinafter referred to as "Broker") agreement to designate a sales associate affiliated with Broker to act as an agent of the Buyer for the purpose of identifying and negotiating to acquire real estate for _____ ("Buyer"), the Buyer hereby grants to Broker a non-exclusive right to represent Buyer in such acquisition. The term "acquisition" shall include the purchase, lease, exchange or option of real estate by Buyer or anyone acting on Buyer's behalf.

SECTION 1: REPRESENTATION
Broker designates and Buyer accepts _____ ("Buyer's Designated Agent") as the legal agent(s) of Buyer for the purpose of representing Buyer in the acquisition of real estate by Buyer. Buyer understands and agrees that neither Broker nor any other sales associates affiliated with Broker (except as provided herein) will be acting as legal agent of the Buyer. Broker shall have the discretion to appoint a substitute designated agent for Buyer as Broker determines necessary. Buyer shall be advised within a reasonable time of any such substitution.

Buyer agrees to work with the Broker and Buyer's Designated Agent in the acquisition of property with the understanding that this relationship is **non-exclusive**. Buyer understands that Buyer may **not** enter into an **exclusive** representation agreement with any other real estate agent or broker. Buyer represents that he/she has not entered into any exclusive buyer representation agreement that is currently in effect.

SECTION 2: TERM
This Contract shall be effective until 11:59 p.m. on _____, 2____, when it shall then terminate. This Contract is irrevocable and can be terminated prior to the termination date only by written agreement of the parties.

SECTION 3: BUYER'S DESIGNATED AGENT'S DUTIES
(a)   To use Buyer's Designated Agent's best efforts to identify properties listed in the multiple listing service that meet the Buyer's specifications relating to location, price, features and amenities, as identified on the attached Buyers Information Checklist.

(b)   To arrange for inspections of properties identified by the Buyer as potentially appropriate for acquisition.

(c)   To advise Buyer as to the pricing of comparable properties.

(d)   To assist Buyer in the negotiation of a contract acceptable to the Buyer for the acquisition of property.

(e)   To provide reasonable safeguards for confidential information that the Buyer discloses to Buyer's Designated Agent.

SECTION 4: BROKER'S DUTIES
(a)   To provide Buyer's Designated Agent with assistance and advice as necessary in Buyer's Designated Agent's work on   Buyer's behalf.

(b)   To make the managing broker, or his/her designated representative, available to consult with Buyer's Designated Agent as to Buyer's negotiations for the acquisition of real estate, who will maintain the confidence of Buyer's confidential information.

(c)   To make other sales associates affiliated with Broker aware of Buyer's general specifications for real property.

(d)   As needed, to designate one or more sales associates as designated agents of Buyer.

SECTION 5: BUYER'S DUTIES
(a)   To complete the buyer's checklist which will provide Buyer's specifications for the real estate Buyer is seeking.

(b)   To work with Buyer's Designated Agent to identify and acquire real estate during the time that this Agreement is in force.

(c)   To supply relevant financial information that may be necessary to permit Buyer's Designated Agent to fulfill Agent's obligations.

(d)   To be available upon reasonable notice and at reasonable hours to inspect properties that seem to meet Buyer's specifications.

(e)   To pay Broker according to the terms specified in Section 8 of this Agreement.

SECTION 6: REPRESENTING OTHER BUYERS
Buyer understands that Buyer's Designated Agent has no duty to represent only Buyer, and that Buyer's Designated Agent may represent other prospective buyers who may be interested in acquiring the same property or properties that Buyer is interested in acquiring.

SECTION 7: DISCLOSURE AND CONSENT TO DUAL AGENCY

NOTE TO CONSUMER: THIS SECTION SERVES THREE PURPOSES. FIRST, IT DISCLOSES THAT A REAL ESTATE LICENSEE MAY POTENTIALLY ACT AS A DUAL AGENT, THAT IS, REPRESENT MORE THAN ONE PARTY TO THE TRANSACTION. SECOND, THIS SECTION EXPLAINS THE CONCEPT OF DUAL AGENCY. THIRD, THIS SECTION SEEKS YOUR CONSENT TO ALLOW THE REAL ESTATE LICENSEE TO ACT AS A DUAL AGENT. A LICENSEE MAY LEGALLY ACT AS A DUAL AGENT ONLY WITH YOUR CONSENT. BY CHOOSING TO SIGN THIS SECTION, YOUR CONSENT TO DUAL AGENCY REPRESENTATION IS PRESUMED.

The undersigned _____
                                          (insert name(s) of Licensee undertaking dual representation)
("Licensee"/"Buyer's Designated Agent"), may undertake a dual representation (represent both the seller or landlord and the buyer or tenant) for the sale or lease of property. The undersigned acknowledge they were informed of the possibility of this type of representation. Before signing this document please read the following:

Representing more than one party to a transaction presents a conflict of interest since both clients may rely upon Licensee's advice and the client's respective interests may be adverse to each other. Licensee will undertake this representation only with the written consent of ALL clients in the transaction.

Any agreement between the clients as to a final contract price and other terms is a result of negotiations between the clients acting in their own best interests and on their own behalf. You acknowledge that Licensee has explained the implications of dual representation, including the risks involved, and understand that you have been advised to seek independent advice from your advisors or attorneys before signing any documents in this transaction.

WHAT A LICENSEE CAN DO FOR
CLIENTS WHEN ACTING AS A DUAL AGENT

1. Treat all clients honestly.
2. Provide information about the property to the buyer or tenant.
3. Disclose all latent material defects in the property that are known to the Licensee.
4. Disclose financial qualification of the buyer or tenant to the seller or landlord.
5. Explain real estate terms.
6. Help the buyer or tenant to arrange for property inspections.
7. Explain closing costs and procedures.
8. Help the buyer compare financing alternatives.
9. Provide information about comparable properties that have sold so both clients may make educated decisions on what price to accept or offer.

Form 339 REVISED 7/6/05   Copyright by Illinois Association of REALTORS

Courtesy of the Illinois Association of Realtors

This form complies with the laws of the State of Illinois and should not be used in other states.

Non-Exclusive Buyer Representation Contract

WHAT LICENSEE CANNOT DISCLOSE TO
CLIENTS WHEN ACTING AS A DUAL AGENT

1. Confidential information that Licensee may know about a client, without that client's permission.
2. The price the seller or landlord will take other than the listing price without permission of the seller or landlord.
3. The price the buyer or tenant is willing to pay without permission of the buyer or tenant.
4. A recommended or suggested price the buyer or tenant should offer.
5. A recommended or suggested price the seller or landlord should counter with or accept.

If either client is uncomfortable with this disclosure and dual representation, please let Licensee know. You are not required to sign this section unless you want to allow the Licensee to proceed as a Dual Agent in this transaction.

By initialing here and signing below, you acknowledge that you have read and understand this form and voluntarily consent to the Licensee acting as a Dual Agent (that is, to represent BOTH the seller or landlord and the buyer or tenant) should that become necessary.

_____   _____   _____
Buyer's Initials   Buyer's Initials   Date

SECTION 8: COMPENSATION
Broker and Buyer expect that Broker's commission will be paid by the seller or the seller's broker for Broker's acting as a cooperating agent. However, if Broker is not compensated by seller or seller's broker, or if the amount of compensation paid by seller or seller's broker is not at least_____ % of the purchase price, then Buyer agrees to pay Broker the difference between_____ % of the purchase price and what seller or seller's broker actually paid. This Section applies if the Buyer, as a result of Buyer's Designated Agent's efforts and during the term of the Broker's representation on Buyer's behalf, enters into a contract to acquire real estate and such contract results in a closed transaction. Any modification to this Section, including the commission to be paid to Broker, shall be by a separate written amendment to this Contract.

SECTION 9: PREVIOUS REPRESENTATION
Buyer understands that Broker and/or Designated Agent may have previously represented the seller from whom you wish to purchase the property. During the representation, Broker and/or Designated Agent may have learned material information about the seller that is considered confidential. Under the law, neither Broker nor Designated Agent may disclose any such confidential information to you.

SECTION 10: FAILURE TO CLOSE
If a seller or lessor in an agreement made on behalf of Buyer fails to close such agreement with no fault on the part of the Buyer, the Buyer shall have no obligation to pay the commission provided for in Section 8. If such transaction fails to close because of any fault on the part of Buyer, such commission will not be waived, but will be due and payable immediately. In no case shall Broker or Buyer's Designated Agent be obligated to advance funds for the benefit of Buyer in order to complete a closing.

SECTION 11: DISCLAIMER
The Buyer acknowledges that Broker and Buyer's Designated Agent are being retained solely as real estate professionals, and not as attorneys, tax advisors, surveyors, structural engineers, home inspectors, environmental consultants, architects, contractors, or other professional service providers. The Buyer understands that such other professional service providers are available to render advice or services to the Buyer, if desired, at Buyer's expense.

SECTION 12: COSTS OF THIRD PARTY SERVICES OR PRODUCTS
Buyer agrees to reimburse Broker for the cost of any products or services such as surveys, soil tests, title reports and engineering studies, furnished by outside sources immediately when payment is due.

SECTION 13: INDEMNIFICATION OF BROKER
Buyer agrees to indemnify Broker and Buyer's Designated Agent and to hold Broker and Buyer's Designated Agent harmless on account of any and all loss, damage, cost or expense, including attorneys' fees incurred by Broker or Buyer's Designated Agent, arising out of this Contract, or to the collection of fees or commission due Broker pursuant to the terms and conditions of this Contract, provided the loss damage, cost, expense or attorneys' fees do not result because of Broker's or Buyer's designated Agent's own negligence or willful and wanton misconduct.

SECTION 14: ASSIGNMENT BY BUYERS
No assignment of Buyer's interest under this Contract and no assignment of rights in real property obtained for Buyer pursuant to this Contract shall operate to defeat any of Broker's rights under this Contract.

SECTION 15: NONDISCRIMINATION
THE PARTIES UNDERSTAND AND AGREE THAT IT IS ILLEGAL FOR EITHER OF THE PARTIES TO REFUSE TO DISPLAY OR SELL SELLER'S PROPERTY TO ANY PERSON ON THE BASIS OF RACE, COLOR, RELIGION, NATIONAL ORIGIN, SEX, ANCESTRY, AGE, MARITAL STATUS, PHYSICAL OR MENTAL HANDICAP, MILITARY STATUS, SEXUAL ORIENTATION, UNFAVORABLE DISCHARGE FROM MILITARY SERVICE, FAMILIAL STATUS OR ANY OTHER CLASS PROTECTED BY ARTICLE 3 OF THE ILLINOIS HUMAN RIGHTS ACT. THE PARTIES AGREE TO COMPLY WITH ALL APPLICABLE FEDERAL, STATE AND LOCAL FAIR HOUSING LAWS.

SECTION 16: MODIFICATION OF THIS AGREEMENT
No modification of any of the terms of this Contract shall be valid and binding upon the parties or entitled to enforcement unless such modification has first been reduced to writing and signed by the parties.

SECTION 17: ENTIRE AGREEMENT
This Contract constitutes the entire agreement between the parties relating to the subject thereof, and any prior agreements pertaining hereto, whether oral or written have been merged and integrated into this Contract.

This Contract may be executed in multiple copies and my signature as Buyer hereon acknowledges that I have received a signed copy.

_____   Accepted by:
Buyer

_____   _____
Buyer   Broker

Buyer's Address: Date:_____

_____   _____
                                Buyer's Designated Agent

_____
Date:_____   Date:_____

Disclosure and Consent to Dual Agency Form

ILLINOIS ASSOCIATION OF REALTORS

DISCLOSURE AND CONSENT TO DUAL AGENCY
(DESIGNATED AGENCY)

NOTE TO CONSUMER: THIS DOCUMENT SERVES THREE PURPOSES. FIRST, IT DISCLOSES THAT A REAL ESTATE LICENSEE MAY POTENTIALLY ACT AS A DUAL AGENT, THAT IS, REPRESENT MORE THAN ONE PARTY TO THE TRANSACTION. SECOND, THIS DOCUMENT EXPLAINS THE CONCEPT OF DUAL AGENCY. THIRD, THIS DOCUMENT SEEKS YOUR CONSENT TO ALLOW THE REAL ESTATE LICENSEE TO ACT AS A DUAL AGENT. A LICENSEE MAY LEGALLY ACT AS A DUAL AGENT ONLY WITH YOUR CONSENT. BY CHOOSING TO SIGN THIS DOCUMENT, YOUR CONSENT TO DUAL AGENCY REPRESENTATION IS PRESUMED.

The undersigned _____, ("Licensee"), may undertake a
(insert name(s) of Licensee undertaking dual representation)
dual representation (represent both the seller or landlord and the buyer or tenant) for the sale or lease of property. The undersigned acknowledge they were informed of the possibility of this type of representation. Before signing this document please read the following:

Representing more than one party to a transaction presents a conflict of interest since both clients may rely upon Licensee's advice and the client's respective interests may be adverse to each other. Licensee will undertake this representation only with the written consent of ALL clients in the transaction.

Any agreement between the clients as to a final contract price and other terms is a result of negotiations between the clients acting in their own best interests and on their own behalf. You acknowledge that Licensee has explained the implications of dual representation, including the risks involved, and understand that you have been advised to seek independent advice from your advisors or attorneys before signing any documents in this transaction.

WHAT A LICENSEE CAN DO FOR CLIENTS WHEN ACTING AS A DUAL AGENT

1. Treat all clients honestly.
2. Provide information about the property to the buyer or tenant.
3. Disclose all latent material defects in the property that are known to the Licensee.
4. Disclose financial qualification of the buyer or tenant to the seller or landlord.
5. Explain real estate terms.
6. Help the buyer or tenant to arrange for property inspections.
7. Explain closing costs and procedures.
8. Help the buyer compare financing alternatives.
9. Provide information about comparable properties that have sold so both clients may make educated decisions on what price to accept or offer.

WHAT A LICENSEE CANNOT DISCLOSE TO CLIENTS WHEN ACTING AS A DUAL AGENT

1. Confidential information that Licensee may know about a client, without that client's permission.
2. The price the seller or landlord will take other than the listing price without permission of the seller or landlord.
3. The price the buyer or tenant is willing to pay without permission of the buyer or tenant.
4. A recommended or suggested price the buyer or tenant should offer.
5. A recommended or suggested price the seller or landlord should counter with or accept.

If either client is uncomfortable with this disclosure and dual representation, please let Licensee know. You are not required to sign this document unless you want to allow the Licensee to proceed as a Dual Agent in this transaction.

By signing below, you acknowledge that you have read and understand this form and voluntarily consent to the Licensee acting as a Dual Agent (that is, to represent BOTH the seller or landlord and the buyer or tenant) should that become necessary.

CLIENT:_____   CLIENT:_____

Date:_____   Date:_____

                                       LICENSEE:_____

                                       Date:_____

Form 335 2/2000 !!!!!!!!!!!!!!!!!!!!!!!!!   Copyright by Illinois Association of REALTORS

Courtesy of the Illinois Association of Realtors

This form complies with the laws of the State of Illinois and should not be used in other states.

ILLINOIS ASSOCIATION OF REALTORS®
EXCLUSIVE BUYER REPRESENTATION/EXCLUSIVE RIGHT TO PURCHASE CONTRACT
(DUAL AGENCY DISCLOSURE AND CONSENT INCLUDED)

In consideration of _____'s (Brokerage Company hereinafter referred to as "Broker") agreement to designate a sales associate affiliated with Broker to act as an agent of the Buyer for the purpose of identifying and negotiating to acquire real estate for _____ ("Buyer"), the Buyer hereby grants to Broker the relationship as marked in Section 1 of the Contract.

SECTION 1: TYPE OF REPRESENTATION
(Instruction: check the box next to desired choice):

___ **Exclusive Representation** Buyer understands that this exclusive right to represent Buyer (Exclusive Representation) means that if the Buyer makes an acquisition of property, whether through the efforts of Broker and his agents or through the efforts of another real estate office or agent, Buyer will be obligated to compensate Broker pursuant to Section 8 of this Contract. This Exclusive Agency shall be effective for the following area: _____. The term "acquisition" shall include the purchase, lease, exchange or option of real estate.

___ **Exclusive Right to Acquire** Buyer understands that this "exclusive right to purchase" means that if Buyer acquires any property, whether through the efforts of the Buyer-Broker and his agents, another real estate agency besides Broker's or other third party, Buyer will be obligated to compensate Broker pursuant to Section 8 of this Contract. This exclusive right to acquire shall be effective for the following area: _____. "Acquisition" shall include the purchase, lease, exchange or option of real estate.

Broker designates and Buyer accepts _____ ("Buyer's Designated Agent") as the legal agent(s) of Buyer for the purpose of representing Buyer in the acquisition of real estate by Buyer. Buyer understands and agrees that neither Broker nor any other sales associates affiliated with Broker (except as provided for herein) will be acting as legal agent of the Buyer. Broker shall have the discretion to appoint a substitute designated agent for Buyer as Broker determines necessary. Buyer shall be advised within a reasonable time of any such substitution.

SECTION 2: TERM
This Contract shall be effective until 11:59 p.m. on _____, when it shall then terminate. This Contract is irrevocable and can be terminated prior to the termination date only by written agreement of the parties. If within ____ days after the termination of this Contract (i.e. the protection period), Buyer purchases any property to which Buyer was introduced by Buyer's Designated Agent, then Buyer agrees to pay Broker the compensation provided for in Section 8. However, no compensation will be due to Broker if, during this protection period, Buyer enters into a separate buyer representation agreement with another broker.

SECTION 3: BUYER'S DESIGNATED AGENT'S DUTIES
(a) To use Buyer's Designated Agent's best efforts to identify properties listed in the multiple listing service that meet the Buyer's specifications relating to location, price, features and amenities, as identified from the attached Buyer's Information Checklist.
(b) To arrange for inspections of properties identified by the Buyer as potentially appropriate for acquisition.
(c) To advise Buyer as to the pricing of comparable properties.
(d) To assist Buyer in the negotiation of a contract acceptable to the Buyer for the acquisition of property.
(e) To provide reasonable safeguards for confidential information that the Buyer discloses to Buyer's Designated Agent.

SECTION 4: BROKER'S DUTIES
(a) To provide through Buyer's Designated Agent, those brokerage services set forth in Section 15-75 of the Illinois Real Estate License Act of 2000.
(b) To provide Buyer's Designated Agent with assistance and advice as necessary in Buyer's Designated Agent's work on Buyer's behalf.
(c) To make the managing Broker, or his /her designated representative, available to consult with Buyer's Designated Agent as to Buyer's negotiations for the acquisition of real estate, who will maintain the confidence of Buyer's confidential information.
(d) To make other sales associates affiliated with Broker aware of Buyer's general specifications for real property.
(e) As needed, to designate one or more sales associates as Designated Agents of Buyer.

SECTION 5: BUYER'S DUTIES
(a) To complete the Buyer's checklist which will provide Buyer's specifications for the real estate Buyer is seeking.
(b) To work exclusively with Buyer's Designated Agent to identify and acquire real estate during the time that this Contract is in force.
(c) To supply relevant financial information that may be necessary to permit Buyer's Designated Agent to fulfill Agent's obligations under this Contract.
(d) To be available upon reasonable notice and at reasonable hours to inspect properties that seem to meet Buyer's specifications.
(e) To pay Broker according to the terms specified in Section 8 of this Contract.

SECTION 6: REPRESENTING OTHER BUYER
Buyer understands that Buyer's Designated Agent has no duty to represent only Buyer, and that Buyer's Designated Agent may represent other prospective buyers who may be interested in acquiring the same property or properties that Buyer is interested in acquiring.

SECTION 7: DISCLOSURE AND CONSENT TO DUAL AGENCY

NOTE TO CONSUMER: THIS SECTION SERVES THREE PURPOSES. FIRST, IT DISCLOSES THAT A REAL ESTATE LICENSEE MAY POTENTIALLY ACT AS A DUAL AGENT, THAT IS, REPRESENT MORE THAN ONE PARTY TO THE TRANSACTION. SECOND, THIS SECTION EXPLAINS THE CONCEPT OF DUAL AGENCY. THIRD, THIS SECTION SEEKS YOUR CONSENT TO ALLOW THE REAL ESTATE LICENSEE TO ACT AS A DUAL AGENT. A LICENSEE MAY LEGALLY ACT AS A DUAL AGENT ONLY WITH YOUR CONSENT. BY CHOOSING TO SIGN THIS SECTION, YOUR CONSENT TO DUAL AGENCY REPRESENTATION IS PRESUMED.

The undersigned _____, ("Licensee"/"Buyer's Designated Agent") may undertake a dual representation (represent both the seller or landlord and the buyer or tenant) for the sale or lease of property. The undersigned acknowledge they were informed of the possibility of this type of representation. Before signing this document please read the following:

Representing more than one party to a transaction presents a conflict of interest since both clients may rely upon Licensee's advice and the client's respective interests may be adverse to each other. Licensee will undertake this representation only with the written consent of ALL clients in the transaction.

Any agreement between the clients as to a final contract price and other terms is a result of negotiations between the clients acting in their own best interests and on their own behalf. You acknowledge that Licensee has explained the implications of dual representation, including the risks involved, and understand that you have been advised to seek independent advice from your advisors or attorneys before signing any documents in this transaction.

Courtesy of the Illinois Association of Realtors

This form complies with the laws of the State of Illinois and should not be used in other states.

Exclusive Buyer Representation Contract

WHAT A LICENSEE CAN DO FOR CLIENTS WHEN ACTING AS A DUAL AGENT

1. Treat all clients honestly.
2. Provide information about the property to the buyer or tenant.
3. Disclose all latent material defects in the property that are known to the Licensee.
4. Disclose financial qualification of the buyer or tenant to the seller or landlord.
5. Explain real estate terms.
6. Help the buyer or tenant to arrange for property inspections.
7. Explain closing costs and procedures.
8. Help the buyer compare financing alternatives.
9. Provide information about comparable properties that have sold so both clients may make educated decisions on what price to accept or offer.

WHAT LICENSEE CANNOT DISCLOSE TO CLIENTS WHEN ACTING AS A DUAL AGENT

1. Confidential information that Licensee may know about a client, without that client's permission.
2. The price the seller or landlord will take other than the listing price without permission of the seller or landlord.
3. The price the buyer or tenant is willing to pay without permission of the buyer or tenant.
4. A recommended or suggested price the buyer or tenant should offer.
5. A recommended or suggested price the seller or landlord should counter with or accept.

If either client is uncomfortable with this disclosure and dual representation, please let Licensee know. You are not required to sign this section unless you want to allow the Licensee to proceed as a Dual Agent in this transaction.

By initialing here and signing below, you acknowledge that you have read and understand this form and voluntarily consent to the Licensee acting as a Dual Agent (that is, to represent BOTH the seller or landlord and the buyer or tenant) should that become necessary.

_____   _____   _____
Buyer's initials   Buyer's initials   Date

SECTION 8: COMPENSATION

Broker and Buyer expect that Broker's commission will be paid by the seller or seller's broker for Broker's acting as a cooperating agent. However, if Broker is not compensated by seller or seller's broker, or if the amount of compensation paid by seller or seller's broker is not at least _____% of the purchase price, then Buyer agrees to pay Broker the difference between_____% of the purchase price and what seller or seller's broker actually paid. This Section applies if the Buyer enters into a contract to acquire real estate during the term of this Contract or the protection period, and such contract results in a closed transaction. Any modification to this Section, including the commission to be paid to Broker, shall be by a separate written agreement to this Contract.

SECTION 9: PREVIOUS REPRESENTATION

Buyer understands that Broker and/or Designated Agent may have previously represented the seller from whom you wish to purchase property. During that representation, Broker and/or Designated Agent may have learned material information about the seller that is considered confidential. Under the law, neither Broker nor Designated Agent may disclose any such confidential information to you.

SECTION 10: FAILURE TO CLOSE

If a seller or lessor in an agreement made on behalf of Buyer fails to close such agreement, with no fault on the part of Buyer, the Buyer shall have no obligation to pay the commission provided for in Section 8. If such transaction fails to close because of any fault on the part of Buyer, such commission will not be waived, but will be due and payable immediately. In no case shall Broker or Broker's Designated Agent be obligated to advance funds for the benefit of Buyer in order to complete a closing.

SECTION 11: DISCLAIMER

The Buyer acknowledges that Broker and Buyer's Designated Agent are being retained solely as real estate professionals, and not as attorneys, tax advisors, surveyors, structural engineers, home inspectors, environmental consultants, architects, contractors, or other professional service providers. The Buyer understands that such other professional service providers are available to render advice or services to the Buyer, if desired, at Buyer's expense.

SECTION 12: COSTS OF THIRD PARTY SERVICES OR PRODUCTS

Buyer agrees to reimburse Broker the cost of any products or services such as surveys, soil tests, title reports and engineering studies, furnished by outside sources immediately when payment is due.

SECTION 13: INDEMNIFICATION OF BROKER

Buyer agrees to indemnify Broker and Buyer's Designated Agent and to hold Broker and Buyer's Designated Agent harmless on account of any and all loss, damage, cost or expense, including attorneys' fees incurred by Broker or Buyer's Designated Agent, arising out of this Contract, or the collection of fees or commission due Broker pursuant to the terms and conditions of this Contract, provided the loss damage, cost, expense or attorneys' fees do not result because of Broker's or Buyer's Designated Agent's own negligence or willful and wanton misconduct.

SECTION 14: ASSIGNMENT BY BUYERS

No assignment of Buyer's interest under this Contract and no assignment of rights in real property obtained for Buyer pursuant to this Contract shall operate to defeat any of Broker's rights under this exclusive representation contract.

SECTION 15: NONDISCRIMINATION

THE PARTIES UNDERSTAND AND AGREE THAT IT IS ILLEGAL FOR EITHER OF THE PARTIES TO REFUSE TO DISPLAY OR SELL SELLER'S PROPERTY TO ANY PERSON ON THE BASIS OF RACE, COLOR, RELIGION, NATIONAL ORIGIN, SEX, ANCESTRY, AGE, MARITAL STATUS, PHYSICAL OR MENTAL HANDICAP, MILITARY STATUS, SEXUAL ORIENTATION, UNFAVORABLE DISCHARGE FROM MILITARY SERVICE, FAMILIAL STATUS OR ANY OTHER CLASS PROTECTED BY ARTICLE 3 OF THE ILLINOIS HUMAN RIGHTS ACT. THE PARTIES AGREE TO COMPLY WITH ALL APPLICABLE FEDERAL, STATE AND LOCAL FAIR HOUSING LAWS.

SECTION 16: MODIFICATION OF THIS CONTRACT

No modification of any of the terms of this Contract shall be valid and binding upon the parties or entitled to enforcement unless such modification has first been reduced to writing and signed by the parties.

SECTION 17: ENTIRE AGREEMENT

This Contract constitutes the entire agreement between the parties relating to the subject thereof, and any prior agreements pertaining hereto, whether oral or written have been merged and integrated into this Contract.

This Contract may be executed in multiple copies and my signature as Buyer hereon acknowledges that I have received a signed copy.

_____   Accepted by:
Buyer

_____   _____
Buyer   Broker

Buyer's Address: Date:_____

_____

_____   _____
                                                     Buyer's Designated Agent

Date:_____   Date:_____

Form 338 Revised 7/6/05   Copyright© by Illinois Association of REALTORS®

acceptance: A seller's consent to enter into a contract and be bound by the terms of the offer.

adjustable-rate mortgage (ARM): A mortgage that permits the lender to adjust its interest rate periodically on the basis of changes in a specified index.

amortization: The gradual repayment of a mortgage loan by installments.

amortization schedule: A timetable for payment of a mortgage loan. An amortization schedule shows the amount of each payment that is applied to interest and principal as well as the remaining balance after each payment is made.

amortization term: The amount of time required to amortize the mortgage loan. The amortization term is expressed as a number of months. For example, for a thirty-year fixed-rate mortgage, the amortization term is 360 months.

annual percentage rate (APR): The cost of a mortgage stated as a yearly rate; includes such items as interest, mortgage insurance, and the loan origination fee (points).

appraisal: A written analysis of the estimated value of a property, prepared by a qualified appraiser.

appraised value: An assessment of a property's fair market value, based on an appraiser's knowledge, experience, and analysis of the property.

appreciation: An increase in the value of a property due to changes in market conditions or for other reasons. The opposite of *depreciation*.

assessment: The process of placing a value on property strictly for the purpose of taxation. May also refer to a levy against property for a special purpose, such as a sewer assessment.

association fee: Amount of money required to be paid by the unit owner in a multifamily building or complex for "common" areas in that building. These common areas might include elevators, swimming pools, or air-conditioning systems in a clubhouse.

assumable mortgage: A mortgage that can be taken over ("assumed") by the buyer when a home is sold.

balloon mortgage: A mortgage that has fixed monthly payments for an initial period but provides for a lump sum payment due at the end of an earlier specified term.

bidding war: A multiple-bid situation in which the seller of a home may counter the best offers to see which prospective buyer will pay the most.

bridge loan: A form of second mortgage that uses as collateral the borrower's present home (which is usually up for sale). The anticipated proceeds from the sale of that present home are used for closing on a new house, before the present home is sold. Also known as *swing loan*.

broker-associate: A real estate agent who is employed by a real estate brokerage and licensed by the state real estate commission as a broker-associate upon completing specified courses and passing specified examinations.

buyer's agent: A real estate professional responsible for representing the buyer's interest in a real estate transaction.

cash-out refinance: A refinance transaction in which the amount of money received from the new loan exceeds the total amount needed to repay the existing first mortgage, plus closing costs, points, and to satisfy any outstanding subordinate mortgage liens. In other words, this is a refinance transaction in which the borrower receives additional cash that can be used for any purpose. Cash-out refinance offers are sometimes used by predatory lenders to take advantage of vulnerable homeowners.

certificate of title: A statement provided by an abstract company, title company, or attorney, stating that the title to real estate is legally held by the current owner.

clear title: A title that is free of liens or legal issues as to ownership of the property.

closing: A meeting at which the sale of a property is finalized by the buyer signing the mortgage documents and paying closing costs. Also called *settlement*.

closing-cost item: A fee or amount that a home buyer must pay at closing for a single service, tax, or product. Closing costs are made up of individual closing-cost items, such as loan origination fees and attorney's fees. Many closing-cost items are included as numbered items on the HUD-1 statement.

closing costs: Expenses (over and above the price of the property) incurred by buyers and sellers in transferring ownership of a property. Closing costs normally include a loan origination fee, an attorney's fee, taxes, an amount placed in escrow, and charges for obtaining title insurance and a survey. The percentage of a sale price dedicated to closing costs varies according to the area of the country where the home is located. Lenders or REALTORS® often provide estimates of closing costs to prospective home buyers.

closing statement: See *HUD-1 statement*.

commission: The fee charged by a broker or agent for negotiating a real estate or loan transaction. A commission is generally a percentage of the price of the property or loan. (These are not to be confused with *state real estate commissions*, which exercise ongoing oversight of the real estate industry.)

commitment letter: See *mortgage commitment*.

common areas: Those portions of a building, land, and amenities owned (or managed) by a planned unit development (PUD) or condominium project's homeowners' association (or a cooperative project's cooperative corporation) that are used by all the unit owners, who share the cost of their operation and maintenance. Common areas include swimming pools, tennis courts, and other recreational facilities, as well as common corridors of buildings, parking areas, means of ingress and egress, and so on.

comparables: See *market comps.*

comparative market analysis (CMA): A study of properties currently on the market or recently sold to determine the fair market value of a home. These properties should be located within a certain distance of the home under consideration and should also bear some similarity to that home, in terms of their features.

condominium: A real estate project in which each unit owner has title to a unit in a building and a shared interest in the common areas of the project.

contingency: A condition that must be met before a contract is legally binding. For example, home purchasers often include a contingency that specifies that the contract is not binding until the purchaser obtains a satisfactory home inspection report from a qualified home inspector.

conventional mortgage: A mortgage that is not insured or guaranteed by the federal government, as opposed to a government mortgage, such as one backed by Fannie Mae or Freddie Mac.

cooperative (co-op): A type of multiple ownership in which the residents of a multi-unit housing complex own shares in the cooperative corporation that owns the property, giving each resident the right to occupy a specific apartment or unit.

counteroffer: An offer made by the buyer or seller that includes changes to the original or the latest offer of the other party.

covenant: A clause in a mortgage that obligates or restricts the borrower and that, if violated, can result in foreclosure.

credit report: A report on an individual's credit history, prepared by a credit bureau and used by a lender in determining a loan applicant's creditworthiness.

deed: The legal document conveying title to a property. See *property deed.*

deed of trust: The document used in some states instead of a mortgage; title is conveyed to a trustee.

deposit: A sum of money given to bind the sale of real estate, or a sum of money given to ensure payment or an advance of funds in the processing of a loan. See *earnest money deposit.*

depreciation: A decline in the value of property; the opposite of *appreciation.*

detached property: A property standing apart and separate from other properties.

discount points: Money paid to the lender when a loan is originated, allowing buyers to "buy down" the cost of the mortgage by paying a certain amount of money up front in lieu of paying interest over the life of the loan. Each point is equal to 1 percent of the original loan amount.

down payment: The part of the purchase price of a property that the buyer pays in cash and does not finance with a mortgage.

dual agent: A real estate agent who represents both the buyer and the seller in a transaction. This agent is legally required to disclose the "dual" nature of the relationship to the parties involved.

earnest money deposit: A deposit made by potential home buyers to show that they are serious about buying the house.

endorsement: A provision added to a contract that alters the original contract in some way, such as adding earthquake insurance to a standard homeowner's insurance policy.

equity: A homeowner's financial interest in a property. Equity is the difference between the fair market value of the property and the amount still owed on its mortgage.

escrow: An item of value, money, or documents, deposited with a third party, to be delivered upon the fulfillment of a condition. For example, a borrower may put money in escrow with the lender of funds; that money is earmarked for tax payments and insurance premiums when they come due. Or funds or documents may be deposited (that is, "placed in escrow") with an attorney or escrow agent to be disbursed upon the closing of a sale of a property.

exclusive buyer's agent: An agent who acts solely on behalf of the buyer. Neither that agent nor any agents in his or her brokerage firm take any listings.

Fannie Mae: Fannie Mae is a New York Stock Exchange–traded company and the largest nonbank financial services company in the world. It operates pursuant to a federal charter and is the nation's largest source of financing for home mortgages. Over the past thirty years, Fannie Mae has provided nearly $2.5 trillion in mortgage financing for more than 30 million families.

Federal Housing Administration (FHA): An agency of the U.S. Department of Housing and Urban Development (HUD). Its main purpose is to insure residential mortgage loans made by private lenders. The FHA sets standards for construction and underwriting, but does not lend money or plan or construct housing.

fiduciary duties: A legal obligation to deal honestly and represent a party's interests in a transaction. Usually established between two or more parties, most commonly between a "fiduciary" or "trustee" and a "principal" or "beneficiary."

firm commitment: A lender's agreement to make a loan to a specific borrower on a specific property.

fixed-rate mortgage: A mortgage in which the interest rate and the monthly loan payments do not change during the entire term of the loan.

flood insurance: Insurance that compensates for physical property damage resulting from flooding. It is required for properties located in federally designated flood areas.

foreclosure: The legal process by which a borrower in default on a mortgage is deprived of his or her interest in the mortgaged property. This usually involves a forced sale of the property at public auction, with the proceeds of the sale being applied to the mortgage debt.

For Sale by Owner (FSBO): An arrangement in which a property is being sold directly by the owner. The owner has not retained a real estate agent to sell the home.

Freddie Mac: A corporation chartered by Congress in 1970 to keep money flowing to mortgage lenders in support of homeownership. It helps lower housing costs by backing loans with a government guarantee and provides better means to home financing.

good-faith estimate: An itemized approximation of the costs (including the seller's cost) to close a mortgage loan. This is not an exact figure, but rather an estimate of the amount of money the buyer will need to bring to the closing table.

gross monthly income (GMI): Consistent income that an individual receives each month, averaged over a specified period. GMI includes an average of any bonuses, commissions, overtime pay, and income from interest or dividends.

guarantee certificate: A bond combined with an investment in an underlying value. The risk is limited with a guaranteed certificate, because at the end of the lifetime of the certificate you receive a part or all of the nominal value of your investment.

high-end home: A high-priced, luxury home. High-end homes typically feature certain desirable amenities, such as attractive views, higher-end appliances, walk-in closets, wine cellars, indoor or outdoor pools, and the like.

home equity loan: A mortgage loan, which is usually in a subordinate position, that allows borrowers to obtain multiple advances on the loan proceeds at their own discretion, up to an amount that represents a specified percentage of the borrowers' equity in a property.

home inspection: A thorough inspection that evaluates the structural and mechanical condition of a property. A satisfactory home inspection is often included as a contingency by the purchaser. Contrast with *appraisal.*

home-loan underwriter: A trained professional who reviews loan information, evaluates the creditworthiness of the prospective borrowers, and decides whether the lender will extend a loan to them.

homeowners' association: A nonprofit association that manages the common areas of a planned unit development (PUD) or condominium project. In a condominium project, the association has no ownership interest in the common areas. In a PUD project, it holds title to the common elements or areas.

homeowner's insurance: An insurance policy that combines personal liability insurance and hazard insurance coverage for a dwelling and its contents.

HUD-1 statement: A document that itemizes the funds that are payable at closing. Items that appear on the statement include real estate commissions, loan fees, points, and initial escrow amounts. Each item on the statement is represented by a separate number within a standardized numbering system. The totals at the bottom of the HUD-1 statement define the seller's net proceeds and the buyer's net payment at closing. The blank form for the statement is published by the Department of Housing and Urban Development (HUD). The HUD-1 statement is also known as the closing statement or settlement sheet.

index: A number used to compute the interest rate for an adjustable-rate mortgage (ARM). The index is generally a published number or percentage, such as the average interest rate or yield on Treasury bills. A margin is added to the index to determine the interest rate that will be charged on the ARM. This interest rate is subject to any caps that are associated with the mortgage.

interest: The fee charged for borrowing money. See *interest rate*.

interest-only mortgage: A mortgage that requires borrowers to repay only the interest accumulated on the principal amount borrowed, until they reach the end of the term of the loan. The principal amount of the mortgage is then repaid at the end of the term of the loan.

interest rate: The rate of interest in effect on a loan; this rate sometimes fluctuates depending on the type of loan the borrower obtains.

interest-rate lock-in: A written agreement in which the lender guarantees a specified interest rate if a mortgage goes to closing within a set period of time. The lock-in also usually specifies the number of points to be paid at closing.

joint tenancy: A form of co-ownership that gives each tenant equal interest and equal rights in the property, including the right of survivorship.

lien: A claim of monetary value against a property before the sale is finalized. Liens, which must be filed with a court of law, must be settled before the property title can be legally transferred to a new owner.

listing: An agreement between a property owner and a real estate agent. The agent agrees to secure a buyer for a specific property at a certain price and under specified terms in return for a fee or commission.

listing agent: See *seller's agent*.

loan commitment: See *mortgage commitment*.

loan default: Failure to make mortgage payments on a timely basis or to comply with other requirements of a mortgage.

loan origination fee: See *points*.

loan-to-value (LTV) percentage: The relationship between the principal balance of the mortgage and the appraised value (or sale price, if it is lower) of the property. For example, a $100,000 home with an $80,000 mortgage has an LTV percentage of 80 percent.

luxury home: See *high-end home*.

margin: For an adjustable-rate mortgage (ARM), the amount that is added to the index to establish the interest rate on each adjustment date, subject to any limitations on the interest rate change.

market comps: Also known as comparables, an abbreviation for comparable properties; used for comparative purposes in the appraisal process. Comparables are properties similar to the property under consideration; they have roughly the same size, location, and amenities, and have recently been sold. Comparables help the appraiser determine the approximate fair market value of the subject property.

mortgage: A legal document that pledges a property to the lender as security for payment of a debt.

mortgage banker: A company that originates mortgages exclusively for resale in the secondary mortgage market.

mortgage broker: An individual or company that brings borrowers and lenders together for the purpose of loan origination. Mortgage brokers typically charge a fee or take a commission for their services.

mortgage commitment: A formal offer by a lender, stating the terms under which the lender agrees to lend money to a home buyer. Also known as a *loan commitment* or a *commitment letter.*

multifamily home: A property with separate housing units for more than one family, although it requires only a single mortgage.

negative amortization: A gradual increase in mortgage debt that occurs when the monthly payment is not large enough to cover the entire amount of principal and interest due each month. The amount of the shortfall is added to the remaining balance to create "negative" amortization.

origination points: A one-time charge by the lender for originating a loan. A point is 1 percent of the amount of the mortgage.

PITI: See *principal, interest, taxes, and insurance (PITI).*

point: See *discount points* and *origination points.*

prepayment penalty: A fee that may be charged to a borrower who pays off a loan before it is due. Some states make it illegal for lenders to charge prepayment penalties.

preapproval: A guaranteed mortgage approval secured by potential home buyers before they make an offer on a house. A lending institution guarantees, in writing, to approve a loan for a specified amount. However, this guarantee may not apply if the home appraises for lower than the mortgage amount, for example.

predatory lending practices: Methods used by dishonest lenders, appraisers, or mortgage brokers to sell, for example, properties for more than they're worth by using false appraisals. These fraudulent—and often illegal—practices also include lending more money than a borrower can afford to repay (so the home-owner loses both the down payment and the property itself in a foreclosure) or encouraging buyers to lie about their income to obtain a mortgage for more than they can afford.

prequalification: The process of determining how much money prospective home buyers will be eligible to borrow before they apply for a loan.

principal: The amount borrowed or remaining unpaid on a mortgage. The part of the monthly payment that reduces the remaining balance of a mortgage.

principal, interest, taxes, and insurance (PITI): The four components of a typical monthly mortgage payment. Principal refers to the part of the monthly payment that reduces the remaining balance of the mortgage. Interest is the fee charged for borrowing money. Taxes and insurance refer to the amounts that are paid into an escrow account each month for property taxes and mortgage and hazard insurance.

private mortgage insurance (PMI): Mortgage insurance that is provided by a private mortgage insurance company to protect lenders against loss if a borrower defaults. Most lenders generally require mortgage insurance for a loan with a loan-to-value percentage in excess of 80 percent.

property deed: A document that transfers ownership of real estate. It contains the names of the old and new owners and a legal description of the property. The individual transferring the property signs it.

property disclosure: A document that specifies material facts—including details about the condition or legal status—of a house being sold.

property value stability: A measure of whether homes in a specific area are increasing in, maintaining, or losing value. Property values fluctuate based on the demand for and availability of homes in a particular neighborhood.

purchase price: The sale price or the amount that is paid for something that is bought. The price paid for a home.

purchase and sale agreement: A written contract, signed by both the buyer and the seller, stating the terms and conditions under which a property will be sold.

qualifying ratios: Calculations that are used in determining whether a borrower can qualify for a mortgage. They consist of two separate calculations: a ratio of housing expense as a percentage of income and a ratio of total debt obligations as a percentage of income.

real estate agent: A person licensed to negotiate and transact the sale of real estate on behalf of the property owner.

real estate broker: A person who, for a commission or a fee, brings parties together and assists in negotiating contracts between them. The real estate broker is the person who handles (or "brokers") the transaction between buyers and sellers.

Realtor®: A real estate broker or an associate who holds active membership in a local real estate board that is affiliated with the National Association of Realtors®.

refinance: The process of paying off one loan with the proceeds from a new loan, using the same property as security.

repayment mortgage: A mortgage that involves the repayment of both principal and interest in monthly installments within a specified term of years.

reverse mortgage: A financial tool that provides homeowners (commonly senior citizens) with money from the equity in their homes. Under this arrangement, homeowners or buyers receive cash in return for a mortgage on their home. The property is used as collateral for the loan, which is paid off when the owner either dies or sells the property and moves to another home. To be eligible, applicants must be at least sixty-two years old, and they must own and live in the home.

seller's agent: An agent who represents a home's seller. Usually referred to as the *listing agent*, this agent is empowered by a property owner to find a buyer for the property.

servicer: An organization that collects principal and interest payments from borrowers and manages borrowers' escrow accounts. The servicer often services mortgages that have been purchased by an investor in the secondary mortgage market.

settlement: See *closing.*

settlement sheet: See *HUD-1 statement.*

share loan: An agreement entered into by a member of a cooperative housing corporation and a lender to finance the member's purchase of the member's cooperative interest.

showing: An opportunity for potential buyers to walk through a home for sale, scrutinize its interior and exterior, and determine if the house is potentially right for them.

single-family home: A home that sits on its own piece of land and is not attached to anyone else's residence.

spec home: A house built before it is sold. The builder speculates that he can sell it.

subagency: An agency whose broker brings the buyer to a property. Subagents are paid by the seller and have a financial responsibility to the seller.

subprime lender: A lender who charges a finance rate that is higher than the prime rate offered by conventional lenders. This type of lender approves loans for individuals who may have poor or no credit history.

term: The duration of a mortgage.

title: A legal document specifying a person's right to or ownership of a property.

title company: A company that specializes in examining and insuring titles to real estate.

title insurance: Insurance that protects the lender (lender's policy) or the buyer (owner's policy) against loss arising from disputes over ownership of a property.

title search: A check of the title records to ensure that the seller is the legal owner of the property and that there are no liens or other claims outstanding against that property.

townhouse: A single-family dwelling built in a group of attached units in which each unit extends from foundation to roof and is minimally attached to another townhouse. Owners of townhouses generally own both the townhouse structure and the land that it sits on.

transactional brokerage: Limited agency that represents neither the buyer nor the seller. This brokerage only facilitates the sale.

valuation: The estimated worth or value of something, such as a property.

walk-through: A visit to a home to be purchased that takes place before the closing and before the property ownership is transferred. It is an opportunity to make sure that the house has been left in the expected condition.